# Riding West

Jim in his outfitter's costume at Lunch Mound in the West Elk Wilderness Area. Photo by Stan Urban.

# Riding West
## An Outfitter's Life

JIM GREER

as told to
CHARLES MILLER

Drawings by
SCOTT YEAGER

University Press of Colorado

Copyright © 1999 by the University Press of Colorado
International Standard Book Number 0-87081-525-3

Published by the University Press of Colorado
P.O. Box 849
Niwot, Colorado 80544

The University Press of Colorado is a cooperative publishing enterprise supported, in part, by Adams State College, Colorado State University, Fort Lewis College, Mesa State College, Metropolitan State College of Denver, University of Colorado, University of Northern Colorado, University of Southern Colorado, and Western State College of Colorado.

The paper used in this publication meets the minimum requirements of the American National Standard for Information Sciences–Permanence of Paper for Printed Library Materials. ANSI Z39.48-1984

Library of Congress Cataloging-in-Publication Data

Greer, Jim, 1939–
    Riding west : an outfitter's life/by Jim Greer as told to Charles Miller
      p. cm.
    ISBN 0-87081-525-3 (alk. paper)
      1. Greer, Jim, 1939– 2. Outfitters (Outdoor recreation)—West (U.S.)—Biography. I. Title. II. Miller, Charles, 1931–

GV191.52.G74 G74 1999
796.5'092—dc21
[B]                                           99-041474

08 07 06 05 04 03 02 01 00 99    10 9 8 7 6 5 4 3 2 1

For Marilyn and Marlene

Although this book portrays real people, places, and events,
the names of most (but not all) of the people have been changed.
Many of the place names have been left intact, while others,
for various reasons (some legal, others environmental)
have been changed. The descriptions of events, though,
are as close to reality as I can make them.

Cowboying is a state of mind.

—LARRY MAHAN

I'd rather live on the side of a mountain
Than wander through canyons of concrete and steel
I'd rather laugh with the rain and sunshine
And lay down my sundown in some starry field.
I think I'd rather be a cowboy
I think I'd rather ride the range
I think I'd rather be a cowboy
Than to lay me down in love and lady's chains.

—JOHN DENVER

# Contents

# Preface

EVERY SUMMER when I was outfitting I used to take clients on trail rides over East Maroon Pass into the Maroon Creek valley and Aspen. Leading rides isn't the most glamorous or exciting part of an outfitter's job—in the trade they're referred to as tending the dudes—but they're an outfitter's bread-and-butter, the professional equivalent of cowboys mending fence or bartenders pouring beer.

The trailhead was in Gothic, a ghost town on the East River a few miles north of the Mt. Crested Butte ski area. We'd climb the abandoned road up Copper Creek to Copper Lake, eat lunch on top of the pass, then follow the trail across the scree and through the woods beside East Maroon Creek. If things worked out, we'd be down on Forest Service Road 125 by late afternoon, pasture the horses at the Lazy K Resort, and catch the Maroon Lake shuttle into Aspen for Mexican food at Toros and a night on the town.

Nothing to it, except that once in a while something would go wrong. A horse might pick up a rock or throw a shoe, and we'd have to stop while I fixed it. Or a client would start feeling faint (the elevation on the pass is about 11,000 feet), and we'd take a break while he rested. Sometimes an August storm drove us to cover, and we'd crouch under our yellow slickers, eyes wide, flinching as lightning stabbed and thunder slammed back and forth among the peaks. But a delay could be critical, because if we missed the last shuttle, we were looking at an eight-mile walk into town.

One afternoon storms held us up on the trail, so the sun was already behind Pyramid Peak and the Maroon Bells when we reached the blacktop. I flagged the last bus, put the dudes on board with instructions to check into the motel in Aspen, then led the string down to the Lazy K by myself. A ranch hand helped me strip the horses, give them a quick rubdown, and turn them out to pasture.

So far, so good: things were under control. By now the clients had taken showers at the Ore Bucket Motel and were off to Toros, comparing their various aches and pains. Afterward, some of them would hit the bars, while others would limp around downtown admiring the Victorian streetlights, gasping at price tags in shop windows, and gawking for celebrities. "Look over there: isn't that Jill St. John?" Or: "Did you see that couple we just passed: wasn't that Don and Melanie?" The clients would get to bed early, though, because tomorrow we'd be off at first light for the ride back over the top to Gothic and the resort.

If I had a problem, it was me. That morning I'd rolled out before dawn, fourteen hours ago, so by now I felt like I'd already done a day's work, and I wasn't through yet. I started walking. After the last shuttle ran, they closed the road to everything but local traffic, and I knew there wasn't much chance of my thumbing a ride. A few early stars winked on. The air was cold, the shadows saturated with milky twilight reflecting off the crown of Highland Peak. To my right, Maroon Creek broke the silence, crackling over the rocks like dice in a cup. I was hiking along in my riding boots feeling sorry for myself when a heavy, black Harley with a chrome sissy bar roared by. Some rich guy with a big house hidden back in the trees, I figured—the kind who'd take one look at a guy like me and keep going. Instead, he hit the brakes, spun the motorcycle around, and came back. He needed a shave, and he was wearing a watch cap and black navy peacoat, just like he did in *The Last Detail*—only at that time I'd never seen the movie, or any other movie Jack Nicholson had made.

When he said, "You want a ride, cowboy?" I told him sure, I'd love a ride, and climbed on the saddle behind him. I was wearing my hat and chaps, and carrying my saddle bags over my shoulder, so he must have thought I was the real thing. I was also carrying my pistol, a .357 Magnum, and I remember thinking, "I hope this guy's not some kind of Hell's Angel, because if he tries something, I'll have to shoot him."

Since then I've heard that Nicholson, in spite of the way he looks and acts sometimes, is a decent guy without a mean bone in his body. He's the kind who'd rather hang out with real people, who work real jobs, instead of a bunch of imitation tough guys or phony Hollywood celebrities. I know when I've seen him being interviewed on television or receiving some kind of award, he's exactly the way he was that night on the road to Aspen.

When we got to town, he offered to buy me a drink, but I told him no, I wanted to buy *him* a drink because he'd saved me a hell of a walk. We went to a bar where he liked to hang out, one of your typical upscale Aspen dives—a gutted Victorian-era hardware store with exposed ceiling beams and century-old cement oozing like last week's oatmeal from between the bricks. There was a long, golden-oak bar with brass fittings, and beveled glass mirrors everywhere so the clientele could watch themselves and each other while they talked and drank.

When I ordered whiskey, I noticed the bartender looking at me kind of funny, but I figured it was because of the pistol. A lot of bartenders get nervous when they see you wearing a gun, afraid you might get careless, or somebody might ask to see it and start fooling around with it, and get somebody hurt. To save trouble, I slid it across the bar and asked him to keep it for me, and I saw that Nicholson—who'd identified himself simply as Jack—was getting a kick out of this.

It was Friday night. The room was jammed with a loud, laughing, happy-hour crowd, but suddenly an empty table appeared, and when I tossed my saddle bags down I noticed everybody staring at us. People stood up. Guys in black T-shirts and leather vests, or gray Armani sportcoats, turned their chairs around to watch. Beautiful women, with shampooed hair and lots of makeup, came over to say hi and kiss Jack, smiling at me curiously, like, Who is this handsome stranger? Before long, there was a crowd sitting and standing ten deep around us, hanging on our every word, and I was sure it was because of me. I figured these Aspenites had taken one look, decided they had a real live cowboy on their hands, and were impressed as hell. I'd never experienced that kind of attention and admiration before, and I was loving it. Maybe I've been too hard on Aspen, I thought; maybe it's not such a bad town after all.

With an audience like that, it wasn't long before me and my new friend Jack got involved in a good old-fashioned male pissing contest. I bought him a drink, and he bought me a drink. I told

him a story, and he told me a story. It was like raising the ante in
a poker game, except that because he was traveling incognito,
Jack couldn't use any of his show-biz material. Finally, when I
started interrupting him, like I do everybody, and topping his stories, he leaned back with the pained expression of an actor who
knows he's being upstaged but can't do anything about it.

I decided that if these people wanted a cowboy, that's what
they'd get. But I cleaned up my act by leaving out a number of
inconvenient facts—that I'd graduated from Denver University, for
instance, or that I'd taught six years in Denver's inner-city schools,
and put in another six as an executive in the governor of Colorado's
budget office. Or that the combination of me and the job had driven
me to the edge of a nervous breakdown, and that I'd walked away
from a couple of marriages leaving behind more children, and more
heartache, than I could ever forget.

Instead, I made myself sound like a simple child of nature,
some good old boy who'd been raised on a ranch and outfitted all
his life. I told stories about guiding big game hunters after elk and
bear; about bow-hunting antelope in Wyoming; about leading pack
trains, and breaking horses and mules. I told them about the ego-
driven, larger-than-life persona that goes with being an outfitter—
about rivals ready to stab you in the back over customers and permit areas, about game wardens breathing down your neck, waiting
for you to commit a game violation. I described the peace and
beauty of the high country, where you go along and start taking it
for granted, and all of a sudden it jumps up and bites you on the
ass. I told them about mistakes that could cost you or your clients
their lives—about rescuing lost hunters, and getting lost in snow
storms myself; about saloon fights, and breaking fingers and toes
and ribs; about crawling through lightning cells, where your hair
crackles and stands straight up on your head.

And the longer I talked, the more it sounded like some kind of
Wild West show. I was having a ball—I figured I had this crowd in
the palm of my hand—and all the time Nicholson's watching me
with that sharp-eyed, tight-lipped smile you see in his movies. Finally he leans across the table and says, "You really *don't* know
who the fuck I am, do you?"

The room got quiet. It surprised me, but I said, "Sure I do,
you told me; you're Jack." And the place broke up—first the people

near us, and then, when they passed the word back about what I'd said, everybody in the room. I just sat there trying to figure out what was going on until finally Jack explained who he was: he's Jack Nicholson, the movie actor, and he mentioned some of the movies he'd made. *Easy Rider?* Nope. *Five Easy Pieces?* Never heard of it. *One Flew Over the Cuckoo's Nest?* Loved the book, never saw the movie—and at each reply, the crowd broke up: Can you believe that? What a putz!

Nicholson's playing me like a fiddle, and everybody's eating it up. Even if I hadn't seen his films, though, I'd heard his name before, so I didn't know whether to believe him or not. But all these people said yes, absolutely, this was Jack Nicholson, the famous movie star, and they thought it was hilarious that I hadn't recognized him.

Finally I said goodnight, collected my saddle bags and gun, and headed across town to the Ore Bucket to rejoin the dudes. I'd learned a lesson that I'd been taught before: never play against a stacked deck. Nicholson and his fans had set me up, and I'd walked in with my eyes wide open, like I usually do. Since then I've seen a lot of his movies and enjoyed them, but in those days I didn't have a clue. I'd spent so much time in the high country and become so wrapped up in my own life, that I'd lost touch with what other people thought was important. In my own way, I considered myself to be just as much a celebrity—and just as much a performer, in a drama of my own making—as the crowd in that bar considered Jack Nicholson to be. And of course I wouldn't have had it any other way.

—JIM GREER

# Riding West

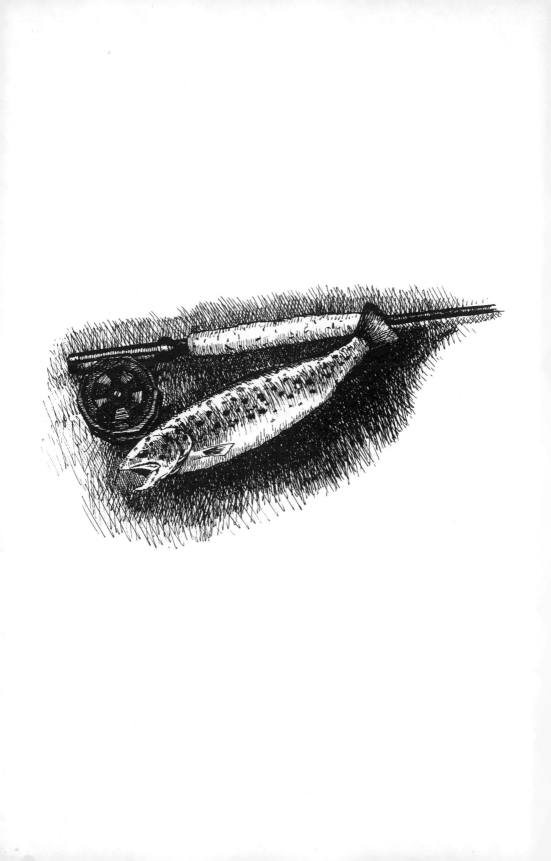

# 1

## *Keeping a Saloon*

THE BREAK WITH MY OLD LIFE occurred one spring morning while I was driving to work at the state capitol in Denver. It was Monday, about six AM, and I was getting an early start on my job as performance auditor for the Colorado legislature. Rain was falling, turning to ice. Traffic-watch choppers buzzed an inbound flow stacked six lanes wide for miles along I-25. Ahead there was a wreck, probably a couple of wrecks. Lights flashed, sirens howled, cops waved flashlights: they were carrying out the dead and wounded.

Around me cars crept forward and stopped, then moved and stopped again. My heart pounded in the back of my throat. Doctors had warned me about my blood pressure, and I knew it had to be running one-ninety over eighty. Suddenly I realized that I'd been making this commute, and working in state government, for so long that this was beginning to seem perfectly normal, and I thought, "My God, I'm on the verge of going as sane as the rest of these poor bastards!"

In those days there was a filling station at the Colorado Boulevard exit, a Texaco station with a red-and-white star as big as Christmas on a tall, white pole. In front of the station was a phone booth, the old-fashioned kind with an accordion door that folds, the kind Clark Kent used to enter only to emerge seconds later as Superman. And just like that I knew what I was going to do. I phoned my office, dictated a letter of resignation to my secretary, and told her to forward my check, because I was through.

A couple of months later I crossed the Continental Divide at Monarch Pass in a second-hand Volkswagen mini-bus. On board was everything I owned; everything else I'd sold or given away, or lost in a divorce agreement with my wife. It was one of the best feelings of my life. Not owning much makes you feel wonderful; you can pick up and go anywhere, anytime you want to, and no-body gives a damn. It felt so good that over the next few years I got rid of things until finally I could tie just about everything I owned behind my saddle. That's when I really felt free.

My wife—my second wife—hadn't been very sympathetic when I told her I'd quit my job and wanted to do something else. I'd changed wives and careers before, so she had a right to be suspicious. The first marriage had broken up about the time I left a job with the Denver school system teaching inner-city kids. I'd loved the job and my students, but not their parents and the public school bureaucracy. After five years, I realized that the only way to change the system was to become an administrator myself and—as a late-night phone call from a sympathetic but helpless school board member informed me—I was the wrong color, the wrong gender, and had the wrong ethnic background for that to happen in Denver, at least during my lifetime.

As a student of Betty Freidan's *The Feminine Mystique*, my second wife and her friends had no problem diagnosing what was wrong with me when I told her I'd resigned. In those days, feminists were promoting the idea that there was something called "the male menopause," and the phrase "midlife crisis" was popular with the media. Between them, they amounted to religious and secular explanations of the same event. It was like being handed your choice of suffering from a plague of locusts or an Oedipus complex.

It depressed me, though, to realize that what I believed was the most important decision of my life could be dismissed with such smug contempt. I preferred to think that what I was doing was taking a "midlife retirement"—another term that was popular at the time. The idea was that instead of waiting until you were old and decrepit, you retired in middle age, when you were still able to enjoy yourself, and did what you wanted to do—something exciting, something physically demanding. Then when your time and money ran out and your retirement was over, you resumed the career you'd abandoned or else found some other job.

None of this made sense to anybody but me. Doctors I consulted assured me that my symptoms—depression, fits of anger followed by guilt, high blood pressure, ulcers, an irregular heartbeat—were not unusual. Many of their patients had some or all of them. The trick, they said, was to learn how to live with them through the judicious use of medication. Several of my doctors confessed that they were dealing with these very symptoms themselves.

When I told my wife I wanted to leave Denver, she made it plain that if I left, I was going alone. We were at the kitchen table, where middle-class couples usually have their most serious conversations. We'd talked for quite a while, getting nowhere, until suddenly she stood up and walked out of the room. I was sitting there, trying to figure a way out of our dilemma when she reappeared in the doorway. "You'd better lie down and take a nap," she told me. "And when you wake up, if you haven't changed your mind, I can recommend somebody for you to talk to."

She meant a shrink, and she was probably right. If I hadn't already decided to leave, counseling would have been the next logical step. We hadn't been getting along for years, and as I got desperate, and my behavior became more and more erratic, she'd learned to withdraw and focus on her own career. She was a pretty woman, part Osage Indian. She had grown up in a small reservation town in Oklahoma and had worked hard to escape that environment—learned the proper way to walk and talk and dress, attended college, and jumped through all the hoops required to get a degree in education. Now she had it made: a job teaching in the Denver school system, a split-level house in the suburbs, friends, her own European sports sedan, a Saturday bridge group. Her husband had a respectable job, our children attended the right schools. She loved the city as much as I hated it. She'd worked hard; now she had everything she wanted, and I was talking about taking her away from it.

Everybody agreed with her: the neighbors, our friends, my colleagues at work. Either I'd lost my mind, they decided, or I was having a nervous breakdown. I was forty years old, with everything a successful, middle-class American man is supposed to want. In another twenty-five years or so (assuming I survived), I would be able to do what they planned to do themselves: retire to a life of golf, fishing, and low-stakes gambling in Florida, Arizona, or Southern California. I suppose there was an implied threat in my decision to walk away: either I was crazy or they were.

I left Denver with no idea of becoming an outfitter. All I wanted to do was escape before the life I was leading there killed me. I drove a thousand miles through half a dozen Western states, scouting locations. First through Wyoming to the Big Sky country in Montana, west of Yellowstone Park. In those days that part of the state was just opening up, and it seemed like a wonderful place to be. I drove through Idaho and Utah to see the slickrock country around Moab, then south to the desert around the Four Corners area. It was all beautiful, but coming through the Gunnison valley I suddenly started to feel at home. When I was a boy, my grandfather had taken me hunting and fishing all over the Gunnison country. Later, with my own family, I'd vacationed at some of the resorts along the river, fishing and hiking trails into the high country.

Now I checked into a motel and started talking to people at the Chamber of Commerce and merchants along Main Street, trying to get a sense of the place. In those days, Gunnison still had the look and feel of a small mountain town. Except for paved streets, it hadn't changed much since the end of World War II, and smelled of sagebrush and hay meadows and cattle. It reminded me of Morrison, Colorado, where I grew up in the 1940s.

There were big, long-leafed cottonwood trees that had been transplanted as saplings from the river bottoms before the turn of the century. Downtown, brick and stone business buildings dating back to the 1880s clustered around the intersection of two highways. At city hall, they blew a whistle at noon and five o'clock, and at odd hours to summon volunteer firemen. Irrigation water diverted from the Gunnison River ran through the gutters along both sides of Main Street, and I watched small boys catch fingerling trout, swept away by the current, with their bare hands. Improbably, a small, public liberal arts college—a mix-and-match collection of brick and stucco buildings—straddled an ancient fault at the base of some hills at the northeast corner of town. Ranchers still drove cattle through streets and across vacant lots (and an occasional lawn) in spring and fall. At night, skunks perfumed the air, and midwinter temperatures of thirty and forty below zero (without benefit of the so-called wind-chill factor) chased flatlanders back to Texas and California after the snow melted every spring.

It might seem funny now, but the question of how I would earn a living in Gunnison never occurred to me. All my life I believed I could go anywhere and land on my feet: I believed that's what this country was about and what I was about. I knew what I set my hand to might not be the job of my dreams, but I never doubted that I could feed myself, and keep a roof over my head and clothes on my back, no matter where I was.

Back in Denver, I got a break. A friend of mine, a woman who'd worked with me in the state government, told me that her husband and his brothers had bought a saloon called the Ramble Inn on the Gunnison River. They were looking for a manager, somebody who could keep a straight set of books, deal with a staff of employees and a mixed bag of customers, and build a business. The Ramble had been mismanaged for years and closed for several more, but the brothers believed it had possibilities. The only drawback I could see was that the Ramble was located a couple of miles from the college campus—but it had a 3.2 beer license and it sounded like a gold mine to me. After talking to the brothers, I took the job.

I had been driving through rain all the way across South Park, but on top of Monarch Pass, I climbed out of the clouds into moonlight so pure it obliterated every trace of stars. South and west other peaks, still snow-capped, appeared like icebergs encountered in midocean, and I took that to be a good omen … probably because I needed one.

West of the pass the clouds closed in again, and I followed the highway down the valley to Gunnison—forty miles of darkness interrupted by occasional headlights. Sagebrush-covered hills rose on one side; on the other, my headlights reflected from water overflowing the banks of Tomichi Creek, gleaming like oil in the meadows. Yard lights illuminated tin-roofed ranchhouses with empty feed lots and dented stock tanks. Finally, between a gap in the hills, the lights of town appeared, gleaming like campfires through the rain.

Rain is rare in the Gunnison valley. Most precipitation falls as snow, but moisture of any kind is uncommon; less than twelve inches a year is normal. The town's most prominent structure sits on a rise on the east side of town—a three-story, red-brick college administration building called Taylor Hall. Working out of the governor's budget office, I'd paid business calls there for years, inspecting the books and advising college administrators on finances. But that night, when I drove by, Taylor Hall looked as foreign to me as the Taj Mahal or the ruins of Angkor Wat.

Gunnison streets are wide, Western-style. The houses are low, one or two stories, some frame, others brick. Many remain from the mining days, the product of frequent renovations, their once-shingled roofs covered with metal, their original log walls disguised by stucco or siding and paint. In those days, the town had a single traffic signal at what was known as "the stop-light corner": the heart of town at Highway 50 (which becomes Tomichi Avenue inside the city limits) and Highway 135 (known as Main Street for a dozen blocks). Turning north, I drove through town and followed the highway to the bridge over the Gunnison River.

The water was high. Runoff swirled through willows and cottonwoods along both banks. On the north bank stood my new place of business, the Ramble Inn—a wide, low building of varnished logs with a low stone chimney and an asphalt shingle roof. A sign identifying the place lay in a pile of last year's weeds. In the past, on vacations, I'd stopped for a drink at the bar. Now, unable to resist a symbolic gesture, I got out of the van to hoist the sign into place. I was struggling to lift it when a pickup truck stopped, backed up, and a voice called:

"You fixing to reopen the Ramble?"

When I told the guy yes, that I was the new manager, a couple of cowboys, returning to the ranch after a night on the town, joined me. Lifting the sign in place, we set the posts back in their holes and propped them with rocks. Then, shaking hands, the cowboys wished me luck and drove off into the darkness.

Standing there, shivering and soaked to the skin, I felt like I'd come home.

My cabin was in a grove of cottonwoods across the parking lot. The key worked, but when I tried to light the propane stove, the hissing valve blew out my matches. Finally I spread my sleeping bag on a bare mattress and laid there for a while listening to rain pounding the roof and field mice scampering among the floor joists. Suddenly a noise roused me, a crash from outside. Through the window, I saw a huge, century-old cottonwood, undercut by the river, swing downstream in the current and disappear.

Next morning the parking lot had six inches of water in it and the boiler in the Ramble was out. I went to work fixing it.

In spite of my talk about midlife retirement, I worked hard and put a lot of thought into promoting business at the Ramble Inn. For entertainment, I organized a series of what, in the 1960s, were called "happenings." For the dancing crowd, I stocked the jukebox with country swing, and twice a week I booked Western bands willing to play for nothing more than a piece of the gate. A popular movie at the time featured a mechanical bull that drugstore cowboys tried to ride to impress their girlfriends. I bought one from a local outfitter who'd been using it to train his sons for the professional rodeo circuit, banked mattresses around it to cushion the customers' falls, then hired a pretty girl in a silk cowboy shirt to operate it. Three-minute rides were a dollar and a half—which, in view of the time most customers stayed in the saddle, worked out to about a thousand dollars a second. Wednesday was cash-rodeo night, and when entrance fees kicked the prize money into the thousands, we had participants coming from all over the state, not to mention complaints from the highway patrol about cars parked along the highway for a quarter of a mile in both directions.

Another happening I promoted was a buffalo-chip throwing contest. A rancher east of town was raising the animals for meat, and I traded him a case of beer for a dozen bushel baskets of chips. There were two parts to the contest, accuracy and distance. In the accuracy event, you sailed a chip backhand, like an overgrown Frisbee, through a swinging automobile tire suspended by a rope from a tree limb. Both sexes participated, but I handicapped the boys by hiring pretty girls to swing the tires. For the distance event, accuracy was irrelevant, but if the contestant overpowered the chip (some of them were greener than we wanted), he got a muzzle-burst in the face.

I also hijacked a happening the college sponsored, a kind of local imitation of the old Woodstock festival called Springfest. It was really an excuse for a beer bust, so I thought the students might as well celebrate it at the Ramble with my beer. In the past, Springfest had been relegated to city parks and ranchers' cow pastures, anyplace the students could get permission. There was live entertainment, both professional and amateur, and games like tug-of-war and two-legged sack races. Wet T-shirt contests and women's mud wrestling were also popular at the time, but I drew the line at events I considered degrading to women, even when the decision didn't increase my popularity with the students. The centerpiece of Springfest was a raft race down the Gunnison River on anything that would float, from inner tubes to bathtubs to twelve-man rafts. That time of year, the water was high with spring runoff, and contestants emerged half-drowned and blue with cold.

I don't know who had the most fun with all this, me or the customers. Most of my life I'd been tied up with school board policies and bureaucratic regulations, so it felt good to be on my own. If I had a new idea for the business—like a hot-air balloon ride, or a kite-flying contest—I tried it. If it worked, we did it some more; if it didn't, I could stop without asking anybody's permission.

It was my first experience with private enterprise since I'd sold fishing worms from a roadside stand in Morrison, where I grew up. After all those years, I'd forgotten how good it felt to make money. It was like small-stakes *Monopoly*, with real cash and real risk, even if they weren't mine. The Ramble's owners had bought the place on credit, and they'd warned me that their finances couldn't afford much failure. So I could enjoy myself, but I had to be careful; otherwise I'd put all of us out of business.

The combination of a 3.2 beer license and a college town proved unbeatable. In Colorado, eighteen-year-olds can't buy beer with a higher alcoholic content, and so large numbers of underage college students depend on such establishments for their drinking. Cowboys aren't averse to 3.2 beer, either, particularly in the company of college girls. My interpretation of free enterprise was to make the most of every opportunity, so I followed the only instruction the Denver brothers gave me: "Get after it."

I knew one of my hardest jobs would be keeping the peace, so to make people feel welcome, I met them at the door and introduced myself. Not only was it good for business, but a lot of times I could spot trouble coming, or head it off before it started.

Ranch hands and college boys tangled over a lot of things, but one thing that surprised me was how little trouble there was between them over the coeds who frequented the place. Most cowboys grow up on ranches in traditional family settings a lot like mine where they're taught to treat their mothers and sisters with respect, and that attitude carries over to their relations with women in general. As a result, if a college boy and a cowboy asked a coed to dance, and she chose the college boy, the cowboy would accept her decision and walk away. One of the reasons cowboys are as popular with women as they are is because they treat them like ladies. (Of course, this is not to say that after closing time the college boy wouldn't find the cowboy waiting for him in the parking lot to discuss the matter further.)

When playing host seemed to work, I started dressing the part in riding boots and jeans, a Western shirt, and a big white Stetson hat. I grew a beard, and before long, when I looked in the mirror, I wouldn't even recognize Mr. Greer of the third grade, much less the director of the governor's budget office. Which suited me fine, of course, because I'd seen all of that guy I wanted to for a while. I went back to being "Jim"; then, because I used to patch up various nicks and bruises for the employees, they started calling me "Doc," a nickname that stayed with me when I started outfitting.

By the middle of summer, I felt well enough established to throw a party. Inviting friends among the customers and people I'd met in the community to the cabin, I served beer, slaw, potato salad, and barbecued beef under the trees. It was one of those classic days: cool breeze, not a cloud in the sky, the river rattling along over the rocks. I set up a keg of beer and played classical music on the stereo. Then after we'd eaten, I brought out the last links with my old life in the city—a handful of silk neckties. When I left Denver, I hadn't been able to make myself throw them away; now, one at a time, I fed them into the fire. I didn't tell anybody why I was doing it, but they understood it was some kind of ceremony, because when they saw me come out the door, they gathered around to watch. I had everything I needed; now I was letting go. What the hell did I want with a necktie in the Gunnison country?

I met the guy who was to be my partner in the outfitting business when he showed up one morning at the Ramble Inn bar. Stu Wagner was operating a rafting service out of a resort farther up the river. With its location between the highway and the river, and its large parking lot, the Ramble offered a perfect place for him to pick up passengers after their ride. We worked out a deal: in return for landing rights on my sandbar, he would steer his customers inside for beer, soft drinks, and sandwiches before busing them back up the river.

We hit it off right away. Wagner was strong and slender, about my age, with steel-gray hair and the chiseled features you see on actors in Western films. He didn't smile much, but when he did, it lit up his whole face. He dressed Western style, and like me wore a Stetson hat cocked on the back of his head, only his was black. One of the few things we didn't agree on was our taste in whiskey: I liked bourbon, Stu preferred scotch.

It turned out that Wagner's rafting business was my stepping stone into outfitting. Rafting is a high cash-flow business, so when tourist season ends there's usually a lot of money burning holes in a rafter's pocket. Most of them head for winter vacations in Mexico or the Bahamas, but it's possible for somebody with a little ambition to convert a rafting license into something less seasonal. A lot of the equipment overlaps with big game hunting, and if a raftsman can wangle a Forest Service permit, with a few more months work and a little luck he can promote his investment into a career.

Not long after Wagner and I worked out our arrangement to use the Ramble's sandbar, he invited me on a float trip down the Gunnison. While we drifted along talking, he operated the oars and I fished. It was a beautiful, golden day. I'd brought beer along, and once in a while we'd land on a gravel bar and watch the water slide by. I hadn't been rafting in years and realized what I'd been missing. Back at the Ramble we sat in the bar and compared our pasts.

Wagner had been born in the Gunnison country, but when he was still in his teens his mother abandoned the family, and his father, unable to support the kids, turned them over to relatives to raise. Stu grew up in Utah with a wealthy Mormon aunt and uncle. Instead of finishing high school, he married, moved to Texas, and over the next twenty years made a lot of money selling farm machinery. All the while he'd dreamed of returning to the valley and making a big splash—the prodigal son returns from exile among the heathen. Only things hadn't worked out, he told me. After selling out in Texas, he'd paid too much for his resort. Now a Middle Eastern oil crisis was driving up prices and ruining the tourist business, and he was in the process of going broke.

He must have been hurting, but you couldn't tell it, especially when he turned on that big, wide smile. He was amazing with animals, and women and children loved him. Nothing seemed to bother him, and when he was around, I always felt like a kid again myself. There was always a sense of adventure, a feeling that something was about to happen, that anything was possible. He was the kind of guy you'd want backing you up in a fight, because you knew he'd be there.

Not long after our fishing trip, Wagner picked me up to go rafting again. Only this time, when we arrived at the bank behind his resort, there was a crowd of customers gathered around three big twelve-man rafts. Since there were two raftsmen in addition to Wagner, I sat down in the last raft and watched while he pushed the others off, expecting him to take the oars. Instead, he flashed that big smile, gave the raft a shove, and called, "See you at the Ramble!"

So there I was with a raftload of people, all of them looking at me like: "Okay, get busy and do something." I'd watched Wagner's technique with the oars on our fishing trip, but I'd never taken a raft down by myself, much less one with a dozen passengers weighing it deep in the water. Now I didn't have much choice, so I grabbed the oars and rowed us out in the channel.

It was disaster all the way. That time of year, the river is shallow, and we hung up on one gravel bar after another. When we ran aground, everyone rocked back and forth while I poled us free with an oar. If that failed, we all piled out and waded, dragging the raft into water deep enough to float it—until we hung up on the next bar. It can take as much as a quarter of a mile to set up for

curves, and I didn't even know where they were. We'd come bar-
reling down the channel, spinning like a top, and the current would
throw us into a whirlpool. When one of those holes undercuts the
bank, it can fill up with brush and tree roots, and if you get in there,
there's no getting out. Women were screaming, little kids cried. I
pulled on the oars, praying they wouldn't break. It was pure luck
somebody wasn't killed.

By the time we got to the Ramble, we were cold and wet and
exhausted. The passengers were ready to kill me, and I was ready
to kill Wagner. But he met us on the bank with that big smile, handing out beer, and I had to laugh—I couldn't help myself. It was a
typical Wagner deal.

While Stu was trying to keep his resort from going under, his
son, Bill, was managing a little ranch on Dry Creek for some Texans. Stu had set him up in the business of taking clients out for trail
rides and overnights into the West Elks. Like his dad, Bill was an
athlete—he'd skied in high school and competed on the pro rodeo
circuit. He planned to outfit that fall, so he'd applied for a license
and a permit area. One morning Stu showed up at the Ramble
with another proposition: he and Bill were planning to round up a
herd of half-wild ranch horses; would I like to go along?

I loved horses, but I hadn't ridden in years. At the ranch we
walked the herd against a corner of the fence, and then with nothing but halters and ropes, we each caught one and mounted. Wagner
whispered: "Move yours up front and head him toward the gate.
We'll ease the rest of them along behind you."

Instead, when I reached the front of the herd, Wagner and Bill
let out a wild *Yahoo!* and the herd stampeded. My horse almost
jumped out from under me. I grabbed his mane and the halter and
clamped him tight with my knees. Ahead of us a shallow wash
crossed the pasture, with banks two or three feet high; beyond it
stood a four-strand barbed wire fence.

Whooping and laughing, Bill and Stu were having a great time,
but I was riding bareback in front of a herd of stampeding horses.
I made it down the near bank, up the far bank to the fence, and got
the horse stopped before we went through, but by that time I had
my knees in his ears.

Again it was typical Wagner, another example of the practical
jokes we played on each other, right up to the end. We called it

"testing the dude" or "leveling the dude." It was supposed to be all in good fun, but sometimes it took a lot of effort, on both sides, to consider it less than serious.

Before long I was pulling a pair of oars and recruiting customers on my own. Finally, when the oil crisis and his debts drove Wagner's resort under, he started operating the rafting business out of a back booth at the Ramble.

By this time I was getting pretty tired of saloon keeping. It was an easy business to build, but hell to run. One problem was that I never knew how far, in good conscience, to push the sale of alcohol. When they hired me, the owners had made it clear that I was to sell as much booze as I could to anybody with the money to buy it. Nevertheless, I didn't want to cross the line of selling a customer too much.

A lot of people didn't take kindly to my cutting them off. One guy, a big roustabout cowboy named Buck, would show up every Friday night and blow his week's paycheck buying drinks for the house. Finally I'd had enough and took his wallet away from him. He was hot. He told me he was going to whip my ass, and I told him he could come back the next day for his wallet and whip my ass then, but tonight he was going home without it. Next day here he comes, looking shamefaced–him and his missus and little girl. The wife was real sweet. She thanked me and said, "You know, Buck's got this problem …"

I told Buck I didn't want to see him in the place again on payday. So he went someplace else, where somebody else took his money. But at least he didn't spend it with me.

I also operated on the theory that saloon keeping is like classroom management: either you're in charge or you're not. I'd done some fighting as a kid (the usual schoolyard stuff at recess, or after school on the streets), so I thought I could handle myself. Besides, I figured that because I looked like a nice, harmless, middle-aged gent, the students and cowboys would cut me some slack and show me a little mercy, if not respect. So, on the theory that I wouldn't ask somebody to do something I wouldn't do myself, I decided instead of hiring a bouncer, I would keep order myself. Sometimes it worked, too. I'd hear a couple of kids talking, ragging each other, ready to fight, and then one would say: "I'd whip your ass, but that old fucker at the door would jail my ass."

One thing I didn't know at the time, though, was that the Ramble Inn's long-standing nickname was the "rumble in," and that it was well deserved. The tipoff came when I was putting up posters on campus to advertise the bucking machine. I met an old friend, a guy from my home town, who worked at the college. When he asked if the football team had been out yet for a visit, I told him no, and he grinned and said, "They will be."

When they showed up—five carloads full—I was waiting at the door with my white Stetson clamped on extra tight. I pointed to a sign which read: "Doc says: 'If you fight in here, you don't pass go, you don't collect $200, you go directly to jail.'"

"This is my place," I told the biggest lineman in the front rank. "It's not your place. And that sign means just what it says."

"Yes, sir," the lineman said. "We'll be good. This is the last place left in town where we can drink."

And they were good, too—at least most of them were, most of the time—especially after I threatened to tell the coach if they gave me any trouble. When they weren't good, I referred them to the parking lot to get better acquainted. I even experimented with a little social engineering. At the time it was popular among both football players and cowboys to cut the ponytails off some of the rope-haired hippies we had running around. Hippies were the common enemy, and they looked to me for protection. Sometimes I'd have three or four following me around everywhere I went, even into the men's room.

More often than not my program for keeping the peace worked, but when things got out of hand, they could become frightening. One afternoon a guy came in high on something—angel dust and beer, the cops said later—and got rowdy. When I told him to leave, he gave me a strange look and marched out to his car. I figured that was the end of it, but a couple of minutes later I saw him coming back and met him at the door. All I saw were those absolutely empty eyes as he blasted me in the head with a quart bottle of beer. I didn't even see it coming.

My hat absorbed some of the shock, but the beer blinded me, and to keep the guy from using the broken bottle on my face, I took him to the floor. I was fighting for my life. I couldn't believe how strong he was—it was like the stories you used to hear about guys high on drugs acquiring superhuman strength.

We rolled over and over, punching, until I got on top and smothered his fists with my arms. The bartender was a football player, a big linebacker I hoped might be of some use in a fight. He and a couple of guys piled on, trying to help, but all they did was pin my arms to my sides so I couldn't move. And with the floor for leverage, the guy punched up at me so hard I almost passed out.

They finally dragged him off, but next day when I dressed for work, I was black-and-blue from collarbone to groin. When I walked into the Ramble, the bartender was on a ladder picking pieces of broken bottle from the ceiling tile.

Another time, while the local rodeo, Cattlemen's Days, was in progress, two cowboys, one a local and the other a friend visiting from Wyoming, threw beer in a woman's face. I ordered them out, but they went off to drink at another bar and then came back. I told them to get out, but this time they weren't about to leave. The local guy grabbed me while his friend started throwing punches.

This time the bartender was one of my rehabilitation projects, a guy I'd vouched for to get him out of jail after he'd been charged with drunk-and-disorderly. He jumped the bar carrying a baseball bat and delivered a home-run cut to the Wyoming cowboy's head. I never saw anything like it. The cowboy went down, the side of his face blowing up like a balloon. But instead of staying down, he just grinned, shook his head, and got up. When I saw that, I thought: "Oh, shit. Now I *am* in trouble."

My bartender vaulted back over the bar and the cowboys stretched me across a pool table. While one held me, the other one tried to smash my face with a pool cue. I kept fighting, but every blow shattered table slate beside my head. The bartender phoned 911, but the sheriff, operating on the Western theory that people fighting in bars should settle matters themselves, said he wouldn't come. Only if shots are fired would he take a hand, he told the bartender.

By now the cracks of the pool cue on the table sounded like small-arms fire, and when the bartender yelled, "Yeah, yeah, they're shooting!" the sheriff dispatched help. Before it arrived, though, the local cowboy broke the pool cue across my back, rupturing a kidney and tearing the ligaments. Finally, when the hospital orderlies carried me out to the ambulance on a stretcher, the parking lot was full of law. The sheriff had even called the highway patrol. I spent the night in the hospital and the next month barely able to walk.

Later, I heard one of my competitors downtown had paid the cowboys to rough me up. I guess I should have expected it, but I hadn't. I was naive enough to think that free enterprise meant everybody was in competition with everybody else, and the winner was the guy who put the most time and talent and energy into his business. Obviously that wasn't how it worked. What I was doing at the Ramble had created too much competition for this guy, so if he couldn't beat me in the marketplace, he'd beat me some other way.

My days as manager at the Ramble ended when the three owners showed up to question me about the profits—or what they considered to be the lack of profits—I'd been reporting. They had talked to a Coors distributor in Denver, and he'd told them how many cups of beer are available, at least in theory, from a keg of beer. They decided I must be holding out on them. Of course, what they didn't understand was that I wasn't selling beer by the cup, I was selling it by the mug and the pitcher and keg, so their arithmetic didn't work.

When they came in, I asked if there was a problem. No, they said, no problem; they just wanted to see the books. So I brought the books to a booth and sat down, ready to answer questions. They looked at them for a few minutes, then said they wanted to take them back to Denver to study. I told them not a chance, there was no way that was going to happen, because I was the book-*keeper*, and that meant I *kept* the books. I told them the books were what I figured taxes on at the end of the year, and if anything happened to them while they were out of my possession—if they had been doctored or something—then I was responsible. I said, "Okay, you can take the books, but they're not my books anymore, they're your books. And I don't work for you anymore; you're on your own."

We really had it out. "Hell," I told them, "you know I just quit a job where I handled millions, and I never touched a fucking dime. And you come in here and accuse me of skimming what? A lousy thirty-five dollars a month? Jesus Christ, talk sense."

The last time I was accused of stealing something—the only time I ever stole anything—was in Morrison, which was so small you couldn't fart in church without everybody in the congregation knowing what you'd had for dinner. I was a little kid, maybe nine or ten years old. I was in the drugstore with some other kids and saw a candy bar I wanted, and I put it in my pocket. Ben Snyder, the druggist, saw me do it and told my dad. I spent the next six months cleaning the drugstore after school, and my dad introduced me to everybody he knew as "my son the thief."

The first time it was true, but that was the last time.

By now it was nearly fall. Before long, the college would be in session, and the war between the football players and cowboys and hippies would start over again. Insurance rates for the mechanical bull were going up, and the bands I had hired in the spring wanted more to play a gig than just a share of the gate. Besides, the country music my customers liked was getting on my nerves, and late one night I learned I could clear the bar by playing classical music.

I found out by accident. It had been a hard day, and I was cleaning the pipes from the draft beer kegs. To soothe my nerves, I put on a Beethoven symphony, and when I turned around, the place was empty. After that I started doing it on purpose. Any kind of classical music will run cowboys and college kids out of a bar, but Brahms, Beethoven, and Bach never miss.

Even before the Ramble's owners showed up, I was training the staff to operate without me. I thought maybe I could manage the place on a part-time basis while I tried something else. I didn't know what it would be—anything, I figured, just as long as it wasn't saloon keeping. That summer Bill Wagner, Stu's son, discovered he couldn't stand working with dudes and gave up the idea of outfitting. That left Stu with some horses and equipment that he could either sell at a loss or, in partnership with me, use to turn a profit. So outfitting wasn't something either one of us planned, it just sort of happened.

Looking back, I realized I'd been tap-dancing around the outfitting business all summer, and suddenly it seemed like the most natural thing in the world. Saloon-keeping had been a bust, and I knew my midlife retirement wouldn't last forever. Someday I'd have to go back to the real world—but until then, I couldn't think of anything I'd rather do. I knew I wouldn't make much money outfitting, but I couldn't think of anything where I'd have more fun.

# 2

## 𝒯he 𝒲alking 𝒲rangler

I WAS RAISED IN A TRADITIONAL FAMILY, with all the gains and losses that implies. It was the kind of family sociologists refer to as a "nuclear family," with live-at-home father and mother and kids, surrounded by a constellation of grandparents, aunts and uncles, and cousins. The various members may not get along with one another, or even like each other, but they're always in contact, and if something goes wrong, help is available. In spite of what feminists claim, it's probably the most primitive social arrangement in the world, and goes back at least as far as the cavemen. To my knowledge, among the Greers it had been operating since the family emigrated from Scotland in the eighteenth century and worked its way west through Ohio to Kansas, and eventually to Colorado.

Our home base was Morrison, a small town in the mountains west of Denver. In the 1940s, following World War II, the Rocky Mountain West was still recovering from the effects of the Great Depression, and the traditional division of labor still applied. Men and boys worked outdoors, hunting and fishing to supplement the family income. Game was plentiful and poaching was common—and as long as it was a matter of feeding your family, game wardens looked the other way. Women and girls kept house and raised chickens and rabbits, milked cows, and tended gardens.

The Greers were a patriarchal tribe. My dad was a contractor, and we followed him up and down the Rocky Mountains as his work took him from one construction site to another. Subject to negotiation—and there was not much of that—his word was the law we lived by. He was a stern disciplinarian who took no chance of spoiling the child by sparing the rod. If we were whipped at school, we would be whipped again at home that night to make sure the fault was sufficiently punished. My dad was an officer in the union who voted a straight Republican ticket most of his life, but worshipped the memory of Franklin Roosevelt. In spite of his ardent Republicanism, though, he was so effective in his conduct of union business that at one time (during the ascendancy of Joe McCarthy) he was accused of being a Communist.

My dad was also the breadwinner in the family. The rest of us, according to age, necessity, and ability, contributed our share to the common good. My mother was a country girl who never had a job outside the home. A wonderful fisherman and horseback rider, she never had a driver's license or wrote a check in her life. On Monday morning, my dad gave her money for the week's groceries, in cash, and it was up to her to make the most of it. If she didn't, or Dad thought she didn't, there was hell to pay. The children—my older sister, my younger brother and sister, and I—learned it was better to be seen rather than heard around the house, and usually better not to be seen at all.

Primarily defensive in nature, the nuclear family resembles a tribal unit gathered around a campfire, with spears pointed out toward the darkness. Its greatest strength lies in the protection it offers its members from the larger world, but it's less effective in responding to problems from within. And though it may be the ideal arrangement for ensuring the nurture and survival of children, it doesn't do much to provide for anything so esoteric as the happiness or self-fulfillment of its members.

By any reasonable standard, my parents were decent, hardworking people who were so profoundly incompatible that they had no business marrying in the first place. But the ethic that prevailed in those days—till death do us part, even if it kills us—required people to practice more persistence than was good for them. You stayed together for the sake of the children and a promise you'd made to God, no matter what the cost.

My parents' relationship eventually became so destructive that one summer when I came home from college, I found my mother incoherent, barely able to function. Years of fighting with my dad had driven her to a nervous breakdown. Yet her condition was of such long standing that people around her hadn't known anything was wrong; they thought she was suffering from premature senility and nothing could be done about it. I got her admitted to the state hospital, and when they released her, she was fine. But at a family meeting, we decided they had to stop living together.

After that, I swore to myself I'd never get trapped in a dead-end marriage like theirs, and I never did. But when you break the rules, there's a price to be paid, and by the time I left Denver, I was convinced that I was a failure and that my life was an irredeemable mess. I'd hurt and disappointed too many people, including myself. Managing the Ramble had helped revive my self-esteem, but it hadn't really solved the problem. Now, as an outfitter, I hoped I could get things straightened out.

Have you heard of poets or musicians who believe that it's their lives, rather than their works of art, that are their finest creations? That their poetry or music simply provides them with the means to focus on their real art, themselves? I know that in school, when I first ran across the idea, it seemed strange, but while I was outfitting, that's how I felt about myself. It had never happened to me before, and it hasn't happened since, but when I was outfitting I believed I was creating something–I felt like I was an artist, and every day my life was a play, or a scene from a play, that I was inventing as I went along. It was like being Lee J. Cobb on Broadway in *Death of a Salesman*. I was the hero, Willie Loman, and the people I met were the other characters. All of us were acting a story with a beginning, a middle, and an end, and every performance required a new interpretation.

The theme of the play was education. The high country runs a hard school, and if you're going to survive up there, you avoid making mistakes. It only takes one time for a lesson to get imprinted on your mind, and you pay such a high price for doing something wrong–you suffer so much–that the learning curve is steep. Or, as they used to tell us in education classes when they talked about motivation, the learning is "accelerated." You don't use white gas inside a tent to get wet wood started—or if you do and live to tell the tale, you don't do it again. You don't put horses out on grass and let them eat their fill. A full horse gets frisky, and even with hobbles, they'll take off on you, and it can be a long walk back to the corral.

Every year I got better at composing my play. The acts became smoother, more natural, better "written," if that makes sense. Every day I learned something new about my role and got deeper into my part. That's why, when the business shut down for the winter, it was hard for me to stop. I felt like I was putting my play on hold, that I was stepping out of character until spring came around and I could perform again.

That first year, when we didn't start until late summer, the experience felt unnatural. Act I should have taken place in March and April. That's when outfitters hit the road to sell their services at national sports shows. Some years, when I could afford it, I loaded a van with food and extra clothes, a portable booth with boxes of brochures and a videotape setup, and followed a route from Chicago to Phoenix, two thousand miles, with stops in major cities along the way. Riding the circuit isn't outfitting—it's more an actor's exercise, a kind of warmup for the acts to follow—but at least you're in character. I always thought of it as something like the old vaudeville companies and circuses blowing into town and handing out playbills and putting up posters.

In my day, Act II was bear season and took place in April and May. Today, a change in Colorado law has eliminated the spring hunt, but in those days, as soon as roads and trails into the high country opened, outfitters started taking clients up after bear. Bears are strange, elusive animals—you almost never walk onto one in the mountains—so they're hunted with dogs, or else baited with garbage (the worse-smelling the better) to bring them in front of a blind. There, hunters photograph them or kill them with some kind of weapon—anything from a bow and arrow to a high-powered rifle.

Summer was Act III. This was my favorite part of the play, not only because of the season, but because I got to play teacher again. City people would show up with their kids and everything we did turned into an educational experience. I always said I guided for bears in the spring and elk in the fall, and for wildflowers in the summer. We hiked and rode horseback, we rafted the rivers and fished streams or high mountain lakes. By the time summer was over, though, I was usually glad to get away from playing babysitter, guidance counselor, and family physician all rolled into one.

Act IV was big game season. Colorado still has a fall bear season, but I was always too busy with other game animals–deer and elk, antelope, mountain lion, bighorn sheep–to do much with them. Act IV is the most physically demanding as well as the most dangerous act in outfitting. It's also the most profitable; outfitters generally earn up to 80 percent of their incomes in the fall. They also play what is probably the essence of their role as outdoorsmen, so if they start to resemble frontiersmen like John Coulter or Davy Crockett, or Liver-Eating Johnson, clients shouldn't be surprised.

My own favorite model was the kind of white hunter Ernest Hemingway wrote about in his African stories. So many of the men I got along with–men I liked, and who liked me–had read him, that sooner or later his name came up in conversations. I guess that today Hemingway's reputation isn't very good. Literary friends tell me he's not politically correct, and that a lot of people object to the independent, masculine code he promoted. There was a neurotic side to his personality that might get him locked up today, but he said things about how to live and about values that are important. At least I know they were important to me when I was outfitting, and I still respect them today.

To the extent that there's an Act V in the drama of outfitting, it takes place during winter, when the weather shuts you down. Then it's time to hustle the groceries and figure out ways to survive. Clients go home, snow closes the trails, and you have to live by your wits. It's a real change of pace for a guy who's spent the last six months playing the great white hunter for a bunch of admiring dudes.

Some years I found a job where I could use my pre-outfitter skills, some years I didn't. One winter I managed the food service concession at a ski area; another winter I wrote copy and took photographs for a county shoppers' guide, then sold advertising door-to-door. Most years I took whatever I could find, which meant frying hamburgers, swamping restaurant kitchens, tending bar, driving a tow truck, starting frozen diesel buses at below-zero temperatures, selling firewood, working as a ranch hand. Some years I held down two or three jobs, hustling from one to the other. Sometimes I was unemployed, and the temptation to resort to food stamps was almost irresistible. Instead, I tightened my belt until bear season began in the spring.

Our first year in business, Stu Wagner and I didn't understand any of this. Stu was a pragmatist and figured on learning whatever we needed to know by the seat of his pants. I was more cautious and tried to find out as much as possible from people who were already in the business. Not that I had much luck. Outfitters are a close-mouthed, competitive bunch; with a few exceptions, not many of them are willing to give a new guy a break. There are a lot of prima donnas in the woods, and I suppose it's good for the ego if you can make it when the other guy can't.

I also searched the local libraries and read everything I could find about guiding and outfitting. In the West, the business started toward the end of the nineteenth century as a spinoff from ranching. What happened was that as the country was settled, people from cities appeared looking for someone to show them the sights and where to hunt and fish. Ranchers discovered that after the hay was cut and their cattle were down from the high country, they could lead hunters and fishermen back into the mountains after wild game. Sometimes these hunting parties carried camping gear and slept and cooked in line cabins or tents, or on open ground; sometimes they returned to the ranch at night to eat in the kitchen and sleep in the bunkhouse.

Those early rancher-outfitters were pretty successful. Game was so abundant that (at least according to the ranchers) it threatened the survival of their herds. Ranchers insisted on exclusive use of the land, and state and federal governments gave it to them. Regulations protecting game were nonexistent. High-powered repeating rifles that had been developed during the Civil War were used against wildlife in the post-war era. The near-extermination of the Great Plains bison is simply the best known of these slaughters, but it had its counterparts among other species, too. By the turn of the century, deer, elk, antelope, and bighorn sheep, as well as predators like wolves, grizzlies, and mountain lions, had pretty well been eliminated all over the West. In libraries of some of the old ranching families, you can see photographs of hunters lined up behind rows of animals laid out like the aftermath of some royal European game preserve hunt. Even more destructive were the market hunters, the guys who made their living killing game by the wagonload to feed crews laying railroad track and working the mines.

Ranch-based outfitters are still in business today, but a more common arrangement, at least for many full-time professionals, is to work through a dude ranch or resort. Typically, outfitters have exclusive recreation rights to the resort's customers, as well as the use of the stables and corrals and bunkhouses. In return, the outfitter pays the resort a flat rate, normally about 20 percent of his take; everything else is profit.

A lot of the trouble Stu and I had that first year was due to our location. We set up headquarters at the Dry Creek Ranch managed by Bill Wagner. The ranch was located about twenty miles from town, backed up against the National Forest, and so isolated that people had trouble finding us. It was a small place, so we were always short of corrals and work space and beds to sleep clients. And because Bill was leasing the property from some people in Texas, we were guests and never felt really comfortable there.

Another problem was our lack of capital. Stu had the horses and camping equipment his son had been using for pack trips, but after the bankruptcy, his credit rating was worthless. I was better fixed, but not by much. I'd saved some of my salary from the Ramble, but the most important thing we had going for us was a credit rating I'd been building for the last twenty years. Against it, we were able to borrow enough money to buy the supplies and equipment, and lease the stock, that got us through that first year.

Stu and I enjoyed planning the business. We were like adolescent boys figuring out how to seduce girls—arguing about what appeals to make, how much to promise, what to spend and where we could save. Both of us had hunted and fished all our lives, but neither of us had ever been on a guided hunt. Relying on anecdotes heard in bars, stories we'd read in books, and our imaginations, we pretty much invented the business for ourselves.

After studying the other outfitters in the basin, we decided there was a niche in the market. At the time, most of them were relying on volume and offering cheap deer and elk hunts to Joe Blow from the factory. We decided that, because our competitors were blue-collar guys themselves, they were afraid to deal with wealthy clients—afraid they couldn't measure up. We believed that instead of selling 100 trips for $300, we could sell 30 trips for $1,000. Either way, the overhead was the same, and so was the profit.

We called ourselves "Executive Expeditions, Unlimited" and gave our address as "Suite #1, Trophy Island." We chose the term "executive" to warn blue-collar hunters that our service was different: not only was it going to be the best, it was going to be expensive. We were after high-dollar guys who were used to being treated well and who demanded first-class service.

As it turned out, we discovered that people with money were easy to deal with because they weren't afraid to pay, sometimes extravagantly, for the best service available. I always felt sorry for the poor joker who dreams of hunting in Africa, who saves all his life to go there, and then the experience is ruined for him because it rains. Rich people know things aren't perfect all the time, no matter how much you want them to be or how much they cost. They realize you've just got to hunker down and make the best of it.

That first summer, Stu and I started sorting out our individual responsibilities. He preferred to run the business end down at the ranch, so I took the high country side. That meant I had to learn what was up there, so at night I read books on local geology and studied USGS maps spread out on the floor. I talked to outdoor professionals—people who worked for the Forest Service, or the Park Service, or the Bureau of Land Management—and questioned ranchers and local hunters and fishermen. And every chance I got, I'd pull a horse out of the string and go off exploring.

In unfamiliar country, I kept track of where I was on a topographic map, but I never used the map to find my way. Instead, I tried to trust my instincts and sharpen my wits by watching for landmarks—a shiny rock face, a dead tree, a mountain peak. Often I'd stop and turn around and look back the way I'd come, because things are always different when you look at them from the reverse angle.

I also learned a lot about the basics of packing. My first solo effort—a trip up the Butterworth Trail to establish a fishing camp on

Diamond Creek—was a disaster. Because I'd never been in the Diamond Creek country, I couldn't make heads or tails out of the topo map. When I asked Wagner for directions, he wasn't much help, either. "Nothing to it," he told me. "You pass two lakes and turn left. You can't miss it."

For the occasion, I wore my Ramble Inn costume—jeans and white Stetson, a pair of cheap cowboy boots and a dime-store bandanna. I was riding a horse I'd just bought—a black gelding I named Morgan after the breed and the pirate—and leading a mule named Henry and two burros, Juan and his sister Two. It was my first time out alone, so I was happy and excited when I led my string away from the trailhead. What I didn't realize was that this was a deal that wouldn't work. Horses and mules and burros don't mix: they have different personalities, different leg lengths, different gaits. Plus they don't like each other, and when things go wrong, that shows up.

I didn't know much about packing, either, so a couple of miles up the trail, my outfit began falling apart. An unbalanced pack on the last burro, Two, slipped, and when she started fighting it, I ran back to boost it into place. Only while I was gone, my new horse started up the trail, taking Henry and Juan with him. I yelled, but Morgan didn't stop, and I got that sense of panic you feel when things are spiraling out of control.

Securing the pack, I jogged up the trail in my cowboy boots, towing Two. But before I could catch up with Morgan, Henry stopped, brayed a couple of times, and rolled over, smashing everything in his pack.

When you're around a guy who's good with stock, who works on a daily basis with cattle and horses, it looks easy. He's never in a hurry. He doesn't walk, he glides, and his hands are so slow and controlled he looks like he's working underwater. Watch a roper coming out of a chute at a rodeo; he's in a hurry, but it doesn't show, he's as smooth as glass. With a pro, it's not just large animals he treats that way. Watch the same guy cross a chicken yard: he won't raise a cluck.

I was pretty green when it came to dealing with animals, especially mismatched animals—reaching and grabbing, jerking on bridles, spooking the stock. Finally, though, I got them rounded up and in line. Then, what I should have done—what I learned to do later—was stop, unload, and repack everything, and get it right. Instead, I just kind of half-assed things together and went on, hoping for the best.

My string held for about an hour before trouble started again. This time we were crossing a wide talus slope when Henry's pack slipped. He started kicking, braying like a banshee. Because the trail was narrow, and the mountain side was too steep for me to dismount to the left, I stepped off Morgan on the right—the wrong-side. Only Morgan's not having anything to do with that shit. If I don't know how to get off him, he's not going to stick around while I figure it out. He walks right out from under me and leaves me flat on my ass.

Horses hate mules—I didn't know that, then—and Morgan trots off up the trail; he can't wait to get away from there. And the burros are fighting, trying to escape—they don't want anything to do with that bucking mule. So there I am, five hours on the trail and I haven't hardly started. I've still got ten miles to go, I don't know where I'm going, and I'm totally wiped out.

Finally, I just walked away—up the trail into a stand of aspen—and left the animals fighting their packs and each other. I was feeling so sorry for myself that when I found a log, I sat down and cried, I couldn't help myself. Tears were running down my cheeks; I was crying so hard I had trouble breathing. I'd run out on everything that's supposed to mean anything—wives, kids, job, security. I'm up to my ass in debt. I'm lost, I'm hungry, I'm beat, and my feet are killing me. This is what my life's come to, I thought.

I don't know how long I sat there—it seemed like quite a while—but finally I decided I had two choices: I could shoot the stock and forget about becoming an outfitter, or I could go back and fix things right. One at a time, I led Morgan, Henry, and the burros up the trail to the log, tied them, unloaded everything, repacked, got them in-string, and started out again.

It was late that night when I reached what I thought was the fishcamp site. Needless to say, the lakes Stu mentioned had been there; the problem was that there'd been half a dozen others, just as big and just as wet, so I never knew when to turn left. By now I was too tired to build a fire or eat, so I bedded down the stock and went to sleep. Next morning, when I looked around, I had to laugh: as near as I could figure, I was still about five miles from the fishcamp, staked out on some little piss-ant creek in the middle of nowhere. But it looked good to me—or as we used to say at the capitol, it was close enough for government work.

I always considered that trip a watershed in the business for me. I knew I'd never have a worse day ... and I never did.

There were other bad days that first season, though. At least four different times the horses beat me back home. In fact, it got so bad that they started keeping book on me down at the resort. They had a tote board by the desk and would take bets on whether I'd lose all the stock or just some of it, and how far after them I'd be. After a while, they got to calling me "the walking wrangler," and at times it was embarrassing. I'd meet a guy downtown in the bakery—somebody I didn't even know—and he'd say: "Heard your horses come in without you again. What seems to be the problem?"

But I was learning. After that first trip, I kept a pair of tennis shoes in my saddle bags—and I used them, too. I wasn't about to go chasing loose stock in cowboy boots again, not if I could help it.

The next year I got smart, because I was bitten by the pickle bucket syndrome. What I'm talking about is your standard white plastic, five-gallon pickle bucket with extruded handles and lipped lid. Pickle buckets are the greatest packing boon known to man. They can hold anything, liquid or solid, from grain to groceries. Light and strong, they're just about indestructible, and bend without breaking or leaking. Bear-proof, they can be hung in trees with food inside or used as dishpans or washbasins. You can carry water from a stream in them. Upside down, they make comfortable chairs around a campfire at night. With duct tape sealing the lid and a lump of dry ice inside for company, they will keep a ham or thirty-pound roast frozen for days. Filled with cold spring water, they work better than alarm clocks for getting hung-over wranglers out of bed in the morning. During electrical storms, they make wonderful insulators. I've crouched inside a rain-battered tent and ridden out many a storm on the hurricane deck of a pickle bucket. But the best thing about pickle buckets is that they are just the right size to fit inside a pannier, especially if you tailor your panniers to their dimensions, as I started doing.

That first year, though, when I carried supplies in cardboard boxes, things were always a mess. When you cinched a load tight enough to ride, you wrecked the contents. Bread came out squashed, the eggs were broken. The worst thing was that if you carried whiskey you might hear the most terrible sound known to packing: *glug, glug, glug.* There's nothing else that sounds quite like whiskey running out on the trail after a mule sidesteps into a tree.

Pickle buckets also make it possible to pack whole eggs, nested individually in grain, into camp. Most packers simply break eggs into quart jars and serve them scrambled. That works, but there's something classy about cracking an egg with your thumb and dropping it into a skillet of hot grease. It shows the clients what kind of packer you are. I'll tell you the truth: I never could understand how Jim Bridger made it to the Yellowstone without a pickle bucket.

What I did the second year was build two-pickle-bucket panniers for the horses and three-pickle-bucket panniers for the mules. Then I'd use a packer's scale to get the loads exactly right, because even a pound can make a difference. A load starts slipping, and before long you've got an animal fighting his pack and dragging half the string with him. After a while, you learn where the long straightaways are on the trails, and when you come to the head of one, you look back down that row of "X's" formed by the cross bucks of the pack saddles. Maybe you see one cocked out of line. What's pure heaven is if you've got a good wrangler back there, some kid that's sharp, and you hold up four fingers, and he understands what you mean. If he's flexible, he can ride alongside that number four mule, scoop up a rock from beside the trail, drop it in the pack, and the whole string never slows down.

Another lesson I learned that first year was that Wagner's judgment was not to be trusted, particularly concerning distances or difficulties that might be encountered on the trail. Late in the summer, I brought a party of fishermen out of Diamond Creek to find he'd signed a family for a trail ride through the West Elk Wilderness Area. The plan was for Stu to drop us off at the head of Castle Creek and pick us up five days later on the Rainbow Lake road. I'd never been in the West Elks, but Wagner claimed to know the country well. "Don't worry about it," he said. "A blind man could find his way through there."

So, not having any better sense I let him talk me into it. What I got into was a regular rabbit warren. We had to cross three mountain passes, all of them over 11,000 feet high. Two years out of three they're closed all year around. I had a family of five with me—daddy, mamma, two boys, and a girl. We're doing a progressive camp, where you ride all day and set up a different camp every night. We're covering a big circle, crossing those passes—only when we get close enough, I look through my field glasses and they're twenty feet deep in snow. At night I put the clients to bed and get out my maps. As near as I can figure, I can't get to the pickup point on time without a steam shovel.

Another problem was the older boy. He was about ten or eleven, a bright-eyed, button-nosed little kid, the kind who watches every move you make. He figures you're running some kind of scam. He doesn't know what it is, but he's going to figure it out, and he's second-guessing me all the way: "Yesterday you said the horse's name was Smokey." By now I'm starting to sweat.

About noon on the fourth day, the boy yelled: "Are you lost?"

"Naw," I told him, but he insisted I was. "Yes, you are; yes, you are!" he yelled. "I threw that Baby Ruth candy bar wrapper away three days ago!"

Now what do I do? The only thing I could think of was to bluff my way out. "Well, shame on you," I told him. "How many times do I have to tell you about throwing trash around this country?" And I made him pick it up and put it in his pocket. There I am, chewing him out for littering, but I'm lost as shit and I figure they're beginning to see through me.

To distract them, I clamped my Stetson on the boy's head and moved him to the front of the line to guide the rest of the day. The next day, to my relief, we bushwhacked over a ridge and dropped down onto what I hoped was the Rainbow Lake road. Instead, it was the Beaver Creek road, five miles—most of them vertical—to the east. With no sign of Wagner, the family was getting nervous, so I figured I'd lay this on him. "Something's broke down," I told them, "and Stu's having trouble fixing it."

We camped that night, about out of food, and the next morning—the sixth day of a five-day pack trip—I left the clients resting and rode out to the highway. I planned to hitchhike to the nearest phone and tell Wagner where we were. It was about noon when I reached the blacktop and started flagging down vehicles, and who do I see? It's Wagner in the stock truck, driving along without a care in the world. He's got the days wrong—he thinks this is the fifth day and he's right on time. "What are you doing on the Beaver Creek road?" he asks me. Instead of telling him what happened, I said: "This looked like a better way out."

"Well, you should be more careful," he said. "You could get into serious trouble not following directions."

That was another turning point for me. From then on, not for time or distance or location did I trust him.

Another mistake I learned not to make was trusting clients to show any sense concerning the dangers posed by the wilderness. At first I was overwhelmed by the idea of my personal responsibility for the health and safety of so many people. A lot of times we were at least a day's travel from medical help. I remember late that first summer I had three Houston neurosurgeons with me at the trailhead. I was ready to take them fifteen miles into the wilderness to go fishing when it occurred to me what their combined earning power was over the next twenty years or so. "What if a horse stepped on one of their hands?" I thought. I had maybe $350,000 worth of insurance at the time and I was nervous. If one of them got hurt, I figured I'd have to massacre and bury the whole bunch.

The answer, I decided, was education. I put together a safety lecture to explain the dangers they faced and what to do if something went wrong. Then I tried to make a game of it by suggesting things that might go wrong, including situations in which something happened to me. Children, I learned, were more likely to pay attention than their parents. "How would you get out of here if you had to?" I'd ask them. "How did we get in here? What would you do if you couldn't find your way back to camp?"

I also put together an emergency kit containing fire-starting equipment, a map and compass, granola bars, a space blanket, and a mirror and whistle they could use to signal their locations. But no amount of education, I discovered, could prevent some people from making serious mistakes.

Early that first fall, I packed half a dozen big-city guys into Diamond Creek to fish and hunt blue grouse. Setting up tents at the fishcamp, we followed a broad, plainly marked trail about three miles into a wide meadow surrounded by timber. In the morning we hunted grouse around the edge, jump-shooting them out of sagebrush and deadfalls, then returned to camp for lunch.

That afternoon, three of them decided they preferred to fish the creek. The other three voted to take another crack at the grouse, so I had to decide which way I would go. The creek was rough, broken up into all kinds of channels; there's down-timber and willows. I'd never seen these guys fish, but I'd seen them hunt and they seemed to know how. The trail was a highway and they'd spent most of the morning in the meadow. So I stayed with the fishermen, warned the grouse hunters again about being careful, and sent them on their way.

The hunters tied their horses at the south end of the meadow and broke rule number one. Because it was a warm, sunny day, they left their hats, sweaters, and jackets, and the emergency kits slung from the saddle horns. Circling the timber at the west side of the meadow, they broke rule number two ("Stay together") when two of them, moving faster, left their companion, a dentist from Kansas, behind. While they continued around the meadow, the dentist saw a grouse, pursued it into timber to the west, shot it, then shot another grouse still deeper in the woods.

By now clouds obscured the sun, and without a map or compass, the dentist had no idea how to rejoin his friends. So then he broke rules number three and four: three, "If you're lost, always walk downhill"; four, "Never, under any circumstances, walk uphill."

Those are pretty good rules. Water runs downhill. If you go downhill long enough, you'll find a stream where you can get a drink and follow it down to a trail or a road. If you go uphill, you're looking for trouble.

The dentist, confused about directions, climbed the ridge and saw a meadow. As it happened, it was a different meadow, longer and narrower, with timber blocking both ends, but it looked good to him. Meanwhile, his friends finished their hunt, waited a while, and then rode back to camp. Unsaddling their horses, they turned their birds over to the camp boy to clean and went to their tents to take naps. As a result, I added a rule five that had never occurred to me before: "Always tell Jim if something goes wrong."

A short time later, I brought the fishermen into camp. By now the wind was blowing and the air was getting colder. Before starting dinner, I followed what was to become standard camp practice: counting heads. When I came up one short, I realized there was trouble.

"Where's your friend?" I asked the grouse hunters.

He hadn't come in yet, they told me, but he was all right. They'd left his horse for him tied at the edge of the meadow.

By now a rainstorm's coming in big-time. This guy is up there lost without a coat or hat, without his pack, wearing a T-shirt. The wind's blowing, the temperature is dropping fast—it's going to be thirty degrees in another hour or so, and these dumb city dudes are telling me their friend is all right.

I threw a saddle on Morgan and spurred him up the trail to the meadow. The dentist's horse was right where they said he would be. Collecting the abandoned jacket and pack, I followed the line of timber around the west side of the meadow. Occasionally I fired a shot with my pistol and stopped to listen, but most of the time I blew a police whistle. A whistle doesn't carry as far as a pistol in the woods. Stu and I tried it, and forty yards is about as far as a whistle goes. Less than that in a wind. You can hear a .357 over a hundred yards, but ammo's expensive—plus a horse is liable to buck your ass off if he decides you've startled him.

When I reached the south end of the meadow, I stopped to figure this out. These guys had done everything wrong I'd told them to do, so I wondered if they wouldn't do everything wrong I *hadn't* told them to do. I thought: "If I had no sense at all, what is the *last* thing I would do?" And I was right. I rode over the ridge to the west, and there was the dentist wandering around in the wrong meadow, scared to death. The first thing I saw was his white face in the dark. He was so scared he'd even started to think. He was still carrying those two birds, but he told me he was about to throw them away—"so the lions and bears wouldn't eat him." And he'd emptied his shotgun into a pile of twigs a couple of times, trying to start a fire. All he did was blow his kindling to hell, but he was trying.

By now it was dark, raining hard, with lightning and thunder crashing among the peaks. So with the dentist nibbling granola bars and hanging on my back, we rode over the ridge, picked up his horse, and headed down the trail nobody could miss to camp.

I know I shouldn't be too hard on the clients. They just had no concept of what this country can do to you. But that first year,

I had no idea how little they appreciated that fact. After that, before I turned anyone loose, I really gave them a lecture. "Set your ass down—by water—in the open, where I can see you. Build a fire. I'll find you," I told them. "I'll stay out all night, if I have to. I lose points if I don't find you. Hell, if I lose too many of you, they'll take away my license."

That usually got a laugh, but I wasn't kidding.

Another mistake I learned not to make was to trust a client's assurances that he knew the way around country that Stu and I didn't know. "No problem getting in there," they would tell you. So you'd try it, and it was worth your life to get back out. I tried to take a dude into some lakes off Razor Cliffs, and I never did find the lakes. He told me that he'd been in there twenty years ago, as a young man, and that it was an easy trip. We were into bogs and down-timber. I thought I was going to lose the horses. In three hours we made a quarter of a mile, and the guy was pissed at me the whole time, like it was my fault. That was the last time I did that.

We also learned not to use drop camps—camps where you leave a party of clients who've packed their own gear, then come back to pick them up later. Dudes have no idea what or how much they need. We finally learned to tell them that, for the same price, we would do it all. It's a lot easier and cheaper to outfit completely than it is to have to go in later and bail them out.

The only clients who caused more trouble than dentists were doctors, and I'm not sure why. Maybe doctors make more money than is good for them and it addles their brains; or maybe, because doctors are good at something important, they imagine they're good at everything. Once a genius, always a genius. Whatever the reason, it got so whenever I saw either a dentist or a doctor coming, I wanted to run the other way. Still, there are exceptions, and I've got to admit that some of the best outdoorsmen I ever worked with were small-town physicians.

Just before opening day that first hunting season, a doctor from Iowa came in as a last-minute fill-in on a hunt. He was a big guy with a hell of a bedside manner. Because of his clothes, he was what I call an L.L. Bean hunter. He had a German Mannlicher rifle and claimed to have hunted all over the world. In camp the afternoon before opening day, I gave my lecture about safety, first aid, and what to do if you're lost in the woods.

The guy never took his eyes off me. I assumed I'd made a believer out of him, but as soon as I finished, he buttonholed me and said he wanted to go out scouting for elk. That wouldn't be such a good idea, I told him. What would he do if he saw one? The season hadn't opened, so he couldn't shoot anything; all he could do was spook the animals, so they'd be harder to hunt the next day. That was true, he admitted, but he wanted to walk around and kind of get the country fixed in his mind.

You'll just mess things up, I told him. Take it easy, we'll be after them first thing in the morning. So we left it like that, which I assumed meant, "Hell, no, you're not going anywhere."

When he walked away, I figured he was going to take a nap in his tent—until it came time to count heads for dinner that night, and everybody was there but him. We looked all over camp, but he was gone. Not only that, he'd broken every rule in the book: he had no coat, no hat, no emergency kit, not even a rifle or pistol to signal his location. So I threw a saddle on Morgan and rode out to find him.

With the sun down, a cold wind started blowing. The camp was on Gibson's Ridge, between Whetstone and Axtell, south of Crested Butte and west of Highway 135. Later I learned that after wandering for hours, the doctor had broken out of the timber where he could look north and see the lights of town and headlights on the highway. Blundering downhill, he flagged a car driven by a rancher and his wife. When he explained his situation, they took him home and fed him dinner and a few drinks. Then they all spent a pleasant evening in the family room watching television. The doctor slept in the guest room.

Meanwhile, the wranglers and I were riding the mountains in the dark—something I hate like hell to do—looking for him. About four AM I gave up and returned to camp, fixed breakfast, and sent the guides out with the hunters. I figured the guy was down, maybe dead. Morgan was beat, so I saddled another horse and was riding out again when here he comes, walking up the trail. He's had a good dinner, a good night's sleep, and a good breakfast. Now he's ready to hunt. When he told me what had happened, I got an eight-foot-long piece of string from the cook tent and tied one end to his belt and the other end to mine.

"That's as far as you get from me this entire hunt," I told him. "Where you go, I go, and vice-versa." At first he didn't think I meant it, but I did. We stayed tied together all day. We couldn't pee without hitting each other's boots. He's insulted, then he's mad, then he's sorry. He won't talk to me, and then I can't shut him up. Finally, when we got back to camp that evening so I could start cooking, he calmed down. "All right," he tells me. "You've made your point. I understand. I apologize; it won't happen again. What do you say we get rid of this string?"

So I figure okay, maybe I'm making too big a deal out of this. This is an intelligent man, a doctor, a respected member of society. There's no point in treating him like a goddamn kid, so I untied the string and turned him loose. I'm fixing dinner, and one of the wranglers says: "Look, Jim, there he goes again." Sure enough, he's heading downhill through timber about 200 yards from camp, looking for the outhouse, which is uphill from camp. He's absolutely lost, crashing wild-eyed through the trees, completely bonkers. I stayed by his side the rest of the week and never let him out of my sight.

Another thing we learned to do was add a 15 percent gratuity to clients' bills and to be clear that we were doing it. These tips, plus a tip pool for the wranglers and another pool for the guides—the high country pool, or hunting pool—were shared by the employees. In addition, most clients tipped an individual guide as much as $100, often slipping the money into a sleeping bag. Stu and I weren't part of the tip pools, but we shared in the 15 percent gratuity and were frequently tipped individually, too.

But that wasn't the way it worked that first year. I hadn't anticipated a problem, but there was one. The kids were saddling their horses and wiping their butts, and I thought clients would understand that that kind of service is supposed to be tipped. But some of them didn't, and it wasn't their fault. There's a special kind of relationship that develops when you're living together in the high country—you become such good friends. Clients felt like they'd be insulting a friend to leave a tip. It would be like me inviting you over to my house for a meal, and you'd slip a five-dollar bill under your plate to show your appreciation. But it's not that kind of relationship.

After hunting season was over that first year, Stu and I found ourselves without jobs and just about broke. We'd both worked as hard as we ever had in our lives, and we'd lost our shirts. Instead of breaking up our partnership for the winter, though, we decided to start another business.

That fall I'd bought a load of grain from a local feed store, but when I started putting it out for the stock, I found it was moldy. Somebody just made a mistake, I thought. I took a sample back to the store, but the clerk told me there was nothing he could do about it, and when I talked to the manager, he told me the grain had been fine when I bought it, so it must have turned moldy on the trip up the river. I was mad, but the stock had to be fed, so I bought another load.

Then I went to the shoe repair shop to get a cracked boot mended, and the owner told me he didn't do emergency jobs. "Leave it and I'll try to have it ready by next Thursday," he said. It was my only pair, and the crack pinched my foot every step I took.

So driving back to camp, with my foot hurting and a load of feed I'd paid for twice, I decided the bastards could stand some competition. When I told Stu, he agreed, and we decided to start our own feed store and saddle shop. The problem was that our only collateral was the horses and mules and camping equipment—which is not the kind of thing that impresses banks and district sales managers. A big Eastern Slope feed company was looking for a distributor on the Western Slope, so we dreamed up a financial statement and submitted it. When the district manager came to check our credentials, we shaved, put on suits and ties, and borrowed a car—a big Cadillac. Then we took him out to Bill's ranch.

The manager was a shiny little dude, very straight, with a coat and tie, and a shirt pocket full of pens and pencils. There were all these cows standing around in the field eating hay, so it was pretty impressive. In the ranchhouse, we sat down at the kitchen table and discussed the cattle business. "How are the cows doing?" "Fine." "They seem to be putting on weight." "They are." We covered all the important ranching topics—the weather, cow medicines, the price of beef—Stu and Bill with a lot of authority, me faking it the best I could. Finally we signed the contract, shook hands all around, and drove the sales manager back to town.

What we did, of course, was not strictly legal. We knew we were good for the money, but we would have had a hard time convincing anybody else. The manager never asked us if we owned the ranch or the cattle, and of course we never told him we didn't. He just assumed we did, and we didn't do anything to disillusion him.

With the distributorship and the first month's load of feed on the cuff, we rented a store and installed benches where we could work on saddles, tack, and boots. There were chairs for customers, and a potbellied stove provided warmth and hot coffee. Ranchers dropped by with harness and saddles that needed mending, and we talked, drank coffee, and sold them feed from a shed out back. It never turned out that way, but we hoped that someday the store would offer a permanent solution to the problem of earning a living during the off-season.

In spite of the mistakes we'd made that first year, we believed Executive Expeditions, Unlimited, was going to work. We'd done some things wrong, but we'd done some other things right. I'd learned a lot about the country, and I'd found out more about Stu than I wanted to know. I'd also learned a lot about myself. One of the most important things was that, although the work was hard, I loved it. I'd never been so happy in my life.

We'd also found a better location for the business—a resort on the Taylor River a dozen miles north of town, called Harmel's. With a solid, upper-middle-class clientele, good traffic flow, and an established reputation, the place was just what we needed. That next spring I sold all kinds of outfitting at sports shows, so I figured it was just a matter of living up to the old International Workers of the World motto: "Early to bed, and early to rise; work like hell and organize."

# 3

# A Modern-Day Cowboy

OFFICIALLY, IN THINGS LIKE STATE STATUTES and government reports, we were known as "guides" or "outfitters," but we called ourselves "packers" because that's what we did. We transported people and supplies, or else we got ready to do it, or we cleaned up the mess left after we were done. Unofficially, though, what we were doing was what American men and boys have been doing for years: playing cowboy. We looked like cowboys—or at least we tried to—and sometimes we acted like them and associated with them, trying to cash in on their mystique.

It was something that just seemed to happen, but the longer I stayed in the business, the more complete the identification became. I used to think about it when I got dressed in the morning, because it was like you put it on with your pants to play Othello. I'd be wearing Levis, braces, and an old flannel shirt. I'd slip into boots and chaps, and strap on my gun belt with the .357 Mag. I always tied a red bandanna around my neck, and by the time I put the Stetson on my head, I'd feel like somebody else. Sometimes, when I'd see this strange guy looking back at me from the mirror, I'd wonder who he was.

Everything we wore was part of a costume, like the suit of lights bullfighters wear in the ring. I don't know enough about their clothing to be sure, but I've always suspected that all the pieces of a bullfighter's costume—the sashes and sequins, the ribbons and leather—have a history and significance of their own. The same thing is true of Western wear, and making and repairing it yourself are important, because to a cowboy every piece of clothing and equipment has meaning. We talked about it at the store when customers brought things in for repair—about how a saddle wasn't right in a certain place and what could be done to fix it; about how the chaps needed to be cut higher; about why Texas spurs have a size and shape that's right for them but wrong for us.

I liked to think I was good at playing cowboy, but Stu was a master of the game. If anything, he was better at it than I was—or if he wasn't, at least he was more successful with a certain kind of client. My appeal was based on an image people retained from their experience with Western novels and films. I was what some Houston drugstore cowboy thought a cowboy ought to look like; I was what people who didn't know any better expected to see. Stu was closer to the real thing. His appeal was to men and women, a lot of them newly rich, whose parents had lived and worked on Western farms and ranches. They knew from experience what cowboys were like, and as far as they were concerned, Stu was it. Maybe that's what impressed me about him in the first place: he looked and acted like the real-life model for all the heroes of Western books and movies I'd ever known.

The difference between Stu and me and other outfitters was that we knew what we were doing—we were acting a part—and why we were doing it, and they didn't. And if you don't know what you're doing, sooner or later you make a mistake. One fall I was guiding for another outfitter (I'll call him Ed) who was a natural. He was a big, blond, good-looking guy, and the clients loved him. He'd be cruising along as smooth as Gary Cooper, doing everything right, and then he'd blow it. A horse would act up, and Ed would stop right there on the trail and start beating him with a stick. The horse would be lunging and squealing, trying to get away; the clients would freeze, looking at each other with amazement. What had happened to Gary Cooper?

Later, Ed would say, "I shouldn't have done that, should I?" I'd think maybe the light was beginning to dawn, and I'd say, "Why's that, Ed?" And he'd say, "Well, because one of those damn dudes might report me to the sheriff or the A.S.P.C.A."

I'd want to tell him no, Ed, you sure as hell shouldn't have done it, but that's not the reason.

I'm also convinced that dudes go searching for cowboys and the West for the same reason I left Denver—to escape from reality. A lot of the West is fantasy, or an excuse for fantasy. One reason I gave up on marriage and a safe, white-collar career was because they didn't satisfy some kind of imaginative need I had, and no matter what I did, I couldn't function without it.

One of the things I learned over the years was that our most dedicated clients—the ones willing to make the greatest sacrifices to live out their dreams—were those most successful in the commonsense world of business and family. After conquering their portion of the real world, they realize that that kind of success isn't enough. Today the Western wilderness—at least what's left of it—is a kind of Disneyland for adults, and an important part of the fantasy is the presence of a guide. And I don't mean just a hunting or fishing guide, but a mentor the client can believe in who rewards him when he succeeds or punishes him when he fails or falls short.

I admit it: I was as bad as any of them. For years I planned to recruit some of my best clients and take them big game hunting in Africa. The plan never materialized, but if we'd done it, it would have been done right—just like it was in Robert Ruark's books, or in Hemingway's *The Green Hills of Africa.* We would have washed in a canvas basin, and drunk tea and the good, dark German beer with the silver knight's head on the label. And there would have been some steely-eyed son of a bitch, like the white hunter Wilson in *The Short, Happy Life of Francis Macomber,* to shoot a lion just before he jumped my ass.

I believe Ruark's and Hemingway's white hunters and Denys Finch-Hatton in *Out of Africa* had motives very much like my own. They weren't in business for profit, or to build estates to sell or leave to their children; they were there for pleasure, for a way of life that appealed to them above everything else. They made whatever sacrifices were necessary to live that life, and took clients along on their hunts because that was the only way they could afford to go themselves.

Clients also have a mental picture of how things are supposed to be, and they judge their experience by that picture. You knew right away from their reactions if you'd made a mistake or if you'd got it right. They never said anything, but you could tell. I'd no more wear a baseball cap on my head leading a bunch of dudes on a horseback ride than John Wayne would have worn a baseball cap in *Stagecoach.* "Jesus Christ," I used to tell the wranglers, "dress like a cowboy. People don't come out here to have some punk kid lead them on a ride in cutoffs and a spaghetti-strap T-shirt."

If anything, foreigners were even more aware of details than Americans. Germans were particularly observant. They'd look you over, and if they didn't scowl, you knew you had it right. The Japanese are also in love with the West, but they prefer looking to participating. Anytime you heard a *vizzz*-ing sound behind you, it was some Japanese dude videotaping everything in sight.

After I left outfitting to work at the college, I escorted a group of Japanese educators to a ranch south of town. They were negotiating the college's presentation of a summer workshop for Japanese students with the president, and when things slowed down, I suggested that they take a look at our corner of the Wild West. As a treat, I put on my old Western costume, and they went crazy, chattering and pulling out their cameras. I saddled a couple of horses and posed for them, then got some of them up on the other horse to pose for each other. I noticed they were getting a little leery, though. Finally I got their head honcho, the old samurai, up there and told him we were going for a little ride. All we did was jog around the pasture, but he was really pissed at me. He never did loosen up, and I realized that all he wanted to do was take pictures, not ride horses.

When we got back to town, the Japanese were ready to go home—they wanted to get back and show everybody their pictures. The negotiations for the workshop didn't work out. The president, who'd okayed the trip to the ranch, blamed me for the lack of success and wound up pissed at me, too.

It seemed to me that all of us—outfitters and clients alike—were engaged in making our own Western movie, only nobody was actually filming it. Stu and I were the star performers, the clients and guides and wranglers were the supporting cast, and all of us were acting out a story that was familiar before the curtain went up or the cameras rolled. What we were after was an atmosphere for what I call a dream of the Old West. I remember a woman in her mid-thirties, a high-level bureaucrat from Washington, D.C., who'd saved her money and dreamed for years of visiting a Western dude ranch. She'd never been outside the Beltway in her life, but around the campfire one night, with tears streaming down her face, she told us how she'd prepared for the experience by saving brochures and travel agent literature.

When she arrived at the resort, the staff had explained how to go about arranging a horseback ride, so when she showed up at the corral, she looked at me and said: "You must be the man who takes people riding."

I knew right away what was happening. It was a little spooky, but in a way I was hardly there at all for her. I was a dream, some kind of fantasy she'd had for years. I said, "Yes, ma'am, I am."

I was busy till Wednesday, I told her, but if she could wait, I'd take her and a family up for an overnight. Later, a maid who cleaned her cabin told me that the overnight was all she talked about. She liked the resort and the people fine, but she was living for that ride.

Early Wednesday morning we met at the corral. She watched me saddle her horse, and then said, "They jingle," meaning my spurs.

"Yes, ma'am," I said. "And they sound mighty pretty on a cold, frosty morning."

I knew it sounded like something out of Zane Grey, but I said it because I knew that's what she wanted to hear. She wanted some guy who looked like a cowboy to say something like that–something sensitive and kind of simple. That's the way she wanted it to be, and that's the way I played it. It was like being part of a script, a character written by somebody else.

She wrote to me for years, sent me cards at Christmas, but she never came West again. For a while that surprised me, but finally I realized that she didn't want to spoil the experience. It had been perfect the first time; it could never be that good again.

I remember another time leading a line of riders through the picnic ground at Harmel's, bound for the high country. There was a wedding in progress–the bride in veil and long, white dress, the groom and groomsmen in tuxes. They looked up as we passed, and one of the guests, the eighty-year-old grandmother of the bride, called to me: "Are you a cowboy?"

"Yes, ma'am, I am," I told her, and tipped my hat and stopped my horse.

"Well," the old woman said, "I always wanted to kiss a cowboy, so if you're a cowboy, I want to kiss you."

So I dismounted and kissed her on the cheek. Somebody took a picture of us—the woman with her face lifted up, her smile ecstatic; me in chaps and snap-button shirt, my bandanna around my neck, my Stetson on the back of my head.

The language Stu and I used, and the clothes we wore, were part of the dream. Another part was the way we lived and the way we treated the clients—even the way we treated each other. It was rough sometimes, and both of us were often high-handed and arrogant, but the clients couldn't get enough.

I remember talking to a friend, a local game warden named Jim Houston, who made the same point. He claimed that all you had to do to turn even the most decent, modest, self-effacing guy into a raving egomaniac was to make him an outfitter. Dr. Jekyll would become Mr. Hyde. Maybe it's because those old frontier values are latent in all of us, and that much independence inflates the psyche like hot air blows up a balloon. Or maybe part of it is working with horses. People on horseback have always felt superior to pedestrians, just like the cavalry always believed they were better than the infantry. Most outfitters I know are convinced that they have not only the right but also the duty to boss other people around. Houston used to complain that an attitude like that makes outfitters hard to regulate, or even to reason with, because they believe that they're a law unto themselves.

That kind of attitude probably also explains some of the high-handed things that Stu and I used to do. Once a guy fishing in the river behind the resort hooked himself in the scalp above his ear with a big, Japanese-made lure. It was embedded pretty deep, beyond the barb, so he and his wife ran to find a doctor, and one of my wranglers suggested they see "Doc" Greer.

As far as the wranglers were concerned, one sawbones was pretty much like another, so the guy and his wife, who also happened to be a registered nurse, came over to the corral. I'd taken a lot of hooks out of a lot of people, myself included, so I didn't think much about it, but the wife really stared when I took a bottle of whiskey from the desk drawer to sterilize a pair of needle-nose pliers.

"Are you sure you know how to do this?" she asked me.

I told her I did, and that with a few minutes' work, I could save them a trip to town and a hospital bill.

"Aren't you going to excise the hair around the wound?" she asked, but I told her, "No, ma'am; this hair's just fine. It don't need no exercise."

The proper technique for removing a hook is to push the barb all the way through the flesh, clip it off, then work the hook back out. I did the first part okay, but as I withdrew the hook, it snapped off, leaving the metal curve under the skin. So I smiled at her and said: "I hope somebody around here has a fast car."

By this time blood's trickling down the guy's neck and his wife's levitating all over the corral. They drove to Gunnison at high speed. When they arrived at the hospital, the emergency room doctor, a friend of mine, figured out what was going on and went into his act.

"Who botched this excision?" he yelled.

"Dr. Greer," the wife told him.

"Dr. who?" the doctor roared. "Is that maniac at it again? I'll report him to the state commission for practicing medicine without a license!"

When they got back to the corral office, they told me what had happened. I don't know whether they were trying to scare me or wanted me to pay the $50 doctor bill. All I told them was to let that be a lesson to them—from now on, they should use good old American hardware instead of those cheap Japanese imitations.

Sometimes we'd play jokes on the high-dollar dudes, too. In fact, sometimes it seemed like the grander the dude, the more fun it was to level him. One of my favorites was a client from Atlanta (who shall be nameless here)—a former television mogul who'd made his fortune in the early days of the industry and retired young to enjoy the fruits of his labors. He'd heard of me through a friend, a former client, and called to arrange a bow hunt for bear.

When they arrived at the airport, the mogul turned out to be a big guy with white hair rigged up in Abercrombie and Fitch's finest. What really caught my eye, though, was his presentation model, 100X silver-belly Stetson—but he surprised me by being equally impressed with my old white Stetson.

For atmosphere, I perched the mogul and his friend on a bale of hay in the truck bed and took them up the river to the resort. They hiked and fished for a couple of days while I turned off the bait. Bears are nocturnal and prefer to forage at night, but once they get a taste for garbage, they'll break their natural feeding pattern and come after it while there's still enough light to shoot.

When I judged they were in the proper mood, we drove up Spring Creek to a blind I'd built in Deadman's Gulch. Sure enough, about twilight a big cinnamon-colored boar—edgy with hunger and scenting fresh bait—appeared, and the mogul dispatched him with a well-placed broad-head arrow behind the shoulder. To celebrate, we lit Havana cigars the mogul's people had smuggled into the country for him, the friend took pictures of the mogul with his bear, and we passed a bottle of Jim Beam back and forth. Then we loaded the carcass aboard the Jeep and headed back to the resort.

We were bouncing down the Spring Creek road when the mogul started telling me again how much he liked my hat. He wanted to know where I'd got it blocked, and when I told him I'd done it myself, he drawled, "Well, you made a fine job of it. I just wish I could get my hat blocked to look like that. You'll have to do mine sometime."

I don't know what got into me—maybe it was the whiskey and the cigar, or maybe just the sight of this big dude lolling there like the lord of the manor—but I said, "No problem," and snatched his hat and sailed it out the window into the creek. I thought he'd bite his cigar in half.

"My God," he said, "that's a $500 Stetson."

"Sure it is," I told him, "but it's got to have the water treatment. Otherwise it'll never fit right."

For a minute I thought he was going to bail out of the Jeep and go after it. It was nearly dark, but you could see the hat bobbing along on the current like a kid's paper boat. I eased down the road for about half a mile while we watched it. By now I was really getting into this, but the mogul was doing a lot of suffering. Every time the hat went out of sight he'd catch his breath, and when it reappeared, he'd let it out again. Finally the hat drifted into an eddy, and while the mogul and his friend sat tight, I scrambled down the bank. The water was cold, about ankle deep, but I waded in and stomped the living piss out of the hat, then held it up to show them. The silver-belly Stetson looked like a drowned rat.

"No wonder this thing won't fit," I yelled at them. "There's something inside," and I tore the lining out and held it up for them to see. "What do you think? You want to keep this goddamn silk hanky?"

By then they were speechless, so I threw the lining away, climbed the bank, and jammed the Stetson on the mogul's head, pulling it down tight. "There," I told him, "now it's blocked. Don't take it off till it dries."

And he didn't. He slept in it and ate in it all that next day. He was still wearing it when I dropped him and his pal off at the airport. And the hat, of course, was fine. It looked just as good as mine; even the mogul said so.

That next fall I called him at his office to talk about another hunt. He wasn't there, but when I gave my name to his secretary, she said, "Are you the guy that blocked his hat? Do you know he won't even wear it? He keeps it in a specially built glass case on his office wall and tells his friends how you blocked it for him."

For years he sent me boxes of Havana cigars—what we used to call "all-day cigars"—stogies that cost four or five dollars apiece, the kind you have to plan ahead for time to smoke in order to do them justice.

My clowning around with the clients was bad enough, but Stu could be even worse. One night in the cook tent we were talking about weapons and ammunition with a group of men from Louisiana, and one of them noticed the .44 Magnum Wagner carried. "That must make a lot of noise," he said. Stu never hesitated. Hauling it out, he pointed the .44 in the air and fired two shots right through the canvas. "What do you think?" he asked. But the conversation was over, our ears were ringing so loud we couldn't hear ourselves think. We stumbled off to bed, but it was a couple of hours before my ears stopped making so much noise I could sleep.

Stu's high-handed attitude was directed at me as often as it was at the dudes. He owned a black Labrador retriever sent by a grateful client—a pedigreed Lab, one of the old-fashioned kind with a short, powerful body and a head as big as a coal shovel. Originally there'd been two dogs, but when Stu drove to Denver to get them at the airport, he returned with only one.

I was in the bar when he came in with the dog and sat down. "Yours died," he told me. "He got some kind of damned fever on the plane. And you know what? I had to pay $350 for a seat on the plane for this one, so he's one high-dollar son of a bitch."

Stu was sitting with the dog in his lap, playing with his ears. "How do you know it was mine that died?" I asked, and Stu said, "Because he was dead when I got there. And I paid $350 for the plane seat. So this one's mine, and yours died."

I didn't care enough about the dog to make an issue of it, but the remaining one was a wonderful dog, a wonderful hunter. We took him with us everywhere, even into elk camp. We called him "High Dollar Son of a Bitch" because of the price of the plane ticket, and "Dollar" for short. Wagner was crazy about him; he was like part of the family.

That next fall we were camped with a hunting party near Forge Peak. Because there were few good campsites in the area, three independent hunters set up tents in a grove of aspen above us. Early in the day, one of them shot an elk calf and hung it in a tree to cool, then went out to hunt again. When his companions returned and saw the calf, they decided to play a joke on him and cut the backstrap out and cooked and ate it.

The successful hunter was a big guy with a good set of shoulders on him. When he got back to camp and saw the carcass hacked up like that, he got so mad his friends were afraid to tell him what they'd done. Instead, they claimed that the black dog in the camp below must have slipped in while they were gone and eaten the meat.

Our clients were sitting around the campfire drinking and smoking. Stu and I were in the cook tent washing dishes when the hunter and his friends showed up with their rifles. The big guy put his head through the flap and said, "Where's your dog? Because I'm going to shoot that son of a bitch."

Stu wiped his hands on a towel and went outside. "I didn't hear what you said," he told the guy. "Say it again." And when the hunter repeated the threat, Stu nailed him—one punch, bare-knuckle, right on the button. It was impressive. The guy flipped over backward, like an acrobat, both feet in the air, and landed flat on his back with blood all over his face.

The thing that really impressed me, though, was that in spite of the fact that he still held his rifle, and his friends were watching with their rifles in hand, Stu pressed the point. Standing over the guy, he said, "Do you want some more? Because if you do, get up."

But the guy just laid there and shook his head. "Okay," Stu said, "but if you change your mind, you know where to find me."

The hunter and his friends returned to their camp. Meanwhile my heart's going like a trip-hammer, and I'm digging in the tent for my pistol, because I figure they'll talk things over and be back. Our clients haven't moved; they're sitting around the fire dead quiet, their eyes as big as a tree full of owls. This is the Wild West in spades, and they don't want nothing to do with it.

When Stu went back to washing dishes, I told him: "Hey, don't be hitting people with rifles in their hands," but all he said was, "Nobody shoots my dog." It had to be one of the most foolish—or conspicuously brave—things I've ever seen a human being do.

Pretty soon, here comes the hunter back down the hill, alone this time, and without his rifle. He apologizes and explains that his friends had admitted they were playing a joke, and it had gotten out of hand. But do you think Wagner gave him an inch? Not a chance. In his mind there was a line you don't cross: you don't kill another man's dog or even threaten to kill him. It was a line I didn't know was there till then, but I've never forgotten it. I bet that hunter and his friends never forgot it, and I bet those clients of ours haven't either.

Because of the effect it had on people's lives, I always took my part pretty seriously, but sometimes I interpreted the role broadly enough to play it for laughs. I remember taking a party out on a trail ride, and one of the clients, a snooty woman from Boston, said, "What mahvellous terrain you have here, young man." And I told her: "You're dead wrong, ma'am. We ain't seen a t'rain in these parts for fifty years."

Another time I was sleeping at one end of a tent full of men when I noticed a snowshoe rabbit playing with a sealed trash bag in the moonlight outside. He was pretty good sized and making quite a bit of noise with that bag. Everybody else was sound asleep. I don't know what got into me, but I thought it would be a good idea to shoot him. So I took my .357 and followed his shadow along the tent wall, and when he broke into the opening at the flap, I put two rounds on him.

That's when I realized I might have been overreacting. Everybody woke shouting, fighting their way out of their sleeping bags. It was a regular riot and I thought: "Jesus, what have I done?"

I felt a little foolish about it, so instead of admitting I'd fired at a rabbit, I told them I'd seen a bear approaching and taken a shot at him. That made me a hero. "Did you get him?" they wanted to know, but I told them I hadn't been trying to hit the bear, only to drive him away. The next morning, though, they found the dead rabbit near the firepit and a hole drilled through the coffee pot. That .357 round had knocked the rabbit to rags. There wasn't even enough left to bury—and I had to cut a peg for the coffee pot, so we finished the trip that way.

They were a good bunch and I took a lot of kidding from them. "Ain't it funny what a little darkness will do to you—turn a rabbit into a bear," they said. I never did admit it, of course, but they all knew what happened, and they didn't let me forget it.

I never made a secret of the fact that Stu and I were acting our parts. If any of the clients were curious, I talked with them about it, explaining what we were doing and why we did it. It didn't happen often, but when it did, their reactions sometimes surprised me. Some of them were impressed, and we talked about things Stu and I could do to be even more convincing. Other people, though, were indignant; they felt like they'd been tricked. It didn't bother them so much that I was out riding and hunting and fishing every day; they just thought that's who I was and what I did. But when they found out about the other jobs I'd had, and the marriages I'd walked away from, they couldn't believe it. I had been just like them, and now I wasn't. Some of them were so mad they wouldn't talk to me. Others thought I was brave, but I told them no, they were the brave ones: they stayed with their ball-cutting wives and ungrateful kids and the lousy jobs. I was the coward; I was the guy who ran away.

The reaction that surprised me most was from my old man. When he found out what I was doing, he was mad as hell. He told me, "The only reason I didn't take off like you did was because of you kids." And I felt like telling him right there, "You should have gone. You weren't doing us any good. If I'd known, I would have given Mom my last dime so that you could have got the hell out and lived some kind of life of your own, and let me live mine."

# 4

## Horses and Mules

I'VE ALWAYS BEEN FASCINATED by birds and animals of all kinds, but I've had a lifelong love affair with horses. In grade school, other boys wanted to be railroad engineers or firemen, but I wanted to ride. My mother owned the only horse in our family, a white mare named Snowball. She was probably just an old plug somebody had sold my mother, but to my eyes she was beautiful–so big and white that, when I was seven or eight years old, mounting her was like climbing on top of a limestone wall. My mother kept Snowball at a commercial stable near the edge of town, and after school I would ride her until time for supper. She must have been about twenty years old and preferred to stay in the stable, so you had to be careful, because she usually tried to rub you off on the corral.

Two of my favorite mounts were a pair of big white geldings an old Swede kept in a pasture I passed every morning on my way to school. They were as graceful as swans, with ears as delicate as the skin on a girl's wrist. The Swede never rode them; he just liked the idea of having horses on the place, I guess. They were so lonely for human companionship that some mornings, when I was on my way to class, they would nicker at me to come over and ride them.

To accommodate them, I tied a hackamore out of a piece of cotton clothesline and concealed it in the branches of an apple tree in the back yard. When I left home, I'd put sugar in a pocket and slip the hackamore under my shirt. That way, when they called,

I'd be ready. I had to ride bareback, so I needed a log or a rock to mount, and I had to be careful about where I got off because I couldn't get back on without another handy step.

Another problem I had with my morning rides was the fact that Mrs. Bevins, the teacher, owned a telescope. Whenever I was absent from class, she'd take it up to the second floor of the schoolhouse and look out the windows until she spotted me riding across the fields or along some of my favorite trails through the woods. Then she'd phone my folks. My dad always whipped me twice, once for skipping school and once for sweating up the Swede's horses.

When I started outfitting, one of the job's chief attractions was the opportunity to ride and to work with horses. I knew they could be dangerous, but that was simply part of the allure. Over the years, I rode dozens of horses, but there were only four that I considered mine rather than simply part of the company string. The first was a "loaner" from Wagner's original string, a fat little mare named Windy. Next I had the tall black Morgan gelding I named Morgan; then another gelding, this one a big roan I called John C. Fremont; and finally a rangy Appaloosa—another horse salvaged from the string—named Oogley. A couple of years after I quit outfitting, while I was working at the college, I made the mistake of buying a fifth horse, Doc, who almost killed me.

I picked Windy because she seemed to be the best horse available on short notice. I hoped they called her Windy because she was so fast she made the wind blow past when she ran, but it turned out she had the same affliction that troubled Adolph Hitler—she was full of gas. It didn't matter whether she was walking or trotting, or running flat out, she popped and farted like an old two-cycle engine.

She was also hard to control. One of her favorite tricks was a variation on crack-the-whip, where she'd run at full speed, then lower her head and dig in with all four feet. The object was to launch her rider from the saddle with as much force as possible. Before we were married, I took my lady friend, Marilyn, riding and Windy threw her that way. The fall broke Marilyn's nose and glasses and blackened both her eyes. It also put a considerable strain on our relationship.

I don't believe horses deliberately set out to hurt you, but sometimes their conduct seems indistinguishable from calculated malice. Even their expressions, after they've pulled one of their stunts, betray an appearance that I can only account for as satisfaction. It was hard for me to persuade Marilyn that Windy didn't know what she was doing—or that maybe I shared Windy's guilt because I'd put Marilyn up there in the first place.

I replaced Windy with Morgan, a black gelding I bought at a ranch sale north of Gunnison. He had a wild eye, but in the ring seemed calm and appeared to have a good disposition. Buying a horse or mule is a test of character that calls for every bit of wit and knowledge you possess, and is likely to stimulate any paranoia latent in your system. William Faulkner, writing about the Snopes clan's horse-dealing shenanigans in *The Hamlet,* definitively exposed a widespread subculture of rural con men.

When I asked Stu what he thought of Morgan, he wasn't much help. "He might be worth ten cents, or he might be worth ten thousand dollars," Stu told me. In other words, a horse is like beauty: his value lies in the eye of the beholder. To put it another way, I was on my own, because Stu wasn't going to venture an opinion.

When I paid for Morgan, I asked the rancher to board him for a few weeks. He agreed, but said to give him a couple of days notice before I came for the horse. I didn't think much about it at the time, but later I decided it sounded like a peculiar request, so the following Saturday, without giving him any warning, I drove out to the ranch. The rancher wasn't there, but with the help of the stable boy, I roped and saddled Morgan. The horse was acting strange, though—rolling his eyes, sidestepping away from me when I mounted—and by the time I got up on him, he was breathing fire.

The corral was big, the fences six rails high, but Morgan never hesitated. With a lunge that threw me back in the saddle, he charged the fence at a dead run. I saw it coming and bailed out early, afraid he was going to put both of us right through the rails. There's no way he can clear it, but over he goes—or, to be truthful, over he goes partway—because next thing I know, I'm sitting on my ass watching, and he's flopped across the fence like an old mattress, bucking and kicking hell out of it. He can't go forward and he can't go back, but he's still trying to escape that corral.

What happened was that when he put Morgan up for the sale, the rancher had doped him with Butazolidin. It took all the starch out of him, so that in the sale ring he looked like somebody's pet. Then, after I bought him, the guy wanted enough warning to get him medicated again before I picked him up. That way Morgan wouldn't have thrown his first fit until after I got him home. It's a trick not quite Snopesian in nature, but it's old, and I was green enough to fall for it.

The stable boy and I finally untangled Morgan from the fence. When the rancher returned, I questioned him, but he played it straight. What do you know about that? Scratching his head, he told me he couldn't imagine what had gotten into the horse, he'd never done anything like that before. We discussed the matter, but the best deal he offered was to take Morgan back as down payment on another, more expensive animal, if I saw one I liked.

It took Morgan and me about six months to get things straightened out. In the process, we knocked a few corners off each other until finally we reached a mutual agreement: I wouldn't hurt him if he wouldn't hurt me.

When I investigated Morgan's background, trying to learn the source of his problems, I became a little more sympathetic. A wealthy family in the San Luis valley had originally bought him for their daughter to use as a rodeo barrel racer. The girl, though, had lost interest in the sport, and Morgan had spent a year penned in a stall, seeing no one but the stable boy who fed him. He turned out to be a hell of a horse. He was smart as a whip, and he could do it all—rope, lead a string, carry a pack, work in harness pulling a buggy or a light sleigh—you name it, he could do it. A man never had a better partner.

Eventually, though, Morgan developed an allergy to dust and was unable, without medication, to eat the hay that was often the only forage we had for months at a time in the high country. When I found myself spending ten dollars a day on antihistamines, I traded him to a farrier near Delta, Colorado, for another horse, a big roan gelding I called John C. Fremont. To get him, I paid $500 to boot, so the farrier got a hell of a deal. And because Morgan was able to eat grass on a regular basis, he did fine in the low country.

Fremont lasted one season and part of another before dying suddenly. The problem was that he objected to being transported by trailer; to let you know, he spent his time back there trying to kick his way out. He'd get after it like he was playing a drum solo: every trip sounded like I was hauling Buddy Rich or Gene Krupa around with me. One morning, with John C. tied securely, I was taking him to the dropoff point for the ride to Aspen when I became aware of an unaccustomed silence. Maybe he's finally getting used to the trailer, I thought. But when I glanced in the mirror, I saw the left side door swinging open and Fremont's hindquarters dragging on the road. By the time I stopped, he was struggling to climb back inside the trailer. I tried to help, getting behind him to push, but he kicked the hell out of me.

The bed of the trailer was about three feet off the ground, and I had no idea how long he'd been hanging there—ten or fifteen minutes, I guessed. Finally I got him untied, he flipped over and rolled, but he seemed all right. I led him up the ramp and drove on to Gothic, a ghost town that serves as trailhead for the Aspen ride. He still seemed fine, so I saddled him and led a group of clients over East Maroon Pass to the Lazy K Ranch, on Maroon Creek, where I'd arranged for us to spend the night.

Fremont ate and drank without a problem, and when I turned him loose, he ran to join the other horses in the pasture. The next morning, though, when I went to saddle him for the return trip, he was lying dead in the grass. There wasn't a mark on him, but apparently he'd twisted a gut and ruptured the vessels leading to the liver. He looked fine, but short of an operation and a recovery period in some kind of sling suspending him in a pool of water for a couple of months, there would have been no way to save him.

Without a spare horse, I walked back over East Maroon Pass. Not only that, I had to carry my saddle, and I made the walk in cowboy boots. When I got home, Marilyn got after me about it. "Why didn't you just send the saddle back on the bus?" she wanted to know. She knew I could have picked it up in Gunnison the next day. I told her I needed my saddle the next day, that I had work to do. Then she wanted to know if I couldn't have borrowed a horse from the Lazy K? Or bought one?

I finally admitted that I'd done it to save face with the dudes. How would it have looked if I'd sent my saddle home on a bus? Or bought a horse I didn't want, or borrowed one from a guy I didn't know? And before she asked, I told her I couldn't have ridden double with one of the dudes, because the trail was too steep and rough, but she didn't understand that, either.

I remember a scene from one of my favorite movies, *The Electric Horseman.* As Jane Fonda and Robert Redford climb a mountain, Redford, playing a washed-up rodeo cowboy, tells the story of a friend hurt by a Brahma bull who "got up and still rode the rankest mare there." Redford's trying to encourage Fonda to continue the climb; she's exhausted and wants to stop and rest. "I will never understand," she protests, "why you find that kind of behavior admirable."

"Well," says Redford, "it gets you up the hill."

I always liked that, not only because it's a nice illustration of who these two people are, but because the hill is both literal and symbolic. Everyone's got some sort of hill to climb, and you might as well get after it. I never told Marilyn that before we left the Lazy K, I took a pair of pliers and pulled the shoes off John C. and carried them back in my saddlebags. They were brand-new shoes. I could hear the dudes talking: "That son of a bitch is *hard*," they said, which was just what I wanted them to think. But at the same time, I knew I was being irrational, caught up in the death of a favorite horse.

After Fremont's death, I finished the season on Oogley, a horse who'd earned that name because he was tall, long, and spotted, and had a rough, rambling gait. He was so ugly that I couldn't get a wrangler up on him; even the dudes wouldn't ride him. He was adequate, but nothing more.

The last horse I owned, Doc, was named after a famous quarter horse stud, Docalina. I always said Doc was half Impressive—which was the name of his sire—and half unimpressive. When I bought him on a bank sale, they warned me he was an incorrigible bucker, but I thought I could break him of the habit. By now, though, I'd been away from outfitting for a couple of years, and had been spending most days in an office at the college in front of a computer terminal. I was out of condition, but I didn't know how bad until I tangled with Doc.

I saddled him in the corral at Harmel's and took him for a trial run in the sagebrush west of the bunkhouse. It was Doc's first ex-

perience in what wranglers call "the real world"—the world outside the corral. When a horse bucks, what normally happens is
that he signals the pattern he's going to use right away—he plants
his forelegs left-right-left-right—and you pick up the pattern and
react accordingly. But Doc fooled me. He planted left-right-left,
and then when I leaned right, ready for him, he went left again. I
wasn't on him long—a couple of seconds, and I was flat on my
back, with most of the ribs broken loose from my spine. I heard
them pop when I hit, but I hoped it was just my collarbone.

Larry Malloy, a kid who used to wrangle for me, had been
watching from the corral fence. I knew I was hurt, but I didn't
realize how bad until I saw Larry's face. He looked very calm and
cool, but covered up, like he knew something I didn't know and
would rather I didn't find out. Kneeling beside me, he spoke in a
quiet, gentle voice, like he was talking to a child. Finally he said,
"What do you think? You want me to get the meat wagon?"

One of the things you never do around a resort is call the
ambulance. They like to come in with the siren howling loud
enough to wake the dead, and you don't want to panic the clients.
But I knew I better have it, so I told him yes. Then he said: "You
want me to get the gun?" He meant did I want him to shoot that
goddamn Doc, but I told him no, I didn't think I could stand the
concussion. I've always been grateful for what Larry did for me.
It's nice to have one of the kids you've taken care of turn around
and take care of you.

Later, a woman wrangler who worked at the resort—one of
the best riders I ever saw—tried to break Doc, but she never gained
an inch on him. Then Larry and another wrangler, assuming that
I'd simply been too soft, and that a girl wasn't up to the job, tried
and failed. Finally the bank turned Doc over to a professional horse-
breaker, who returned him as incorrigible. Eventually they sold
Doc on another bank sale—bought, I hope, by a younger, tougher,
wiser guy than me. I hope a professional bucking string has him
now, because you can't teach a horse to fight like that. It's a talent,
and Doc might as well buck people off for a living, because I don't
believe there's any way to break him.

Some packers own all, or at least most, of their stock; others lease it from suppliers. A good horse, with two reshoeings thrown in, costs $550 a season. Horses reach their prime between the ages of nine and eleven, mules when they're a few years older. When they reach the high country in spring, horses are in poor condition and have to be ridden from forty-five minutes to an hour a day, sometimes for several weeks, to prepare them for the upcoming season. Like athletes, they've got to be trained and exercised, and because of their size, it's harder to acclimate horses than people to high altitudes. A lot of the horses we got from the Midwest had drunk from stock tanks all their lives and had to be taught to step into and even drink running water. We even had to teach them to walk up and down hills.

One of the things that never failed to amuse the wranglers was the clients' interest in horses. The first thing they wanted to know was their horse's name. The only way we would have been able to remember the names of all the horses we had to deal with was if we'd painted them on their sides. Sometimes, if we couldn't remember the name of a particular animal, we invented one on the spot. Sometimes the name changed from one season to the next, or even from one ride to the next. We always had a Dolly, because that was a name the clients liked. Only sometimes a repeat customer would ask for his old horse, and when we brought it, he wouldn't recognize it.

"That's not Dolly."

"It isn't? You sure?"

Other favorite names were "Ten Minutes to Midnight" and "Sudden Death." We always had a couple of those around, because clients loved them. So did the wranglers. "How is he?" the dude would ask—some smooth guy, very confident, probably been an asshole all his life and always would be.

"Well," we'd tell him, "we don't know. Nobody's been up there long enough to find out."

"What's his name?"

"Ten Minutes to Midnight."

"That's right," the wranglers would chime in. "Ten Minutes to Midnight. Hell of a horse."

It was another example of leveling the dudes. Some of them started pretty high, but by the time we got up on top, in the mountains, we were all even. Actually, the clients were all kinds. Some of them were assholes and some of them were the finest people I ever met, God love 'em one and all. But if it wasn't for the dudes, all of us would have been working for a living, and we knew it. It was an example of what the guys in the science department call a symbiotic relationship: the clients needed us, but we needed them, too.

Occasionally clients wanted to bring their own horses with them into the high country, but the animals were in no condition to handle the work. Whenever somebody asked, we always quoted them two prices: $100,000 if they brought their own mounts, $100 if they didn't. They usually got the message.

One outfitter, new to the business, tried to ride a pair of high-priced Arabians out of Texas over Conundrum Pass without conditioning them first. He got one over, but he had to bring the other one out by helicopter. The night before the ride, I was kidding him in the bar at Harmel's and offered to sell him a map of the area I'd draw on a napkin. Maybe he thought I was kidding, or maybe I hurt his feelings, but he said no, he could handle it. Next day, climbing into unfamiliar country, he took the wrong trail. One of the Arabians, a delicate little mare, slipped and rolled down the side of a mountain and wound up on a ledge overlooking a canyon. When the horse was unable to climb out under its own power, the outfitter returned to town and called for a helicopter.

At that altitude, the pilot couldn't get sufficient lift to raise the mare with a sling, so he persuaded the outfitter to push her off the ledge. It wasn't until she fell several hundred feet that the helicopter blades gained sufficient purchase in the thin air to carry her to safety. She survived, but it cost the outfitter $1,200 to get her out. After that, I always called him "the helicopter outfitter." I told him I would have drawn him a map for a lot less than $1,200, too.

After a full season of being ridden by dudes, horses can turn pretty sour. Inexperienced riders issue contradictory signals and commands, pulling on the reins, kicking their mounts and yelling "whoa" at the same time—which can get pretty confusing for anybody. You warn clients about it, and you watch for that sort of thing and try to straighten them out, but you can't be there all the time.

Accidents with horses are common in outfitting, and because the animals are big and strong, the results can be serious. My first year in the business, I used to get myself in some tough spots and then have a hell of a time getting back out. It's like driving a Jeep: at first you think they can do anything and go anywhere, but they can't. You've got to learn where you can go and get back, and you learn not to go anywhere you can't.

Some people, remembering the old John Ford Westerns, where the cavalry seems to spend as much time walking as riding, think you should try to lead a horse out of a bad place. But that's a mistake. If you get a horse on a steep slope, and he starts lunging, he could run right over you. Horses don't set out to hurt you. They're just trying to take care of themselves, and when they panic, they don't even know you're there. I remember one time Morgan stepped on my foot–broke it in three places and broke a couple of my toes. One of the clients, a woman, heard me yelling and said: "What's the matter with you, young man?"

I guess my language had been a little salty. "Well, ma'am," I told her, tears as big as cow turds rolling down my cheeks, "I'm allergic to horses: whenever one of them steps on my foot, my eyes start to watering." I never took my boot off for ten days, because I knew if I did, I'd never get it back on. A boot makes a pretty good splint, though, and when I finally cut it off, my foot had healed fine.

Cold and snow in the high country present outfitters with a whole new range of problems. Night time temperatures of thirty below zero aren't uncommon in the Gunnison country, so the tack, as well as the horses, takes a beating. In the morning, wranglers have to be careful to heat bits in the cook tent, and carry them to their mounts under the armpits of their coats. If they don't, it's just like putting your tongue on the pump handle when you're a kid. Warm spit quick-freezes your mouth to the metal, and it's hell to get it loose. I remember one wrangler who forgot and thrust a frozen bit into a horse's mouth. Snorting with pain, the animal jerked its head away, caught the wrangler in the face, and relocated his nose alongside his head. The frozen bit tore a piece of skin from the horse's mouth, and he bucked for quite a while before settling down again. We had to take the wrangler to the emergency room at the hospital.

Once in a while, though, all that cold and snow would do you some good. The winter after Fremont died, I was leading a six-horse string packing supplies out of basecamp to some drop camps we were running when a herd of elk, spooked by hunters above us, stampeded down the mountain. When I heard them coming, I assumed it was an avalanche and spurred my horse, trying to lead the string clear. Instead, about twenty head of wild-eyed elk broke out of the trees and crashed into the horses right behind me, sweeping them away down the mountain. All I could do was watch as snow flew, horses screamed, and packs and saddles went flying. Some of those horses rolled and cartwheeled half a dozen times.

When their tie lines broke, four of them made it down through the timber to the bottom of the slope, but the other two got hung up around a tree when their line held. I slid down and cut them loose and they scrambled down the rest of the way. But with Fremont's death fresh in my mind, I thought all of them were finished. Talk about a twisted gut—those horses must have intestines like Chinese rope puzzles.

I climbed back up the slope to my own horse, and when we got to camp, I couldn't believe it. All six horses were lined up where they'd been tied the night before, waiting to be fed. I worked late dragging packs and saddles into camp, and the next morning I went outside expecting to find the whole bunch dead—but they were fine. Apparently all that snow had cushioned their fall, and rolling down the mountain had been like bouncing around on grandma's feather bed. I repacked the loads, lined the string out for another run at resupplying the drop camps, and the horses were as frisky as ever. It was amazing.

I've loved horses all my life, but after outfitting a few years, I became just as fond of mules. One reason was because their gait is usually superior to a horse's gait—they just seem to flow along, and there's a delicacy about the way they stand and move that even the most graceful horse can't match. A horse will come to water and step in right away, trusting his rider to know it's safe, but a mule is a lot more cautious. If there's any reason to doubt a situation, he trusts no one but himself. Before entering a lake or stream, he'll stop and look for the bottom, and he won't move until he sees it. People claim mules are stubborn, and a lot of them are, but some of what appears to be hard-headedness is an awareness of risk that their riders don't recognize but the mule does.

Compared to a mule, a horse is clumsy. On a trail, a horse will bang along, stepping or kicking into anything in its way. A mule will follow a trail like a person, watching at each step where he puts his hooves. A horse will step on a rock, stumble, and catch himself; a mule will see the rock and step somewhere else. Mules may fall down once in a while, but never through any fault of their own. There's an old saying, "As sure-footed as a mule," and it's true.

One of my favorite mounts was a big chestnut Missouri mule named Edith. Wagner and I bought her from a logger who'd been trying to make a living cutting timber in the mountains east of Gunnison. He'd been doing it the old-fashioned way, snaking logs out one at a time, with Edith as his sole means of power and transportation. When the job got to be too much for him, he wanted out in a hurry, and so we bought her for a lot less than she was worth.

The first time I rode Edith was after Morgan, whom I was riding at the time, threw a shoe. We needed fresh meat in camp, so I sent word to Wagner, who had been riding Edith, that I'd meet him on the trail halfway between the resort and basecamp. When Wagner saw Morgan limping, he offered to take him down to be shod, while I rode Edith until we could exchange mounts again.

Mules have all kinds of hangups, but one of the things that bothers them most is being alone. They'll even put up with horses, who don't like them, just so they won't be by themselves. Of course, once they get to know you, everything's fine, since then they're not alone–they're with you. Edith liked Wagner and she didn't want to leave him. Even before I mounted, she laid her ears back in warning and tried to break away to follow Wagner down the trail to the resort. I yelled at him that I didn't think this was going to work, but he called back: "Take a switch to her," and continued down the trail.

A good-sized horse will go about fifteen or sixteen hands, but Edith stood eighteen hands high and weighed more than eighteen hundred pounds. She was so big that getting up on her was like climbing a three-story building, and she was so strong that the idea of switching her wasn't very appealing. But each time I pointed her up the trail, she'd turn and start down again. Finally I realized I didn't have much choice: either I followed Wagner's advice or I was going to walk all the way back to camp leading her—assuming she'd let me. So I rode into a clump of willows and cut a three-foot-long switch.

Edith had been switched before, because she knew right away what that was all about. Mules have eyes set toward the sides of their heads, like zebras, so they can see behind them, and as soon as she spotted the switch, she did what I told her. I didn't even have to touch her—the slightest gesture with the switch was enough. In fact, before long everything was going so well—the birds were singing, Edith was flowing up the trail with that long, smooth, ground-eating mules' gait—I decided we'd reached an understanding. But I no sooner threw the switch away than Edith circled through the trees and started back down the trail. All of a sudden, I realized this goddamn mule is smarter than I am.

Back to the switch again, I decided, but Edith had learned a lesson, too, and refused to let me ride her close enough to a willow tree to cut another one. Finally I stopped, tied her, and walked to a willow thicket to cut my switch. But this time when I approached, she laid her ears back and circled away from me, snorting and raring, refusing to let me mount until she saw me throw the switch away again.

Now what was I going to do? She was so big and strong I didn't have many choices. I had to be careful where I got off her because she was hard to get back on, even when she was cooperating.

Finally I walked to the other side of the thicket and cut another switch. Then I pulled my shirttail loose in back and slipped the switch down inside my collar. This time when I walked up to her, I held both hands out in front, like a magician with his sleeves rolled up. I even did a little pirouette, to show her there were no hard feelings. And it worked: Edith let me mount again, and as soon as she saw me produce the switch, she let me ride her up the trail to camp.

Not only was she smart, but she had quite a memory. As I continued to ride her, she came to accept me, but one day, while we were traveling between the resort and the fishcamp, she refused to follow a section of trail beside a beaver pond. Instead, she crossed a meadow and circled the pond before returning to the trail, and nothing I could do would change her mind.

Puzzled, I mentioned it later to Wagner, and he started laughing. A couple of months earlier, he'd ridden Edith over the same trail, but at the beaver pond he'd circled through the meadow and stopped to fish. Remembering the earlier, roundabout route, Edith had followed it again. It was like she was saying: "You dumb gebronie, you just don't know the trail. I'll have to show you where it goes."

The longer I rode her, the more my confidence in her grew. One fall, the owner of the Lake Irwin Lodge, west of Crested Butte, booked a party of hunters for the second big game season. As he knew nothing about horses or hunting, he contracted Stu and me to guide them. We completed the hunt just in time—a heavy snowstorm struck the mountains the night the season ended, and next morning we woke up to find ourselves knee-deep in fresh powder. Stu had already left with the guides, and the wranglers and I were packing when a report came over our C.B. radio that a hunter with an unguided party was lost in the Dark Canyon country west of us.

Dark Canyon is drained by Middle Anthracite Creek, but the country is so geologically disorganized that you can't find your way out simply by walking downstream. There are few fishermen's trails or logging roads. Broken and rolling, the country is a patchwork of streams that go nowhere, stands of timber, and isolated lakes, many of them no larger than midwestern cow ponds. The country is also extremely isolated—from the Kebler Pass road south of the canyon, it's thirty miles to the next road north, the Crystal River road, and between the roads is the Ruby Range, with peaks over 13,000 feet high.

The hunters had established a camp west of Kebler Pass, then scattered into Dark Canyon. When the storm hit, the others made their way back to the road, but a dentist from Arizona had been missing all night. Search and Rescue was going out, but a second storm was due in a matter of hours. So I put a quilted down coat on over a denim jacket, tied my hat on with a wool scarf, buckled on my emergency kit, and saddled Edith.

I knew that finding the guy was a long shot, but I figured that with Edith I had a chance. There was about three feet of snow on the ground, and the next storm was supposed to be worse than the first one, but when you're working outdoors, you don't really think about weather. It's like heat at the equator—you know it's going to be there, and you work in it. I figured Edith and I had about half a day to find this guy, and then we'd have to get out.

The Search and Rescue teams were working their way north off the Kebler Pass road, hoping to cut the doctor's trail as he walked west, toward Lost Lake. I rode west across Ruby Divide and entered Dark Canyon about five miles north of them. A lot of what's going on with something like that is in your head, and you do it a step at a time. You think: "I'll just go a little farther." And after you've gone that far, you think: "Just a little farther."

The reason you look for somebody who's lost or hurt is because, if something like that happened to you, you hope somebody would give you a hand. Only I wasn't familiar with that Dark Canyon country, and as Edith and I got in deeper and deeper, I started thinking: "What the hell am I doing out here? I don't know this guy."

No horse would have made it in snow that deep and country that rough. Even a mule will try to move only until snow reaches its shoulders, but all those years logging had given Edith tremendous muscular development. She was a big, high-stepping mule—she really made the snow fly—and we kept going, hour after hour.

About the middle of the day, though, when we still hadn't seen any sign of the dentist, I started thinking about turning back. We were losing the light as that next storm filled in west of us, and I remember telling Edith, "Let's give him five more minutes, then we're out of here."

We were crossing an open snow field when we cut his trail. Fresh snow had covered his tracks for miles north of the Kebler Pass road, so Search and Rescue had missed them; but as the first storm went through, and the dentist kept walking deeper into the Ruby Range, he started leaving footprints. But I still had no idea how far ahead of us he was or if we could catch him in time.

On a trail, though, a mule's like a bloodhound, and as soon as Edith figured out what we were doing, there was no holding her. Finally I saw something on the hill ahead of us—just a dark speck on the skyline against the snow—and then it was gone. Edith saw him, too, and really turned it on. We crested the hill, and there he was, lying in the snow. He was a wreck—he didn't even know we were there. In convulsions, he was jerking and shivering from the cold; then suddenly he jumped up and yelled, scaring the hell out of both me and Edith. Eyes rolled back in his head, he started waving his arms and babbling about something.

I pulled him down and talked to him for a while, then got him to drink some water. Finally, when he realized somebody was actually there, he had to talk it out. He told me he'd been moving toward "the shots"—he'd been hallucinating about a rescue party and thought it was up ahead. I waited about half an hour, listening to him and watching that next storm coming in—big black snow clouds ballooning over Mt. Marcellina. Finally I got the guy up behind me and we headed out. Edith never liked to carry double, but after the half-hour wait, she was too stiff and tired to fight about it.

The dentist, it turned out, was suffering from hypothermia and a little frostbite, but otherwise he was okay. He'd had a hell of a scare, though; he'd thought he was a goner. I haven't heard from him in a while, but for years he sent me a card every Christmas to thank me—and Edith—for saving his life.

Another time Edith and I got into it over an umbrella, a farewell gift from my staff at the capitol when I left government service. They knew I was headed for the Western Slope, so the gift was supposed to be a joke—the umbrella was a short-handled, black executive model, the kind that fits in a briefcase. But I figured it would fit in a saddle bag, too, so I saved it, thinking it might come in handy.

When it started raining one afternoon during a trail ride, I decided that instead of putting on a slicker, I'd impress the dudes by using the umbrella. The picture struck me funny—it would be like Robinson Crusoe walking around the desert island under his parasol. Like a lot of ideas, though, it was three-fourths pretty good, with a last quarter that kills you.

Showing off, I opened the umbrella with a flourish—and Edith rolled her eyes, saw this big black thing rising above her, and took off. She thinks it's the biggest vulture in the world and she's trying to get away from it. We were in heavy country—dark timber, rocky ridges, cliffs that dropped a hundred feet without warning—the sort of place where you don't want to fall off, because you're likely to get killed.

The clients are laughing, Edith's bucking and jumping, we take off through the trees. It's a rodeo, me hanging on with one hand and without enough sense to get rid of the goddamn umbrella. It's like water-skiing, where you go under and know you're supposed to turn loose of the rope, but you don't, you hang on thinking, "I ought to let go of this son of a bitch, because if I don't, I'm liable to drown."

Finally, I flip the umbrella in the air, it swoops over a couple of times and comes down behind us, and Edith really takes off. She sees that black thing lying back there, and she's sure as hell going to get away from it. She must have run about half a mile before I finally got her stopped, but I never could get her to go anywhere near the umbrella. Finally I tied her to a tree, walked back and furled it, and stowed it in one of the client's saddle bags. Edith never did umbrella-train, though I admit I never tried it again; it never seemed worth the trouble.

Another of our mules, Buckwheat, also caused me a lot of problems. Buckwheat was small for a mule, tan or buckskin-colored, with a delicate-looking head and long, slender ears. We picked him up at a bargain price from an outfitter near Lake City, south of Gunnison. Of course, buying a mule cheap is like going on a blind date—a guy ought to know better.

Buckwheat had been trained to carry a pack but not a rider. I liked the flexibility offered by an animal that could do both, so I set aside a few days to bring him up to speed. He seemed smart enough and didn't object to carrying a saddle, but he drew the line when it came to being mounted. Whenever I put a foot in the stirrup, he'd start circling away. I tried different methods of cornering him, but finally I resorted to the classic device, the snubbing post in the middle of the corral. With the halter tied in a slip knot, I'd chase him around the post until his neck twisted and his nose was anchored in place; then I'd mount him, slip the knot, and away we'd go.

Once free, I expected him to buck, but he just crow-hopped—rocked back and forth from front to hindquarters, kind of like a hobby horse. It's not the most comfortable gait in the world, but I figured we were making progress, so we headed up the blacktop toward the Spring Creek bridge. Buckwheat's walk was smooth and easy, but when he saw the bridge, he stopped abruptly: it turned out he didn't do bridges. Instead, he stood rigid and then, in spite of everything I could do, he backed down the road to the corral.

We did it over and over. Every time Buckwheat backed away, we'd circle the corral and return to the bridge—and every time, Buckwheat would back away again.

We made quite a sight. People stopped their cars and asked if I needed help. I'd be talking to Buckwheat in a vocabulary made up mostly of four-letter words, and working him over pretty good with a pair of sharp spurs, and he'd be shuffle-stepping backward. "No, thank you," I'd tell them. "I've been training this mule all week to walk backwards, and he's just about got it right."

One thing I learned about training animals is that you can get so locked into your own stubbornness that you stop thinking. Finally, I realized that the Spring Creek bridge wasn't that important after all—there really weren't all that many bridges in that country anyway—so I decided to postpone Buckwheat's education with bridges and try creeks. This time, when we reached the bridge, I reined him down a fisherman's path to the water. But when we reached the bank, he slammed on the brakes—it turned out he didn't do creeks, either.

He stood there staring at the water like he couldn't believe his eyes, and when I applied the spurs, he went into reverse and headed for the corral. While we circled the corral, I called one of the wranglers and then rode Buckwheat back to the creek. The wrangler followed us, and I had him take a dally—two or three wraps of a lariat—around the saddle horn and simply drag Buckwheat out into the water. It worked, too. The wrangler was up on a good-sized horse, and by now Buckwheat's neck was pretty sore. That's what a snubbing post will do to an animal, and by then Buckwheat had been fighting that post for a couple of days.

Once we got in the middle of the creek, everything seemed fine. Buckwheat had calmed down, so I told the wrangler: "Okay, give him to me." The guy retrieved his rope—and for the first time, Buckwheat started to buck. He was good at it, too. We were under the bridge, where there wasn't much room, and I couldn't sit up straight because I was afraid he'd beat my brains out against the beams, so I crouched over the saddle horn and tried to hang on.

Water flying, Buckwheat thrashed downstream from under the bridge out into the Taylor River. The harder he bucked, the more terrified he became. It wasn't the bridge and it wasn't the creek he was afraid of, I realized, it was running water.

Along there, the river's about three or four feet deep on average, with some holes deeper than that. When the main current hit
us, Buckwheat gave a mighty leap and scrambled onto a flat-topped
rock in the middle of the river. It was the first dry place he could
find.

So there I am, an imitation cowboy on a mule that's scared to
death, on a rock in the middle of the river. We must have looked
like an eagle on top of a standard; if we'd had a pole under us,
we'd have been a hell of a sight. We're like two drowned rats.
Buckwheat's shivering and I'm hurting all over; he's beat the hell
out of me. I'm sitting there wondering how we're going to get off,
and then I hear this noise, like cheering, and I look over at the
resort and see the deck full of people, yelling and clapping. They
think it's some kind of trick-riding performance we're putting on
for them!

For me, though, it was life or death. I thought about swimming ashore and leaving Buckwheat to starve to death in front of
the whole resort, but I gave that up as bad public relations. Finally,
I pulled my hat down, tightened my grip on the reins, and drove
both spurs into his flanks. No matter how much trouble he'd given
me, I'd never double-spurred him before, and away we went. Buckwheat gave three mighty bounds, like a flat rock skipped across
water, and made the bank.

Then, with me hanging on, he backed up the slope and across
the road to the corral. Everybody's cheering, like they're watching
a circus. It caught me off guard, I didn't know what to do, but I
smiled my best showbiz smile, tipped my hat, and bowed to ac-
knowledge the applause.

Eventually things got better for me and Buckwheat. Because
he wouldn't cross bridges forward, I made the necessary adjustments and backed him across whenever we encountered one. After that, the whole outdoors was ours. He never did get over his
reluctance about being mounted, though. In the mountains, whenever I got off to stretch or smoke a cigarette, I had to dally him to a
tree. Then, when I went to remount, he did his rotation around the
trunk until he couldn't move, I'd step up and unwind him, and
we'd be on our way.

Buckwheat spent the winter in the low country with the rest of
the stock, and when he came back, he was pretty well cured of his

various phobias. I never had any more trouble mounting him or getting him to cross bridges and streams. One night during the second year, though, he escaped from the fishcamp, hobbles and all, and just disappeared.

I waited a few days, figuring he'd turn up, and when he didn't, I searched the valley but couldn't find him. Finally, after he'd been missing nearly a week, I realized he must be hiding. I set out on foot to cut his trail when he went to the creek for water. It was a hot day, and I walked for miles without a sign of him. I hadn't brought water with me, and I got so thirsty I broke my own rule about not drinking from the streams. Even in the high country the water's polluted, but I took a chance.

A few days later, when I began suffering from stomach cramps and vomiting, I realized I'd contracted giardia. That was enough for me; I knew there had to be a better way to find Buckwheat. I owned a knife the wranglers admired—a handmade Bowie knife with an elkhorn handle and a fifteen-inch blade. I'd made it from a mail-order catalogue blank, but I raised the ante by claiming it had been hand-forged by an old man who made only three a year and tempered the steel in cow's blood. When I passed the word that I'd give the knife to anyone who found Buckwheat, the wranglers started searching for him during their time off.

Finally a Game and Fish guy led Buckwheat into camp. He had done what I had tried to do—cut the mule's sign when he went for water—but instead of walking, the Game and Fish guy'd done it on horseback. He'd also gotten lucky because Buckwheat, when he heard the horse's hooves, had peeked over the tops of the willows where he was hiding.

"It was curiosity that got him," the game warden told me. "Old Buckwheat looked just like a turkey gobbler. His head came up for a second, then disappeared, but by that time I'd seen him." The hobbles were still intact, though during the weeks he was gone they'd worn most of the hair from his forelegs.

Another time my fondness for mules got me into trouble with the law. Stu and I had a mule named Birdy who was too old to work, but because she was gentle and good with colts, we kept her. She didn't have any teeth, so she had to eat constantly, but she still looked like she was starving to death. Finally, a guest at the resort, a woman, noticed Birdy in the corral and complained to me about her condition. I explained the situation, but she wasn't satisfied and called the sheriff. When he also proved unimpressed with my explanation, I got my rifle and offered it to them. "You shoot her," I told the woman. "I can't; I couldn't sleep at night."

But she didn't want to do that, either. She was the kind who'd step over a starving person in the inner city, but she'd bleed all over an old mule in her last days. The sheriff went through the motions of charging me with cruelty to an animal, but he never pushed it, and the case never came to court.

Edith and Buckwheat, along with Wagner's favorite horse, Buddy, died one night in the cattle pens along the old Denver and Rio Grande right-of-way south of Gunnison. We'd trucked them, along with some other stock, down from the resort one Saturday in preparation for a Monday trail ride. Unexpectedly, the weather turned warm. Overnight temperatures stayed in the sixties, and Sunday, when I went to water the stock, I found the other horses standing around, but Edith, Buddy, and Buckwheat were down.

I called Wagner and a vet. His diagnosis was that they'd eaten a rare fungus that had grown suddenly during the unusually warm night. Until the heat triggered them, he told us, the spores had probably been latent in the soil for years. Apparently Edith and Buddy and Buckwheat had been strong enough, and determined enough, to drive the other animals off, and had eaten most of the fungus themselves.

So we lost three of our best animals. We'd paid $1,500 for Edith, and we'd turned down $6,000 for her. She was just exceptional, and everybody who saw her knew it. Buckwheat came cheap, but he'd turned out to be a fine little mule. Stu's horse, Buddy, had been like a family pet. Stu took one look at him stretched out in the corral and started crying. "When lightning strikes," he told me later, "it hits the best you've got." And I had to agree with him.

# 5

## Springtime in the Rockies

STARTING IN MIDSUMMER, as Stu and I did that first year, meant missing what I call Acts I and II in the drama of outfitting. The most serious loss was Act I, where you hit the road to promote your business on the sports show circuit. If you miss the shows, especially when you're starting out, you have to depend on walk-in customers and a lot of luck. Of course, it makes a difference if you're running an established business or are associated with a successful resort, but sooner or later you've got to get out there and sell your service to the public.

The late start also cost us Act II, the spring bear season. That used to be one of the most lucrative, as well as exciting, parts of the business. A few years ago, though, the people of Colorado disregarded the recommendation of the State Wildlife Commission and voted to end the spring hunt. But in my day, a guy could start taking clients into the high country after bear about the middle of April, when the roads dried, and by the end of May (if he knew what he was doing) he could make more money than he had all winter.

Selling the service to clients is just as important as anything else an outfitter does. The biggest problem is that salesmanship isn't much like outfitting, and guys who are good at one aren't necessarily good at the other. An outfitter's real stage is the outdoors, but in Act I, he's performing in big-city arenas–places like

McNichols Arena in Denver, or Kiel Auditorium in St. Louis. I always thought of Act I as a kind of actor's exercise, a rehearsal for the real thing. You came out of winter quarters pretty rusty; Act I gave you a chance to work on your role and recruit your supporting cast.

Usually I left home the end of February and stayed out through March and the first part of April. My route took me through Phoenix, Dallas, Houston, Tulsa, Oklahoma City, Kansas City, and St. Louis—more than 2,000 miles. One year I got as far east as Chicago.

I traveled in my old VW van with a knock-down booth, boxes of brochures, and a TV/VCR so I could show a videotape of the resort and groups of satisfied customers posed with dead bears, strings of trout, or dead deer and elk. I also carried a collection of props—a trophy-sized elk head, a bighorn sheep head. In a local pawn shop, I found a stuffed rainbow trout that must have gone ten or twelve pounds when it came out of the water. From the bar at the resort, I borrowed a bear skin with black marbles for eyes and a mouth full of big ivory teeth.

Late winter's a bad time for an outfitter to be dipping into his savings, but sports shows have to be prepaid. Depending on the location of your booth and the size of the show, space costs between $250 and $1,000, and after a lean winter, making out $5,000 worth of checks came hard. At some arenas, you could park in the lot to unload your gear. Other places, you parked blocks away, paid the daily rate, and carried everything through the streets in your arms.

I took a wrangler along to spell me driving and lend a hand in the booth when things got hectic. I was the lead pitchman, but I counted on the wrangler to hang onto customers till I could get there. To explain the wrangler's duties to him, I borrowed an old rodeo term, "headin'-and-heelin'"—a team-roping technique where one rider catches a steer's head while the other guy ropes the hind legs. Sometimes two or three potential clients would be standing around, waiting their turn. I'm pitching one guy and I see the other two start looking at their watches. They're about ready to walk, so I say, "Hey, why don't you check with Larry about that big bull we took last season on Forge Peak?" And while Larry takes over with the first guy, I jump on the other two.

The wrangler also came in handy when I was trying to sell a summer vacation to a family and a teenage girl was present. She's rolling her eyes, bored out of her mind at the thought of going off to a dude ranch. None of her friends are going to be there, so she's not going to be there either. And then she notices this good-looking cowboy, a little older than she is, and she can't take her eyes off him. He smiles at her, and she smiles at him, and it's, "Oh, daddy, daddy; let's go." Her sales resistance is shot and so's her old man's.

The best salesmen I ever had, though, were former clients. I always carried a list with me, arranged by locale, and when we hit town I'd phone them. "We're here for a show, maybe we could get together for a drink?" I'd mention I was available for a presentation to some organization they belonged to: "You're a member of the Rotary, aren't you? I could show some slides, and you could tell them about that trip we took last year?"

Clients love hearing from you, and the idea of giving you a hand made their day. Sometimes they'd invite us to stay in their homes—which helped a lot, since we were traveling on the cuff—or they'd throw a party for us in their living room or rec room, or at their country club. They considered us celebrities, exotic specimens from another world, and they loved to show us off to their friends. They wanted to prove that though they might look like everybody else—holding dull, traditional jobs and leading the same boring, conventional lives everyone else did—for at least a couple of weeks a year, they were somebody entirely different.

There'd be drinks and dinner, and then I'd do my slide show, talking the guests through various kinds of outdoor vacations. Involving the ex-client and his wife and kids was easy, and before it was over, we'd usually sell a hell of a lot of outfitting.

Sometimes, if a guy was particularly enthusiastic, I'd invite him to be my guest at the show. He'd bring photographs of himself standing with his trophies, and we'd put them on the counter, under glass so they wouldn't walk off or get damaged by handling. To prospective clients, he'd describe how he'd caught those fish or shot that bear, pitching our service and out-selling me and the wrangler every time. Guys like that love to shill for you, and they make wonderful salesmen. After a few hours, they'd work themselves to such a pitch that it was unusual if they didn't sign up with you for another trip themselves.

There was nothing subtle about our sales technique. Because we were eating and traveling on the down payments, the idea was to sign clients on the spot. I'd try for 25 percent down, but I'd take whatever I could get, down to 1 percent. I'd take cash or checks or credit cards, you name it, anything negotiable. "Your watch? Sure, let's see it." I'd tell a guy who was hesitating, "I'm almost full that week, mister. I got three more spots, and I can't hold 'em beyond tomorrow night. You're going to have to let me know."

One of the problems with selling your service is that a lot of pretty fair outfitters aren't any good at it. Sometimes I'd take a break to check the competition and cruise the aisles with a cup of coffee. There were some rough-looking guys pitching the dudes. When somebody asked them a question, the best they could manage was, "Yup," and "Nope." It was embarrassing. Some of them were so ugly they didn't need a gun to kill game. It used to amaze me that I didn't have all the outfitting in the world—they were that bad. I'd get back to my own booth and wonder who would want to go out in the woods with these guys.

Not that there was anything wrong with them. They just weren't cut out to be pitchmen. They were country boys raised on a ranch somewhere and were naturally shy. They didn't have much education and they were scared to death of these city people. They were trying to make a living, trying to make the ranch pay, and not having much fun doing it.

Selling never bothered me. In fact, after a long, hard winter, I enjoyed dressing up like a cowboy again and talking to people about something I loved. Traveling was fun, as long as you didn't let it wear you down, and it was wonderful seeing the country— deserts coming into bloom in the Southwest, the woods and gardens full of color in the Midwest. I'd kid with the men, clown around with the little kids, and flirt with the women.

All kinds of people came by the booth. Some I called "outfitter groupies," who weren't girls but grown men who just wanted to talk to a professional guide about hunting and the outdoors. They'd hang around by the hour asking questions about fishing tackle and rifles and cartridges. They loved to swap stories with you about their experiences. You knew they wouldn't buy a hunt from you in a million years, but they were so needy that it was hard to run them off so you could get to the paying customers.

Another type I enjoyed were what I called "the Big Daddies," because they always reminded me of the character Burl Ives played in that movie, *Cat on a Hot Tin Roof.* They're classics, and every sports show has at least one. You'd see them coming through the crowd with an entourage of wives, friends, girlfriends, and hangers-on. They wore Rolex watches, two or three gold chains, and hundred-dollar haircuts. A lot of times they were shopping for trips for their employees, but sometimes they'd sign up with you to hunt or fish themselves. They were always fun, and some of them worked out pretty well, especially guys with rural backgrounds.

After spending six weeks at sports shows, on top of a winter hustling groceries, it was a relief to get home and back to outfitting again. The first thing I had to do was locate bait-sites and construct blinds in areas I knew were frequented by bears. These were meadows in the transition zone, between 9,000 and 10,000 feet, with aspen forest below and pine forest above. Bears are constantly patrolling treelines at that altitude, because the meadows are full of their favorite foods—cow parsnips and service berries, grub-filled rotten logs and dandelions. In the spring, bears will eat anything—animal, vegetable, or mineral—but they're wild about fresh, young dandelion flowers, and graze on them like hogs on turnips or cattle on sweet clover.

Access roads were important, too. I wanted to drive as close to the site as possible because a five-gallon pickle bucket holds twenty-five or thirty pounds of bait, and I'd be hand-carrying as many as half a dozen buckets a day, seven days a week, into three or four sites. After that, all I needed was a location for the blind: somewhere inside the treeline, with enough down timber available to screen the blind and cover the bait, and a comfortable log for me and the hunter to sit on when he arrived.

It seemed strange, but even in those transition-zone meadows, where bear traffic was heavy, I rarely saw a track. About the only evidence they left would be an occasional lump of bear scat, or else long, black streaks on the pale aspen bark where some big boar had sharpened his claws. Or there'd be marks, like fingerprints, where cubs had climbed when their mothers chased them up trees to get them out of danger. But I always knew that no matter how little evidence I saw, as long as I stayed in those high meadows, I couldn't get it wrong. I don't think I ever put bait out in country like that and missed.

One reason, of course, is because the Gunnison country is full of bears. I used to estimate the population at about 5,000, which at that time meant there were more of them than there were of us. Another reason is because bears give you a lot of cooperation. Their sense of smell is amazing. After they'd come and gone from the site, I would backtrack them and find the place where they'd stopped, turned suddenly, and started toward the bait—and it would be five miles away.

For me, the hardest part of bear hunting was collecting bait, and over the years, it got harder to do. When I started, it was easy to collect cooking grease (which is the basis for first-class bait) from catch-pans in every restaurant and burger joint in town. Cooks were so happy to get rid of it, you felt like they should pay you for taking it off their hands. But after a couple of years, I couldn't touch the stuff, because companies paying premium prices to reclaim grease ran me out of the market.

At first, competition from other outfitters wasn't bad, either, and it was easy to scrounge all the garbage I needed from grocery store dumpsters. The night crew would fill the dumpsters early in the morning, sometime around three and four AM, and I'd get there about dawn, two or three hours later. But as more and more guys began hunting bears, I had to get up earlier, and dig deeper, to find what I needed. Finally, toward the end of my career, I'd have to be parked beside the dumpster when the crew came out the stockroom door or there wouldn't be anything left.

Fresh garbage isn't bad to work with; in fact, it's hardly like garbage at all. It can smell as clean and sweet as greenhouse produce or new-mown hay—but as it ages, it can get pretty rank. My stomach's naturally delicate, and when things got bad, I'd have to soak a bandanna in after-shave, or whiskey, and tie it across my face like an outlaw's mask. Of course, the deeper you dig in a dumpster, the worse things get. Sometimes I'd pick up an innocent-looking object—a lopsided grapefruit, or a loaf of stale bread—and it was like pulling the plug on a charnel house sewer. There were times when I'd see a guy hanging over a dumpster, legs working, and think he was after some culinary treasure, and realize he was unloading his breakfast.

Outfitters scrounging garbage are one of the saddest sights you'll ever see. Dressed in ragged coveralls and dirty jackets, we looked like a bunch of old winos, all of us with buckets and bags fishing for rotten fruit and vegetables and butcher scraps. Most guys wore leather or neoprene gloves; others didn't bother, grubbing around with their bare hands. I remember looking up one time—it was still dark, about ten below zero with a wind blowing—and thinking: "Oh, Jesus, I've come to this."

For me, another good source of garbage was the resort kitchen, especially after a buffet. Busboys would collect plastic bags full of watermelon, cantaloupe, cherries, lettuce and cabbage from salads, plate scrapings of all kinds. Dog food, liberally laced with cooking grease, makes a wonderful base, and old bread—the older, the better—works well. Sometimes I'd throw a fresh-skinned coyote carcass into the freezer to be chopped up later. Another source of high-protein bait was ice at the local reservoirs, where fishermen would keep trout and salmon they'd caught, but throw suckers, which they considered trash fish, away. I used to cherry-pick the ice, collecting rejects in pickle buckets, and store them in the freezer.

Bears love candy, especially candy that's gone bad. They'll roll in it with all the joy and enthusiasm they show for a rotten cow carcass. One of my greatest bait coups was finding 200 pounds of out-of-date chocolates on an after-Christmas sale at a wholesale warehouse in Montrose, Colorado. Later that spring, while I was baiting with the candy, I used to dream of walking over a hill and finding a bear with his pinkies full of chocolate-covered cherries.

Everything edible—or inedible, depending on your point of view—was grist for the bait mill. One night Old Red, a rooster with spurs two inches long and a temperament to match, challenged the stock truck to single combat when I drove in the gate at Harmel's. He jumped out of the darkness into the headlights, and there was no way to avoid him. He went *thump, thump*, and I put him in the bait vat, feathers and all. Apparently the bears found nothing wrong with Old Red's contribution, because for weeks I found various indigestible parts—feathers, beak, a foot—strewn around the mountainside among their scat.

I always considered bears the most fascinating animals I hunted–the most interesting and at the same time the most dangerous. In the West, black bears are smaller by several hundred pounds than their Eastern counterparts, but even a 300- or 400-pound Western bear can be pretty scary. I remember one night returning to a camp on Diamond Creek after a big boar raided my cook tent. His prints were all over, and the canvas had been slashed to ribbons with what appeared to have been a sharp knife. The most serious damage was to an aluminum pressure cooker. After using it to prepare ham and beans, I'd washed it, but enough scent remained to attract the bear. His canine teeth had punched holes so big through that thick aluminum that I could fit my index and little finger past the first knuckles.

Indians believe there's something mystical about bears, and I think they're right. I know that funny things go through your mind when bears are around. In summer, we worked with a window from about 4:00 to 7:30 PM, when it starts to get dark. Before 4:00, bears wouldn't approach a baitsite, and after 7:30, it was too late. It's illegal to shoot them after dark or by any kind of artificial light, and walking away from a blind at night is too dangerous–you can walk right into one.

Once in a while I'd meet a bear in broad daylight, and that was always a thrill. Once I got back to the resort after a camping trip, and when I unpacked, I found I'd lost the valve to my favorite stove. That model was no longer in production, and it was useless without the valve, so I changed into tennis shoes and walked back up the trail toward the camp I'd left that morning. When I found the valve on the trail, I started back to the resort, then decided to take a shortcut through a creekbed. Something was lying beside the stream, so I was careful till I saw it was a dead cow. Sometimes cows eat larkspur, and when the poison starts working, they head for water and die.

I was a few yards away from the carcass when a black bear reared up. He'd been feeding on the other side, crouched with his head inside the cow's stomach. Now, when his head came up, it was so matted with blood and shreds of meat he could hardly see me. My heart started revving like you wouldn't believe. We weren't fifteen feet apart. I don't know how long we stared at each other– it seemed like forever–and then I broke the first rule of conduct when you walk up on a bear: don't run. I went straight up the bank as hard as I could go, and I don't even remember doing it. The next thing I knew, I was about halfway up—maybe thirty yards from the cow—and I stopped to look over my shoulder, to see if he was gaining on me. And there he was on the other bank. He'd run up his side as fast as I'd run up mine. We looked at each other, and so help me, I wasn't even breathing hard.

Finally he snorted and trotted off. I watched till he was gone, then climbed the rest of the way up the bank, and I felt great. I was so high on adrenaline, I floated all the way down to the resort.

Bears are nearsighted, so it doesn't take much to make an effective blind—a screen of branches no more substantial than a garden trellis does the trick. Their noses are keen, but the stench of the bait seems to anesthetize it. Nothing interferes with their hearing, though. One evening I was in a blind taking pictures of a big cinnamon boar, and to test his hearing, I tapped my watch crystal with a thumbnail. To my ears, the sound was barely audible, but at twenty yards, the bear recognized something unnatural and stared right at me. He couldn't see me, but it was like he'd run the sound through his computer and it had come out wrong.

Another thing about bears that impressed me was their silence. No matter how carefully you listened, you never heard them coming to the blind. The only way you knew they were close was that suddenly the woods got quiet. Everything seemed to stop, even the wind, and then there they were. They'd come up on you like a barefoot man. I hunted them for years, but I never saw one before he was right in front of me. Sometimes I used to dream of watching a bear from the distance, kind of ambling along through some open meadow or crossing a stream, but it never happened.

Once in a while, bears will show up in town and cause all kinds of commotion. Usually they're adolescent males with hurt feelings, run off by their mothers to make room for younger siblings. Searching for a territory of their own, they appear in the middle of a street, stopping traffic, or feeding in an alley out of somebody's garbage can. A few summers ago, a thirty-five-pound male appeared in the middle of campus on the college president's lawn while a barbecue was in progress. Startled by the attention he attracted, the bear scrambled up a tree and had to be captured by the fire department. It's my opinion that as a result of the elimination of the spring hunt, we're going to see a lot more bears trying to establish territories in town.

Occasionally bears paid a visit to the resort and caused a lot of excitement among the guests. One night a businessman from Denver and his wife woke to hear a racket on the front porch of their cabin. A bear was banging away at a cooler full of fish, trying to break it open. In response to his wife's demand that he do something, the guy switched on the light, emptied a .32 pistol in the bear's direction, and jumped back inside. Fortunately, the bear decided to run the other way.

Next morning, when I returned from camp, I found bits of blood and fur on the porch. I wasn't sure how seriously the bear had been wounded, but I saddled two horses, and the businessman and I tracked him into the high country. The guy didn't last long, though. He got to bragging about how he'd hit the bear, and I told him all he'd done with that popgun was get the animal pissed off. And if the bear was gut-shot, he'd be up there someplace laying for us with a hell of a bellyache. After that, the guy started hanging back, thinking it over. Finally, when we stopped for lunch, he said, "I don't have to do this—I don't want to do this."

I couldn't blame him—I didn't want to do it, either—but I told him if he pulled a stunt like that, he ought to help clean up his mess.

The guy rode back, and I tracked the bear for three days before giving up. By that time he'd stopped bleeding, so apparently the wound had sealed itself. If peritonitis didn't set in, I figured he'd be okay—and probably be a lot more cautious about picnic coolers, even if they did smell like fish.

Because bears are solitary by nature, they're edgy around baitsites; they find communal feeding unnatural. Years ago, when rangers fed bears at Yellowstone, you could tell from pictures how uncomfortable they were with each other. A sow with cubs will be really grumpy, especially if there's an old boar around, because a boar will eat a cub if he can catch it. Brown bears—grizzlies—hunt black bears all the time, and if they catch them, they'll eat them in a New York minute.

Sometimes—not often, but occasionally—bears kill people or maim them. For some reason no one pretends to understand, this is more likely to happen in the West than back East, where bears are not only larger but less aggressive. A few years ago, a runner who lived in Gunnison was jogging on the Mill Creek trail, about twenty miles north of town, preparing for a marathon race. When he failed to come home one night, a Search and Rescue team went out and found his body. He'd died in a fall from a tree, but his running shoe showed the teeth marks of a bear.

I went up to look and found the runner's tracks on the trail, along with those of an adult bear and several cubs. The bark of the tree was scuffed, the branches broken. The obvious inference was that the runner had gotten between a mother bear and her cubs. She'd chased him up the tree, biting at his heels; he'd lost his grip and been killed in the fall.

One of the reasons I loved baiting bears was that it gave me a chance to watch them and photograph them. I also believed that baiting was beneficial to the population. I know I carried a lot of food up there, and over the years, I saw a significant increase in their numbers–by at least 5 percent–and that was over and above the ones my clients were killing. One reason their numbers increased was because a lot of twins and triplets survived. When times are hard, only the strongest cub in a litter will live; sometimes he won't make it, either. I wasn't baiting sows, but I couldn't keep them off the bait; they were going to get their share, and so were their cubs.

A wildlife biologist did a study of Gunnison country bears a few years ago, though, and came to the opposite conclusion. He argued that hunting was depleting the bear population, but I always thought he had his facts wrong. Most outfitters I know wouldn't let that happen, not in their areas. For an outfitter, bears are money on the hoof. By the time you add the kickback from the taxidermist, a bear is worth $2,000 to an outfitter.

I charged $1,500 for what I called "a shootable bear"; that is, a bear close enough to shoot, whether the hunter killed it or not. But I never *guaranteed* a bear kill. I'd tell my clients, "If you don't get a shot, you owe me nothing–the hunt's on me. But if you get close enough to shoot, you owe me, whether you kill one or not." That's because about as many men miss a bear when they shoot as kill one. I never guaranteed any other big game as shootable, but I guaranteed bears because I knew I could bring them to the bait.

Bears are nocturnal. They feed at night and lay up during the day, so you've got to persuade them to change their natural feeding schedule. The trick is to bait them for three or four days until they're hooked on the smell and taste. But you can't just keep feeding them: you also have to destroy their habitual caution about daytime feeding by turning off the bait. That means that during the two or three days before you take the hunter to the blind, you supply less and less bait. But no matter how impatient a bear becomes, you can seldom get him on the bait—and in front of the hunter's gun—more than an hour before dark.

To get the timing right, I'd bring the client in early and stretch the hunt over three or four days. Sometimes I had as many as half a dozen baitsites going at once, with two or three bears working each of them. While the bear was experiencing withdrawal pains, I'd take the hunter fishing or horseback riding, or send him out hiking. Some outfitters are less conscientious, and that can cause problems not only with wildlife management personnel, but also with the public at large. Some Gunnison outfitters are notorious for the speed and efficiency with which they conduct their hunts. Instead of bringing clients in early, they wait until the bait has been turned off for a few days and then phone them. When the clients step off the plane, the outfitters take them to the blind, they shoot their bear, and a couple of hours later, they're on the plane home.

Outfitters like that will kill as many bears as they can get permits for. Usually that's about twelve or fourteen a year. Of course, an attrition rate like that won't put much of a dent in the bear population, but it's the principle of the thing. It just doesn't seem very sporting to kill an animal that way. It's like shooting a hen sitting on a nest.

There's always been some difference of opinion among wildlife biologists about what rouses bears from hibernation. It's got to be some combination of increasing sunlight or water from snowmelt leaking into their dens. But once awake, they come out hungry and disoriented, like lapsed alcoholics looking for a drink. Early spring is hard on wildlife everywhere, but especially in the high country, where short growing seasons and cold temperatures restrict the amount of available food. The main portion of a bear's diet consists of roots, grasses, and shoots. They dig milk vetch. They search stream bottoms for over-wintered berries emerging from the snow. They eat buds, sedges, and cotton grass tussocks.

Because of their vegetable diets, spring bears have almost no odor. Spring is also the season when their coats are best—thick, clean, and lustrous. Their meat is firm, leaner by at least 30 percent after hibernation. Sometimes I barbecued animals that were so large I could have fed fifty or sixty people from one carcass. People who requested small helpings to begin with always asked for more.

Until it was made illegal, spring bear season lasted from April, about the time high country roads and trails begin to open, until the end of June. Because the fall season overlapped with big game season, I never hunted bears then, but occasionally I skinned fall bears other people killed. It was not an activity I enjoyed. By then their coats were in much worse shape—worn ragged, filled with ticks and lice and burrs, foul with matter from decomposing cows. Sometimes it was all I could do to keep from losing my lunch.

When bears approach a baitsite for the first time, they circle it for a while, as though unable to believe their luck, before they go to work on it. The second day, they defecate the first day's meal within twenty yards of the site, and they continue that pattern until the bait is gone or they're killed.

To protect bait from coyotes or stray dogs, I covered it with logs or trees too large for them to move. When the bear got there, he would simply throw the cover aside with a sweep of his paw. Of course, that got the hunter's heart beating pretty good, because some of those logs weighed a hundred pounds or more, and bears do it with amazing ease, as if no effort at all were involved.

Bear hunters, I learned, are a lot like bears themselves, as far as personalities go. They tend to be solitary, preferring to have as little as possible to do with the regular resort guests. Usually I put them up at the wranglers' bunkhouse and cooked their meals myself. It was funny, but just like bears, you couldn't fill them up. They'd eat at the kitchen table, double portions of everything, then wipe their plates with a piece of bread.

Sometimes they'd drop by the bar across the road for a drink, but they liked to sit by themselves, and it didn't take long for the bartender and the waitresses to learn to leave them alone. Maybe it was because of the risk involved in hunting bears, but they were edgy, too. None of them had much of a sense of humor, and if you tried to kid them, they'd take it just so long before snapping back at you.

For them, bear hunting was the *manly* thing to do. I always thought they were deliberately pressuring themselves, trying to increase the sense of danger that goes with hunting and firearms. There's a big difference between hunting bear, say, and hunting deer. All a deer wants to do is get away from you, but bears are predators themselves. They'll kill and eat anything they can catch—deer and elk, cows and sheep, even chickens. Even hunters, and hunters know it, too. They don't talk about it, but they think about it a lot.

I always considered bear hunting to be the closest thing on the North American continent to African-style safari hunting. Hunting leopards would probably be the closest. Both animals are nocturnal, so they're rarely seen during daylight in the wild. Neither of them get along well with humans, and as a result, they've been driven to the most obscure portions of their habitat. Both also range widely, and because of their shyness and stealth, you have to hunt them over bait or with dogs. Without the services of a guide, they're almost impossible for the ordinary hunter to find and kill. And both, when wounded, are extremely dangerous.

Adding to the air of danger and excitement is the strange physical resemblance between bears and men. Primitive peoples recognized it centuries ago and treated tribesmen who killed bears with a deference that, in some cases, amounted to awe. Bears are about the size, and in many cases, about the weight of humans. They have diets similar to ours. They even smell like men—particularly like some of the unwashed desert Indians I met when I was in Mexico. When a bear becomes excited or angry and rears up on his hind legs with his front legs extended like arms, the resemblance is frightening. Even worse is how much a skinned bear, with its pale, bloody limbs and torso, looks like a naked man on a morgue slab. All he needs is a tag on his big toe.

It didn't take me long to figure bear hunters out. At sports shows, they'd tell me how much they'd always wanted to hunt a bear, then ask what kind of weapon I recommended. I'd play on that macho thing by asking how close they wanted to get. "I like a bow," I'd say, "because that gets you right there on the ground with them. But you can use anything you want—a bow, big game rifle, black powder rifle, or a pistol." In fact, sometimes I'd phony the deal up a little and tell them, "Hey, you're the hunter, I'm just the guide. I can bring 'em to the blind, but you're going to have to kill 'em. I'll be there to back you up, but you want to remember: they're pretty dangerous."

Not that they're really all that dangerous. I remember a hunter asking me in a blind what we'd do if he missed a shot and the bear charged. I told him all the bear would do was panic; he would be trying to run away, and the odds of his coming on the particular compass heading that would lead to us would be 360 to 1. Of course, it can happen. Bears, especially browns, kill people and injure people from time to time, even hunters with rifles that would flatten an elephant.

To give clients their money's worth, I usually stretched the hunt from three to five days while I turned off the bait. We'd get to the blind by late afternoon and sit there waving away mosquitoes instead of slapping them. Unless an exceptional bear appeared, I'd postpone the kill for a day or so by telling the client it was a sow or claiming that we could do better. We'd leave the blind about dusk, in plenty of time not to walk into a prowling bear in the dark.

At the resort, we'd have a drink at the bar, discuss the hunt and the next day's activities, and call it a night. Some outfitters used to turn their bear hunters loose during the day, but I'd take them horseback riding or fishing, or for a Jeep ride. If the client brought his wife or girlfriend along, I'd invite her to accompany us. I always made it a point to give them a look at the high country, because bear hunters were good candidates for a fall elk or deer hunt.

One spring, I arranged a bear hunt for a woman television network photographer. When I tried to prepare her for what was going to happen, she told me not to bother, that she'd photographed lions and tigers in Africa and India, and that she certainly wasn't worried about a 300- or 400-pound black bear. What she didn't tell me was that she'd done her photography standing on a seat through the open roof of a Land Rover.

She was big and blonde, about forty years old, with a hell of a tan. She wore knee-length boots and safari clothes, like something out of Banana Republic. To simplify things, we agreed that instead of using a tripod, she'd shoot with the lens of the camera resting on my shoulder. In the blind, we waited about an hour before a big male appeared. He circled the bait suspiciously, then started demolishing the log cover.

Video cameras don't make much noise, just a little hum, so I could hear it. Then, all of a sudden, it started jumping, kind of slapping against my cheek. It was still humming, but I knew there was no way she could be getting a picture. What the hell was going on, I wondered? Then I knew: she was scared to death; she was shaking so bad she couldn't finish filming.

"Ha-ha-ha," she whispered. "I think I peed my pants." I looked and sure enough, there was a little wet spot, right in the crotch.

We watched the bear clean up the bait, then walked back to the Jeep, making a lot of noise. At the lodge, we looked at the tape she'd shot on a TV set in the lounge. The picture was steady while she tracked the bear to the bait, and it was all right when the bear flipped that first log. But when he started throwing the rest of them around, the picture bounced so bad you couldn't watch it. Which, I always thought, illustrates one of the important differences between shooting from a Land Rover and getting on the ground with game.

Another client, a dentist I met at a Kansas City sports show, told me he'd hunted all over the world with a rifle, but he'd become fascinated with the idea of killing a bear with a revolver. Until he met me, he'd never found an outfitter who'd arrange a hunt under such conditions. Since I preferred to get hunters as close as possible to the game they were after—I considered it part of the experience—I had no objection. "Whatever turns your crank," I told the guy. "We'll jump out of trees on 'em with a jackknife, if that's what you want."

I built a blind in a neck of timber above Jack's Cabin on the Crested Butte road and started the baiting process. Before long, I had a pair of cinnamon bears interested. When the dentist arrived, he showed me his pistol—a reproduction of a nineteenth-century, .44 caliber Colt Dragoon revolver chambered to a modern .44 Magnum cartridge. With an octagonal barrel and rosewood grips, it looked like something that belonged in a museum instead of on a bear hunt. I'd never seen anything like it, but the guy claimed he'd shot it at targets, and it worked fine.

Baiting earlier each day, with progressively smaller portions, I got the bears coming in while the light was good enough to shoot. When the dentist and I entered the blind, he sat against a tree trunk across from me, his back to the bait. I always signaled when it was safe (and legal) to fire, so I faced forward, toward him.

All of a sudden things got quiet, like everything was holding its breath. I looked at the dentist, to see if he knew a bear was close. The big Colt was lying in his lap and he'd stopped breathing. He was looking past me, his eyes as big as a tree full of owls, and right away I knew what had happened: the two cinnamons had been coming up a draw in front of the blind, but tonight another bear had come over the hill behind us. He didn't see us or hear us or smell us, so he just stepped right in the blind with us.

Black bears are not particularly aggressive. Give them half a chance and they'll turn and run; but if they're startled, or feel trapped, they may decide to attack. I couldn't see the bear, and I was afraid to turn around, afraid I might spook him. I'm watching the dentist, waiting, and his arm comes up. He's waving that dragoon revolver around, half the time aiming past my head, half the time I'm looking right down that octagonal barrel.

"Jesus," I start to whisper, "take it easy," when b*ang!* a round goes off, right past my face. Powder burns my cheek from the leaky cylinder; I'm deaf as a post from the report. The bear must have been about two yards behind me, but the dentist was shaking so bad, he missed him by ten. I turned just in time to see the bear whirl and disappear.

Next day we tried again, and this time the original pair showed up from the proper direction. They were about twenty yards in front of the blind. The light was perfect, but by now my dentist was shaking so hard, he fired and missed them both.

That was the end of his bear hunt, but he left satisfied. He told me it had been a hell of an experience—and he paid me $1,500, without an argument, because I'd done what I said I'd do: I'd delivered a shootable bear. That first one had just been a little more shootable than he'd bargained for.

Once in a while I met a bear that was more than I bargained for myself. A friend of the Kansas City dentist, who was also an experienced international hunter, came out the next spring. Since he was planning a trip to Alaska that summer for Kodiak bear, he wanted to try out a new rifle—a 300 Weatherby—on something smaller first. After he sighted it in at the local range, we went up to a baitsite on Red Mountain. A big cinnamon showed up and the hunter fired, but the bullet hit him too far behind the shoulder to kill him.

Growling and biting at the wound, the bear stumbled over a rise and disappeared. I drew my .357 and we went after him. He made it as far as a shallow draw about thirty yards down the slope, then collapsed. That big Weatherby had shocked him pretty good. He was lying on his side, eyes closed and breathing hard, but otherwise not moving.

I left the hunter on top and slipped closer. The bear's eyes were partially open, and he looked like he was trying to lift his head—and I got careless. I thought he was paralyzed, so I put the pistol barrel against his head and kind of pushed him down. Because I didn't have a license, I didn't want to kill him, so I turned and yelled at the hunter: "You're going to have to shoot him again." And I see this expression on his face. It's very strange; it's an expression you don't see outside an old Fay Wray movie, like, "Something is about to eat you."

I turn around, and the bear's up on all four feet—and all four feet are working. There was no way I could outrun him—bears are so quick, you don't even want to consider it—so I stood my ground and, at six inches, shot him between the eyes.

Down he goes, and I turn around to look at the dentist. A Weatherby bolt has an unusually long stroke, and because the gun was new, he wasn't used to it. In the excitement, he'd forgotten to chamber another round; now he was jerking at the bolt, trying to eject the spent cartridge.

"Come on," I yelled, "you're going to have to shoot him again." And again when he looked at me, I saw that strange expression on his face. I turned and the bear was up. At point-blank range, I shot him in the head again—only by now it's occurred to me that I must be doing something wrong. Backing away, I yelled at the dentist to hurry. And sure enough, the bear gets up again: that's three times.

I just kept backing away from him, waiting, and finally I hear the big Weatherby crack and the bear goes down for good.

Later, when I skinned him, I examined the skull and found that both my bullets had entered above his eyes, tracked over his skull under the fur, and gone out the back. The brain, though, hadn't even been touched. In fact, I don't know if that .357 even gave him a headache.

A few weeks later, I was talking to some veteran bear hunters and learned that the safest place to shoot one is in the neck. Sever the spinal column, and nothing answers. The next best place is in the mouth, particularly if it's open, so his teeth won't deflect the bullet. Bears have small brains, but the lower brain, which controls the autonomic nervous system, is highly developed. To finish a bear, all of them agreed, you have to put its nervous system out of commission.

A lot of people are worried about bear poaching these days, and they have a right to be. Because of their supposed aphrodisiac qualities, Orientals prize bear gallbladders and paws. In the United States, black-market bladders sell for a couple of hundred dollars, but by the time they reach Korea and some other places in the Far East they may bring as much as $5,000. A bowl of bear paw soup, a traditional dish for Oriental bridegrooms, will cost $500. As a result, bears in the Orient and Russia have been hunted nearly to extinction, and there is increasing demand on the American market.

This situation has put pressure on American game wardens and animal control officers—men for whom I have the highest regard. In the old days, when their jobs were political appointments, some of them weren't much good, but today these guys know their stuff. They have degrees in wildlife biology and game management. They also have a lot of courage—they're out in the woods checking an armed population, a lot of it careless, some of it criminal, and most of it hostile. It's not a job I envy.

I always cooperated with game wardens who worked in my area, because I knew we shared a common interest in the welfare of the forest and the animals. Late one summer, I was scouting the high country on horseback with a warden I'll call Fred Robertson.

I was looking for game, getting ready for hunting season; Robertson was looking for private elk camps and four-wheel-drive tracks where there weren't supposed to be any. Like professional outfitters, free hunters usually return to the same campsites every year, and it was easier for Robertson to check hunting licenses if he knew in advance where their camps had been the year before. The Department of Wildlife had failed to provide him with a horse, so I'd lent him one of mine.

Working our way into remote country near the headwaters of North Willow Creek, we found four-wheel-drive tracks cut in the forest floor and smelled rotting meat. In a meadow, crows and magpies squabbled over the carcass of a bull elk. Somebody was baiting bear. They'd driven in, dropped off the carcass, and got out again.

Robertson and I looked for the permit that was supposed to be in a can hanging from a nearby tree, but found nothing. Robertson also had a list of all the bear permits that had been issued in the county, but there were none for this area. Someone was not only driving off the road and baiting bear, he was doing it without a license.

The idea that it was a fellow outfitter, though, never occurred to me. I figured some flatlander had been tooling around up here where he didn't belong with a rifle. When he spotted an elk, he couldn't resist temptation and killed it. Then, trying to parlay his investment in crime into a trophy bear, he used the body for bait. Now, unless the guy had an attack of conscience (or common sense), he'd be back.

While I went back to town, Robertson set up camp not far from the baitsite to wait for the poacher. I didn't even think about who it might be. I even talked about the situation in a couple of bars around town—how somebody was poaching bear on North Willow. After two days of sitting on the bull, Robertson saw an outfitter from the other end of the basin approach the carcass on horseback and jumped him. But when Robertson accused him of poaching, the guy denied it, claiming he'd simply been "cruising through the country."

You wonder why a guy would do something like that, but it's a combination of desperation and ignorance. They don't realize that the proper technique for baiting bears not only involves feeding them, but also turning off the feed. With deposits in hand, and hunters coming in, they set up an illegal bait and jack-o-lantern one in the dark. Doing it the right way is a lot easier, but it's hard to do if you don't know how.

The wildlife people fooled around with the investigation for months, but could never make a case against him. Finally they dismissed the charge, but the guy was convinced that I'd reported him because Robertson had been using one of my horses.

If they had wanted to get tough about it, they could have taken his license and permit area away from him, putting him out of business. He bad-mouthed me all over town, sure I'd turned him in to get his area. There was some of that in the old days—one outfitter would set up another one, drive him out of business, and take over his territory. But what the hell, I wouldn't have done something like that. As a matter of fact, the guy had a lousy area—I wouldn't have had it on a bet.

The only bear I ever had anything to do with killing in the fall was at the trash dump behind the resort corral. Larry Malloy, the wrangler who used to do the sports show circuit with me, bought a used .54 caliber Hawken black powder rifle that generated a terrific kick and a prodigious quantity of smoke. We experimented with it, shooting at targets, and it was a lot of fun. Larry wanted to see what it would do on something big and tough, and the obvious choice was a bear. A big boar had been raiding the dump, causing a lot of excitement among the guests, so he was elected.

Malloy bought a license, and we built a blind out of sagebrush between the corral and the dump. In addition to the Hawken rifle, Malloy carried a .44 Magnum revolver, and I had my .357 Mag. To be comfortable, we borrowed a couple of lawn chairs and set them up in the blind. Then we opened a carton of beer and opened all the cans, so we wouldn't spook him by popping tops if his timing was bad.

It was a warm afternoon, almost like summer. We could hear kids yelling and splashing in the swimming pool, people walking along talking on the road to the dining room. The bear had been getting there early, but tonight he was later than usual. We sipped beer, tucking the empties back in the carton. The sun was getting lower, stretching shadows across the sage, but we still had half an hour of legal shooting light.

Across the road, we could hear supper being served. It was getting late, I told Larry; maybe we'd better give it up. He agreed, and about that time the bear came swaggering out of the pines, as dark as an ink blot, with that confident air bears adopt when they're on familiar ground. He'd been doing this for weeks, so he had his M.O. down cold. Strolling to the dump, he started throwing trash around to get at the kitchen scraps and picnic leftovers the guests had thrown away.

Larry and I eased to our feet. The bear was so busy, and making such a racket, that he didn't see or hear a thing. Larry leveled the Hawken, then lowered it, hoping the bear would move closer, or stand sideways, so he could get a better angle for the shot. "What do you think?" Malloy kept whispering.

Finally I told him if he was going to shoot, he better do it. This time, when he lifted the rifle, I gritted my teeth and stuck my fingers in my ears, because I knew what was coming. *BAM!* The bear disappeared in a cloud of black powder smoke, but I heard him let out a roar. In fact, later we learned people all over the resort had heard the noise. "What was that?" they asked me. "We thought maybe it was a mountain lion. And what was all that shooting?"

With the smoke, we couldn't see a damned thing, but Malloy dropped the rifle, drew his .44 Mag., and blazed away, blind. Then he dropped the revolver and said, "Give me yours," and emptied my .357, too.

The air was so full of lead, it sounded like a war: Malloy and me versus the bear, only I'm unarmed, and I still can't see a damned thing. We stand our ground but figure he's probably charging our position. I'm supposed to be there to back up Malloy, but I'm keeping old Larry between me and the bear so he can take the brunt of any attack.

When Malloy finally ran out of ammunition, all we could do was wait, our ears ringing. My hunting knife was our last line of defense, but I didn't draw it, because by now I figured if the bear was going to kill us and eat us, he would have done it already.

Reloading the revolvers, we watched the smoke clear, then crept forward. The bear was lying in a pile of cardboard boxes, stone-cold dead. He hadn't taken four steps, and there weren't but two holes in him: one was that .54 caliber round, right through the heart. The other one we were never sure about—some kind of bullet had knocked off a front toe. A total of thirteen shots had been fired, and only two of them did any damage. The bear was deader than a doornail—only he didn't know it, and we hadn't known it, either.

I seldom hunted bears myself with anything but a camera. Once, though, I had a big cinnamon bear—an exceptional bear, with a particularly beautiful coat—working a bait. It was the end of the season, and two hunters—on two different tries, from less than twenty yards—had failed to kill him. Marilyn would love a bearskin rug on the floor in front of the fireplace, I thought, so I decided to go after him myself. To increase the sporting nature of the hunt, I decided to use a bow and arrow.

Wearing a camouflage suit and face-black, I climbed into a platform I'd built in a tree overlooking the baitsite and waited. And waited. All spring the bear had been coming in right on time, but as afternoon faded to evening, it looked like he wasn't going to show up at all. I must have dozed off, because suddenly I woke, stiff with cold. Even from the tree, it was almost too dark to shoot, so I decided to give it up. There was still light up high, but on the ground it was dark and absolutely still. Rather than descend carrying the bow and three razor-sharp broad-head arrows, I followed the safety procedure I recommended to clients: tying bow and quiver to a cord, I lowered them to the ground, then climbed down myself.

I was bending over to pick up the bundle when I smelled him. By the end of June, bears develop a powerful odor from the bait and the rotten animal carcasses they've been eating. It's a strong, sweaty, acid smell, like the odor of an unwashed man. Because there wasn't any wind to speak of, I knew he couldn't be more than ten or fifteen feet away. I couldn't see him, and with the camouflage suit against the tree, I didn't think he could see me. But he could smell me, just like I smelled him, and we both froze.

My revolver was on my hip, but I was afraid of the noise I'd make getting rid of the bow and arrows, turning around, and drawing the pistol. In that situation, the bear had every advantage. Finally, notching an arrow, I drew the bow twice, working up my nerve, then turned and released the string.

The arrow struck. I heard it go in, but from the dull thud it made, I knew I hadn't hit the spine or lungs; instead, I'd probably gut-shot him. There was a wild thrashing in the brush, and then the bear turned and ran in the opposite direction.

Returning to the truck, I waited an hour for the shot to take effect. By now it was dark, so I lit a Coleman lantern and started tracking him. He was hit hard and losing a lot of blood, but it was blood that was hard to see. By the light of a Coleman lantern, blood looks more brown than red, so I got down on my hands and knees and crawled, feeling in the grass and leaves to make sure.

The bear had fled up a creekbed through heavy brush. I'd crawl a few yards, stop, and then crawl some more. Occasionally I backtracked a ways and sat there to consider my options. At a time like that, your imagination gets to working overtime, and all kinds of stories go through your mind, none of them good. The thought of waiting till daylight, I admit, had a powerful appeal.

Then I started smelling the bear again. There wasn't a breath of air stirring, so I knew he had to be close. The question was how bad was he hit, and how much strength did he have left? I was cussing myself, wondering why the hell I hadn't brought a shotgun with me.

Revolver in one hand, lantern extended arm's length in the other, I followed the blood trail, sure the bear was about to charge. Instead, I found him lying dead beside the creek. The arrow hadn't hit a vital spot—it was too far back in his side—but his flight had worked the broad-head back and forth into his liver, and he'd bled to death.

All of a sudden the night got pretty chilly, and I realized how hard I'd been sweating. I'd broken all kinds of rules on that one—something you find yourself doing often with bears, no matter how careful you try to be—and I'd gotten away with it. One of these days, I knew, I wasn't going to be so lucky.

By lantern light, I cleaned and skinned him, then carried the wet, heavy pelt to the truck on my shoulders. When I went back to drag the body out, I was surprised to find that the distance between the tree, where I'd shot him, and the place where I'd found the body wasn't much more than a hundred yards. It seemed like I'd followed him half a mile on my hands and knees.

Later, I sent the pelt to a taxidermist in Grand Junction, but I never got it back. Somehow, no matter how hard I tried, I was never able to get $300 ahead. The taxidermist had quoted me a great price—I was getting the outfitter's discount—but I was always paying bills or I had to buy something that just couldn't wait. At least that's how it seemed at the time. Later, I got to wondering if I really hadn't wanted a bearskin rug around the house at any price. After about six months, the taxidermist gave up on me and sold the skin to somebody else. I don't know who he was, but he got a hell of a nice rug—and he's welcome to it.

Jim in his previous incarnation at the state capitol paying off a bet to then Assistant Attorney General Joe Desraimes.

The sign greeting patrons of the Ramble Inn during Jim's tenure as manager.

Jim and two of his waitresses and customers for the Ramble Inn bucking machine.

The trail to Aspen over the East Maroon Pass. Jim's in the lead, Marilyn's riding drag.

Summer look at Dark Canyon from Castle Pass, where Jim and Edith found the lost hunter. Photo by Stan Urban.

Jim on Morgan forming up guests from Harmel's to ride in the grand entry of the Gunnison Cattlemen's Days Rodeo.

Early morning at Harmel's corral, getting ready to take clients for a ride.

Jim and the big blond bear he wounded and then tracked in the dark.

Jim with Steve and Matt Teter, with a slicked up Morgan in the background.

Jim, Marilyn, Fremont, and Blue the packhorse on top of East Maroon Pass on the Aspen ride.

A well-loaded Fremont at the fishcamp on Diamond Creek.

Perched on a pickle bucket, Jim grills chicken in camp in the Fossil Wilderness Area. Photo by Stan Urban.

Three weeks into the season, a weary cook makes skillet biscuits in hunting camp on the Big Blue.

Guides' tent in hunting camp on the Big Blue.

Jim with a native cutthroat accidentally killed using a Mepps spinner.

Early-morning coffee with one of the guides in Crystal Basin at fish camp.

Horses saddled and ready to go at winter hunting camp on the Big Blue.

Jim on Jack the mule under the Castles.

# 6

## Summer Dudes

ACCORDING TO THE DICTIONARY, the term *dude* was coined in New York City in 1883 to identify "an excessively aesthetic" young man who "affected an exaggerated fastidiousness in dress, speech, and deportment." He was a "dandy," a "swell." When the term was adopted in the West, it meant a non-Westerner, a city dweller who preserved his foreign ways and inappropriate dress. A dude, then, is someone who doesn't belong, and who probably never will no matter how hard he tries.

When I was outfitting, one of the wranglers' favorite songs was "The Rodeo Song." They played it over and over on the resort stereo until even the dudes grew fond of it—or else escaped to their cabins to avoid the noise. To a tune resembling an old country-and-western favorite, "I'm Movin' On," the chorus uses a square-dance motif and four-letter words to criticize the competence of dudes in general. The lyrics don't make complete sense, but they capture the irritation and resentment people who deal with dudes feel about them after a long season.

Real cowboys—the guys who actually mend fences and herd cattle—are suspicious of outfitters who take clients hunting and fishing for a living. Perched on a rail fence or seated in a bar, an authentic cowhand will shake his head in disgust at the thought of being around them. I wish I had a nickel for every time I've heard a cowboy say something like: "I hate the fucking dudes, man. How can you stand them? They're so goddamn dumb and helpless. I seen one of them damn fools walk right up behind a mule—didn't have the sense God gave him."

I always thought the reason for the cowboys' contempt was the disdain of the expert for the untalented but ever-hopeful amateur. Starting as children, cowboys gradually master their riding and roping skills and acquire their expertise with animals. By the time they're adults, these accomplishments have become second nature, and they've forgotten the process by which they learned them. The real source of the antagonism between cowboys and dudes is between the expert who lacks the instincts of a teacher and the pupil who seeks that expertise.

I remember asking a friend from Canada who'd been a hockey player how to skate backward. I'd been watching him, and he was a wonderful skater, but when he tried to explain the process to me, he couldn't do it. He wound up getting mad at me—like it was my fault I couldn't just do it like he could. I remember how, after Doc bucked me off and broke my back, I had to consciously learn how to walk again. I would hate to have to explain to somebody, who couldn't already walk, how it's done.

However, the relationship between outfitters and dudes is more complex, because it's a case of mutual dependence. That first year in business, I tried to use some of the local, ranch-raised kids as help, but they were hopeless. I thought because they'd grown up working with livestock and living outdoors, they'd be easy to train, but they weren't. They wanted to do everything the way they'd always done it, and they refused to follow instructions. They despised dudes and spent their time cowboying the horses—racing them as hard as they'd run—and showing off for each other. I finally realized that they were really cowboys at heart, and that there was nothing I could do about it.

The second year, I discovered that it was easier to take beginners and teach them to ride and work with stock than it was to turn cowboys into teachers. Still, as the season grew longer, and the dudes persisted in making mistakes, even my best hands' patience wore thin.

We also had to be careful around clients, many of whom were poor shots and careless with firearms. Stories of dudes who've shot an outfitter, or a guide or wrangler, are rare, but they make a deep impression. My first year, an outfitter near Steamboat Springs was killed in camp when a hunter dropped a pistol. It went off, and the bullet hit the guy in the back, between the shoulder blades, killing him instantly. Almost everybody in the business can tell stories of near misses.

Some outfitters are baffled and frustrated by clients. I knew a guy who quit the business because one dude, an old man in his seventies, insisted on walking the ten miles back to town after a hunt instead of riding a horse back to camp like he was supposed to. No amount of persuasion from the outfitter or the old man's friends would stop him. Three times he started for town, and three times the outfitter brought him back.

"I couldn't just write him off," the guy told me. "He could have been lost, or hurt, but finally I had just had it. Your run-of-the-mill dude's bad enough, but this old guy was something else. I got to feeling like it was him or me, so I decided I'd had enough. It was that or wind up convicted of murder in the pen at Canon City."

Clients fall into several general categories. First are the low-land guests at the resort, customers who swim and go for a hike, or a raft or horseback ride, and who may, when they meet you in the bar at night, buy you a drink. Next are the family groups—moms, dads, and assorted relatives, often two or more families together—who bring their children and their children's friends to hike and ride and swim at the resort pool.

Then there are the summer sportsmen. They fish, climb mountains, and take longer hikes or more strenuous horseback rides into the high country for an overnight camp. Some of the businessmen we dealt with, who took their entire staffs into the mountains to plan marketing strategies for next year, fell into in this category. Finally, there are the hunters who come for big game season in the fall, or the bear hunters who arrive at the resort during late spring and early summer.

My favorite season to be outfitting was summer, when trips seemed to unfold without effort as everyone—the resort staff as well as the guests—operated in a kind of blissful, unconscious harmony with their surroundings. On trail rides I loved to work with children, just as I'd done years before in the Denver schools—only these were not disadvantaged kids from inner-city slums, but the privileged sons and daughters of the upper middle class. Nine through fourteen seemed to be the years of wonder, when they wanted to know about the outdoors and weren't afraid to ask. Even parents lost their fear of appearing childlike, and asked questions that would have embarrassed them a few years earlier or a few years later.

Not only is each category of guest different, but each requires a different mindset on the part of the guy dealing with them, whether it's the wranglers, or the guides, or the outfitter himself. I enjoyed working with all kinds of people, but I had to make conscious adjustments when I went from one category to another. In fact, sometimes abrupt transitions left me a little disoriented. I'd finish a week in the mountains with a bunch of hard-drinking, rough-talking men, and next day I'd take out a busload of Baptist ladies and their kids and have to watch myself so that something like "Pass the fucking mashed potatoes" didn't pop out.

Some of those Baptist ladies are pretty straightlaced. Outside Crested Butte, I was taking a load of them up a steep hill they call "Son-of-a-Bitch Hill," and the ladies kept calling it "Son-of-a-Gun Hill." At first I thought they hadn't heard me, so I said it again—and then I realized they had.

That same trip a bunch of naked hippies were swimming in Lake Irwin, and when they started waving and yelling at us to join them, I beat it out of there. Then driving back down the mountain, we met a lady naked as a jaybird on a bike. When she waved and smiled, I couldn't think of anything to do but honk and wave back—but when the Baptist ladies saw her, they covered the kids' eyes. One covered the eyes of a thirteen-year-old boy. It was probably the first naked lady he'd ever seen—and maybe the last one, too, if mama had her way. I wanted to tell her to let him look, but I knew it was hopeless.

Some of my summer trips were with groups of high-dollar dudes, men who weren't there vacationing with their families, but who came to the high country on business. Frequently Texas and Oklahoma oilmen arranged camping trips with their employees and seldom left camp. Isolated in the high country, without any kind of interruption or distraction, they planned their business strategy for an entire year.

While they talked, the wranglers and I were busy cooking three meals a day and providing them with drinks and snacks. These were clients who preferred gourmet meals to plain food, and so something more exotic than my standard camp menu was called for. They wanted cloths and silverware on the table; they wanted service, the kind you don't even have to pick up a phone to get. Actually, it was a cheap way for them to get a lot of service and a lot of privacy. It also impressed the hell out of the competition when they got back to Houston or Dallas or Oklahoma City.

It took two full-time wranglers to care for the horses and mules, because the animals had to be on grass two hours, both morning and afternoon. To prevent problems, the wranglers handled them in shifts, but sometimes disaster struck anyway. Once an Air Force jet out of Colorado Springs buzzed camp, and the sonic boom put the whole remuda to flight. It took the best part of the morning to round them up. When I got back to the resort, I called North American Air Defense Command to complain and talked to a polite young captain. When I explained what had happened, he put me on hold for a few minutes, then came back on the line. "Sir, I'm sorry," he said, "but I checked our maps, and you're not there. The map shows the area to be unoccupied."

During summers, trail rides are an outfitter's bread-and-butter. Some years, when the weather was good, I led as many as half a dozen parties over East Maroon Pass for a back-door visit to Aspen. It was on one of these trips that I met Jack Nicholson and swapped drinks and stories with him in his favorite bar.

Once we crossed the pass, it was a downhill ride past Castle and Cathedral and Keefe peaks to the east, and Precarious Peak and Shoemaker Ridge to the west. The old trail, originally established to serve high country gold and silver mines, led down across the shale through heavy stands of aspen and pine.

To make the ride even more pleasant, I used to load one of the mules, Maggie, with a cooler containing wine, cheese, nuts, Danish ham, and hard deli bread. Usually we stopped to eat lunch in a glade north of the pass and drink cold Chardonnay. At that altitude, though, people tend to get dehydrated without realizing it. They may not feel thirsty until they start drinking, but once started, they can't stop. On one trip, a heavy, gray-haired woman in her fifties refused to drink, but when everyone praised the wine, she changed her mind and accepted a glass, then another. We were riding down the trail, picking up speed as the horses sensed the corral ahead, when I heard a sudden *ka-thump!* When I looked, she was lying in the trail, still very elegant, with every hair in place, her eyes closed.

When I revived her, she told me she'd suddenly felt dizzy, but she completed the ride without further trouble. It took me a while to realize that she hadn't fainted from the altitude, though the air's pretty thin up there—she just didn't hold her liquor very well.

Emerging on the road below Maroon Lake and the Bells, we'd follow the trail down the valley and pasture the horses at the Lazy K Resort. Sometimes I made reservations at the Lazy K; other times we took the shuttle bus into Aspen and stayed at a motel.

No matter how many times I did it, though, it was always a shock to the system—all that Aspen glitter and glitz after the high country. We'd spent the day listening to horseshoes rattling and wind in the trees. We'd watched hawks and jays and magpies through my binoculars. Sometimes we'd see bald or golden eagles soaring, riding the thermals over the peaks. Hillsides of wildflowers would be blooming, little spring-fed streams running under the trail on log platforms—bridges laid by miners a hundred years ago to get their ore out. If the wind was right, you'd hear East Maroon Creek at the bottom of the valley. Sometimes a NORAD jet out of Colorado Springs would be practicing bomb runs on Castle Peak or Triangle Peak.

And then you'd hit Aspen, with all those people and prices, all that noise and light, like something out of New York or London or Paris. Ten-thousand-dollar coyote-fur coats hanging in the windows. Art galleries and restaurants with tables under Cinzano umbrellas. Bars and hotels restored for more money than the whole town was worth fifty years ago. Jewelry stores with Swiss watches and sunglasses that cost more than I'd make all summer. I felt like the dog-dirty miner in that Robert Service poem who walks "out of the night that was fifty below and into the din and the glare."

On the Aspen ride, I always carried a pistol. When clients asked why, I told them there were three reasons. They thought at least one was for protection from wild animals, but I said no, the reasons were: "One, because when you cross that gate"—I meant the National Forest boundary—"there ain't no law up there"—and it's the truth. Once you get up on top, you never see a sheriff; you're on your own.

Number two was because a horse might break a leg, and I would have to put him down. When I was a kid, I camp-boyed for a bunch of ranchers and businessmen who rode into the high lakes around Steamboat Springs every fall to hunt. One of the horses broke a leg, and there wasn't a gun or knife of any size around. All I had was a penknife, and I had to kill the horse by hammering it into his brain with a rock. I swore I'd never let that happen again.

When we got to number three, I used to smile and tell them: "The third reason is because it looks good." That's also what I used to tell kids when they asked about my chaps. There are good, solid reasons for wearing chaps, but kids loved the idea that I wore them because of their appearance.

Not everyone was impressed with my outfit, though. My first trip to Aspen, a woman bus driver froze when she saw the .357 on my hip as we got on board. She had one of these pale, stressed-out, citified faces that need makeup to keep from disappearing altogether. When I saw her studying me in the mirror, I knew I was in trouble. She had a two-way radio and called ahead, and when we got off, lights were flashing on an Aspen-style Saab patrol car, and a pair of uniformed cops were waiting.

"What are you doing with that gun?" they asked.

"Packing it," I told them.

"Why?"

"Because," I explained, "I didn't want to leave it with my horse."

"Well, you're not supposed carry it around on your hip like that."

"I thought it was against the law to carry it concealed," I told them.

"You want to turn it over to us?" the cops asked, and I said: "You want to try to take it away from me?"

The dudes were wide-eyed, ready to take off, with a look on their faces like: "Hey, who is this guy? Never saw him before in my life."

"Leave it with us while you're in town," the cops told me, but I told them no, not unless they had a gun ordinance. I knew they didn't have one, none of these Western towns do, not even Aspen, because it goes against their macho image. But I was pissed at them for bracing me right in front of the dudes.

"Tell you what," I told the cops, "you go get your gun ordinance and show it to me. I'm checking in at the motel across the street. I'll wait for you there." So with the clients trooping after me, we crossed the street and marched through the lobby to the desk. The clerk—some hippie kid with his ponytail in a rubber band—had been watching, and when I said, "Have you got any rooms for Greer?" he raised his hands in a stick-'em-up position and said: "Yes, sir, Mr. Greer—all the rooms you want."

The clients, who were a little tense after our brush with the law, cracked up, and after that everything was all right. We never saw any more of the cops, of course, because they didn't have a legal leg to stand on. Next morning, when we rode the bus back to the Lazy K, the driver gave me a nervous smile, like she thought I still might try to hijack her, but she didn't say anything.

The highlight of the ride back from Aspen to Crested Butte was a visit to what I called, Jim's Bar & Grill. I always started talking it up early, before we got onto the last stretch leading to the top of the pass. "It's down below," I'd tell them, "in the woods on the other side." "We didn't see any bar and grill on the way up," clients would say, and I'd get after them: "You goddamn dudes, what am I going to do with you? You're just not observant."

Jim's Bar & Grill was located in a forest glade with wildflowers and ferns, a stream, and views north to East Maroon Pass and south down the valley toward Gothic. In a thicket of wild rose bushes, I kept a hand-lettered sign with the name of my establishment, and while the clients dismounted, I stood it against a tree trunk. A cooler on Maggie held the bar—ice, glasses, more wine, and for those who preferred it, scotch, bourbon, and gin. "How do you like Jim's Bar & Grill?" I'd ask them, and give them my pitch: "Two tables, no waiting, and I get a kickback from the bartender."

People love kidding around like that, and besides, it softens them up for the tip.

Normally I paid little attention to weather, but around thunderstorms—particularly in the high country, with clients in my charge—I learned to be careful. The Aspen ride was especially dangerous. Around noon, as we climbed toward the pass, thunder cells often came raking across the bare peaks and open bowls. If conditions looked bad from the south side, it was easy to wait or turn back toward Gothic, but the return trip was hard to postpone.

One afternoon, I was leading a party of eight, plus a young wrangler I'll call Carl, toward the pass. I was timing the thunder cells as they moved between the peaks. The cells were lined up one after another, like brass bands in a parade—lightning flashing, thunder roaring like a kettledrum section. They would sweep across the peaks, fill the mouth of the pass for about five minutes, and then blow through. The interval between cells was about thirty minutes—just enough time, I figured, to get the dudes over before the next cell caught us.

At the foot of the last steep pitch, icy blasts of wind hit us in the face, and the air became so charged with electricity that it was hard to breathe. While we waited, putting on our slickers, I explained the situation to Carl and told him that, once we started, he had to push the clients hard. Carl was a tough, low-country kid from Pueblo who'd started wrangling for me that summer. He liked to wear high-topped tennis shoes with a red-and-white checkerboard pattern that made him look like a walking (or riding) advertisement for Purina Mills.

When the storm cell cleared the pass, I spurred Morgan up the trail while Carl pushed the slicker-clad clients close behind. But before we reached the notch, the next cell swooped off Precarious Peak with a spectacular barrage of thunder and lightning. Things were really popping. Bolts hit about every thirty seconds, ricocheting back and forth between the peaks. With the echoes, it never let up: *bam! bam! bam!* Dudes started screaming and crying; the horses were going nuts.

A shallow bowl offered our only protection, so I waved and shouted them into it, and Carl and I collected the reins and led the horses farther down the slope, out in the open. Horses must sense the danger posed by their iron shoes and the resistance provided by their bodies, because they're terrified of lightning. When you stand on two feet, they're about twelve inches apart, so we get that degree of resistance. But a horse's hooves are more like five feet apart—and it's the resistance that kills you.

Deluged with rain and lightning, Carl and I clung to the reins—until suddenly, without saying a word, he broke and ran up the slope and threw himself down among the dudes. I couldn't believe it. I was so surprised I couldn't even yell, plus I was afraid that if I added to the noise, the horses would scatter. Before they realized they were loose, I grabbed the reins Carl had dropped and hung on while the animals jerked me from side to side.

The clients, of course, were scared shitless. Their hair was standing up like fright wigs. Women were crying like it was the deck of the *Titanic*, you could almost hear the band playing "Nearer My God to Thee." Meanwhile, a thought had crossed my mind: what would happen if lightning hit the six rounds in the revolver in my shoulder holster? Would they explode? So with ten sets of reins wadded up in one hand, I drew the revolver and dropped it in the mud.

When the thunder cell finally blew out of the pass, I picked up my gun and led the horses up to the bowl. The clients were getting to their feet, and there was my wrangler with a woman holding onto him, comforting him. I started turning the air blue; I figure I'm going to kill that son-of-a-bitch Carl. I'm trying to think of three ways to parboil a wrangler, because as far as I'm concerned, he's broken the Code of the West and has to pay for it.

Then Carl, bawling his eyes out, explains: earlier that summer, he'd been home visiting his family, and while he was at the country club playing golf with his grandfather, he had seen the old man killed by a bolt of lightning. What could I say? It was all I could do not to apologize. Finally I backed off and tried to make the best of it, telling myself that at least he'd held out for a couple of minutes before he cracked.

Then the dudes started getting after me. "Why did you make us lie down in that terrible hole," a woman demanded, "while you stood out in the open? Why did you abandon us?"

I looked her in the eye and said: "I got insurance on all of you, and I didn't want no witnesses left alive. I figured one strike would get you all."

I thought that was funny, but the dudes weren't amused, and it wasn't a bunch of happy campers I brought back to the resort that night. Tips weren't much, either.

Riding the high country in late summer, I ran into thunderstorms all the time. Sometimes, crossing a ridge, I'd find bodies of deer and elk that had been killed by lightning. Once I counted eight elk in a line—a single bolt had brought them down.

One storm trapped me in a canyon above the fishcamp. I'd left the clients fishing on the stream and taken the horses to graze. I set up a tent and cook stove and was fixing dinner when a thunder cell rolled in. Lightning arcing back and forth between the cliffs crackled like an Oklahoma tornado. It scared the hell out of me, but I remembered that lightning detector towers are equipped with glass insulators to protect the occupants, so I sat down on a pickle bucket and balanced one foot on a catsup bottle and the other on a mustard jar. I even got gutsy enough at one point to flip the chimney off the stove so it fell outside—and then I hopped back on my pickle bucket. When I didn't have a pickle bucket handy, I've stood on one leg to wait out a thunderstorm. I figure without two poles, you can't offer much resistance. It may sound funny, I know, but it works: I'm still alive.

I loved summers in the high country, especially when I could get off by myself. Sometimes, instead of returning to the resort with clients, I'd stay until the wranglers brought the next group up, sometimes for four or five days. I'd hike or ride or fish, or lie in a hammock and read. When you're alone like that, books take on a strange, other-worldly quality. In *The Sun Also Rises*, Hemingway has Jake Barnes think about how vivid things seem when you're drunk, but up there, I was high on loneliness and silence. Even today, I can remember every book I read in camp like it was something that actually happened to me—voyages to Japan, getting drunk in a bar in Tangiers, being lost in the African jungle—and I've never been to any of those places.

After a while, though, I'd start hearing voices above the sounds of rushing water, or echoing from a nearby draw. Sometimes the voices were so convincing I'd slip through the woods for a look, thinking somebody was up there with me. Once, riding along the Butterworth Trail after not seeing anyone for nearly a week, I heard a party around the next bend—laughter, the clink of glasses above a piano, men's and women's voices so clear I could almost understand what they were saying. The illusion was so real that, riding up the trail, I half-expected to find them. Instead, the slope dropped away sharply, and over the tops of the trees I looked into the blue gulf of a canyon. Once, after I'd been alone for a long time, I remember hearing a voice call me by name: "Jim! Jim!" I stopped my horse and thought, "He knows who I am," but when I looked, there was nobody there.

Probably illusions like that are caused by sensory deprivation, the auditory equivalent of witch's water on desert highways. If you don't hear other voices for a long time, you begin to invent them.

Sometimes I'd get clients who objected to being called dudes. This was particularly true with repeat customers. After they'd been out a number of times, they'd start pestering me with questions about how to escape the label. "If you don't want to be called a dude," I'd tell them, "you've got to prove yourself by doing something a dude can't do."

One such group was made up of four friends, bright, corporate lawyers from Philadelphia. They learned about me from another friend, a guy who'd talked to me at a sports show in Chicago. All of them loved the West—at least they loved the idea of the West the way it used to be, just like I did. They were history buffs who read about life in the old days, saw all the movies, studied Louis Lamour and Larry McMurtry and Ivan Doig. For years they'd exercised at gyms to maintain their physical condition and rode at private stables around the city while they dreamed about going West to experience the real thing.

When they phoned, I was in the office and answered the call. Irv was the spokesman, and it was love-over-the-telephone, real big-time corporate lawyer hustle. They wanted to come out for a week at the resort, but there was no way they were going to pay full price. We were going to negotiate a deal. Did I have any legal work that needed doing? They figured they had a simple country boy on the line, and I had to laugh: I was getting a real fucking over the phone. We kept after it, though, negotiating through four or five calls before we finally settled on a price, and they agreed to come out.

I met them at the Gunnison airport. Because I wouldn't know what clients looked like, I always wrote my name and "Executive Expeditions, Unlimited" with a crayon on a piece of cardboard and let them identify me. This time it wasn't necessary. I took one look as they got off the plane and threw my sign in the trash can. They were a sight to behold. If you'd been casting a movie, you couldn't have done any better. One was short and fat, one was tall and skinny, one was dark, about medium height, and one was a blond, burly guy. They were right out of central casting, and they all looked like they'd been dressed by an Eastern cowboy store.

I'd parked Old Blue, my International flatbed stock truck, in front of the terminal. There was room for me and my dog in the cab; the dudes, along with a mountain of luggage, sat in back on hay bales. For atmosphere I borrowed a friend's cow dog–a scruffy little border collie–and put him back there with them. By the time we got to Harmel's, the dog was fine, but the lawyers looked wind-blown and wild.

Before it was over, we all became good friends, and I enjoyed them a lot–they were a great bunch of guys, quick, smart, well-educated. In court they would have eaten me alive, but they were on my ground, so I had the advantage. They were as much in love with the West as I am, and they made a lot of sacrifices to be part of it. Sometimes, sitting around a campfire, they'd start telling stories about how their friends kidded them, and how their wives thought they were crazy, and it took me back to my last few months in Denver.

Our first year out together, I was nearly as green as they were, and against my better judgment, I agreed to take them on an old-style "progressive" cowboy camp–one that moved every day, as opposed to a stationary camp. My plan was to swing through the Fossil Ridge country, staying at a different site every night for five days. The first camp required a long pull to the head of Willow Creek, but it was late by the time I weeded out their excess baggage and got them on the trail. By the time we reached the camp-site, the sun was going down. I unpacked the animals and put the four lawyers to work setting up their tents, which was a show in itself. Then after hobbling the horses, I kicked them out on grass and built a fire to start heating water.

It was dusk. We'd had a good, hard ride up the creek, and I'm standing there with a cup of coffee watching the dudes play with their tents thinking, "My God, it's like a picture book," when I see a bear–an old brown so big and dark he looks like a grizzly–working across the hillside through the aspen. Should I say anything to the dudes, I wondered? I decided not to, afraid they might panic, but all of a sudden Morgan caught the bear's scent and let out a squeal of alarm. Before I knew what he was doing, he rounded up the horses and herded them running down the trail toward the resort.

My tennis shoes were still in my saddle bags, so I went after the herd in cowboy boots for half a mile before I admitted that, even wearing hobbles, they could outrun me. That was the summer I was playing the walking wrangler, so now it was time to do it again.

When I got back to camp, the dudes were owl-eyed and wanted to know what I was going do.

"Fix dinner," I told them. "Build up the fire. Then I'm going to get to bed early, because I'm getting up pretty early in the morning to go after them."

They wanted to go with me, but I told them no. There was plenty of food and water and firewood, all they had to do was wait. I promised I'd be back before dark the following night. In the middle of camp stood a tall, dead pine tree. "Do what you want tomorrow," I told them, "fish or hike around, or whatever, but don't get out of sight of that tree."

With the map, I plotted a course to the nearest telephone—fifteen miles east across the mountains to Parlin, a town on Quartz Creek. At 3 AM, wearing tennis shoes and a denim jacket, I bushwhacked across the mountains using the North Star as a reference point and following game trails when I could find them. By the time the sky got light enough for me to see, I was crossing a series of long, open benches and timbered ridges on the Quartz Creek side. From there, I broke into a dogtrot. By noon I was in Parlin and on the phone to the resort. My ass was beat, my feet were killing me. I told one of the wranglers to have Stu round up the horses and to send another wrangler for me in a fast car.

By the time I got to Harmel's, Wagner had Morgan and the other horses ready, and I head-and-tailed 'em back up the trail to the Willow Creek camp. The sun was just hitting the ridge when I led the string into the meadow. And there they were, all four dudes sitting with their backs against that dead pine tree, every one of them facing out in a different direction, looking for that bear. I thought I'd die laughing.

Because I'd been gone all day, I offered to deduct the price of that day's trip from the bill. I thought they'd say, "Hell, no, Jim, it was an experience," but they didn't. They took me up on it. They were Philadelphia lawyers, all right.

The next year, I let each of them lead his own pack mule on another progressive camp trip, this one up East Beaver Creek. Everything was going fine until we rode into the middle of a cattle drive. One thing you need to know about mules is that they hate cattle as much as horses hate mules. We came around a bend, and all of a sudden, there was the whole Taylor Park cattle pool right in our faces—half a dozen cowhands and a thousand head of cattle on their way down to Highway 50 and their fall pasture.

The mules went crazy. The dudes, caught completely off-guard, lost control of them. Gina, one of my prize mules, pulled Irv's horse down. Edith looked at those cattle bearing down on her and just took off, and the rest of them went with her. I had mules, pack gear, cattle, and dudes scattered from hell to breakfast.

When the dust settled, I started trying to get them straightened out and rounded up, and there were these cowboys—the whole trail crew—sitting up there on the ridge watching. They were kind of squatted down, with their horses behind them, hanging onto the reins. It looked like a movie: you know, the cattlemen watching the wagon train load of emigrants, with all their women and kids and dogs, headed for California. I could see these little grins at the corners of their mouths, but they weren't laughing or hurrahing or anything, maybe because they noticed the gun on my hip.

It took me about half an hour to get my outfit separated from the cattle and lined out on the East Beaver trail again. Until I did, those cowboys never moved. I had to respect them: they took the whole thing in and never offered to help. If they had, I don't know what I might have done ... probably something I'd have been sorry for.

A couple of weeks later, I met one of the cowboys in a Gunnison bar. "That was really something," he told me. "We went out there to do a day's work and got to see a free rodeo."

By the third year, the four dudes were feeling pretty cocky about their ability to handle themselves outdoors. They refused to let any green help from the resort go out with them; only veteran wranglers were acceptable. They were also starting to get surly if I called them dudes when they made a mistake. "All right," I told them, "I'm going to give you your chance—but you only get one. I'm planning a trip no dude could survive. Next summer, if you can do it, you're not going to be a dude ever again."

It was marketing at its best.

That winter, I got out the topographic map and plotted a route that looked like a real pip. By linking up trails and following contour lines, I figured we could get from Crested Butte, across the high country to the head of Dead Man's Gulch and Spring Creek, then into Brown's Canyon and across Doctor Park, and come out at North Bank campground on the Taylor River road. It was some of the highest, roughest country in Gunnison County. I'd been over parts of it, and I talked to people who'd been over other parts, but I couldn't find anybody who knew it all.

There wasn't any point in my asking Stu, of course. On the off-chance that the district forest ranger might know something, I asked him, but he didn't have a clue. Everybody who knew the country agreed, though, that the climax of the ride would be getting from Cement Creek to Spring Creek by way of a horseback climb to the top of Cement Mountain.

The four dudes worked out and rode all winter at commercial stables in the Philadelphia area, so they showed up in top shape. When we rode out of Crested Butte, we had nothing but our bedrolls, and enough camp gear and food for us and the horses, tied behind the saddles. It was a survival march all the way. Even at the end of May, there was a lot of snow up high that year. The wind blew so hard we had trouble getting fires started. We lived in slickers and slept under tarps. A couple of nights, when it really got bad, we built open-faced shelters out of pine boughs. One morning when we woke up, there were six inches of fresh snow over us. The trails were icy, and when a horse fell, we'd all pitch in to help get him up again.

I figured late morning was the best time to climb Cement Mountain, but when we went through the aspen line, I wondered if we could make it. Morgan was taking deep, panting breaths, and the saddle was creaking like a metronome as we plowed through wind-crusted snow. Without footing, it would have been too steep for a horse; with the snow, I thought we might have a chance. Above us, the mountain stood like Everest, with a long, curling plume of snow hanging motionless against the pale sky. Wind had built a ten-foot snow cornice along the top, and where it was broken, avalanche chutes had raked the slope and piled tumbled snow in an alluvial fan across the wind-scoured rock.

I never stopped. We crossed the scree to a steep ridge about eighty yards long and two or three yards wide, with two-hundred-foot dropoffs on both sides. The dudes had been talking nervously about the climb all morning; now, when they saw it, they got quiet. I called them together and said: "No human being has ever had a horse up there, but that's where we're going. So get off and follow me."

Trying to lead a horse out of a bad place is always a mistake—they get to plunging and can trample you—but this time there wasn't any choice. It was lead them or give up, so I started up the ridge and never looked back, post-holing Morgan behind me, then crow-hopping him up the last stretch. Under the cornice, I grabbed my hat with one hand and broke through, towing Morgan after me, onto the top.

Then I looked back, and it was a goddamn legal conference going on down there. Those dudes were huddled up, talking and waving their arms, and I could read everything they said. "I won't go back," Irv's saying, "Jim made it." And Morty was pointing and saying, "Well, I'm sure as hell not going up there." But none of them wanted to lose face with their guide and be dudes for the rest of their lives, and I'm standing on top waiting for them. Finally I see the big one, Al, say, "Fuck it," and lead his horse out on the ridge. The rest of them watched, to see if he meant it, and then they followed him.

They all got to the top except Morty. He was a little, chubby guy with round cheeks and big, dark eyes. He got below his horse, and it rolled on him and punched him right through the snow. He completely disappeared, with the horse on top of him, and I remember thinking: "Oh, shit, I wonder if my insurance covers this?"

When the rest of them reached the top, I went down to give Morty a hand, but by the time I got there, he was up and had the horse on his feet. "Get the hell out of my way," was all he said, and when I saw his face I did.

His buddies cheered him all the way, waving their hats, and when we got on top, we hurrahed and rode figure eights all over the place. It was flat up there, like a butte, and just about the size of a football field. On the backside was a nice, gentle slope down to Spring Creek. The dudes thought I'd known it all along, but I hadn't. I hadn't been able to tell from the topo map how much grade there was on that side, so I was as surprised as they were.

That night was our last night out, and we camped in the Spring Creek valley, ate steak and mustard beans, and drank Jim Beam around the fire. Before we left the resort, I'd gathered four turkey feathers—just in case—like the one I always wore in my hat. Now I presented each of them a feather and told them they'd earned the right to wear them in their hat bands, just like me.

It's hard to describe the setting around that campfire. They'd tested themselves to the limit, and they'd succeeded. They were grown men, successful at their professions, with wives and children and colleagues who respected them, and this was the most important test they'd passed in their lives. For them, it was bigger than passing law school, or the bar exam, or winning their first case.

"We're not dudes," they reminded me. "So what are we?"

"That's right," I told them. "And you'll never be dudes again, as long as you live. You are now … turkeys!"

"Turkeys!" The dudes were delighted. Next day, when we rode into Harmel's, there was a stampede to the single pay phone on the resort porch so they could call home and tell their wives what had happened. "Darling," I heard them announce, "you'll never guess what! I'm no longer a dude—I'm a turkey!"

Even today, I try to picture the expression on those Philadelphia matrons' faces when their husbands told them their new name.

I never did tell the four turkeys about another, easier route from Cement Creek to Spring Creek. Instead, whenever they came out, I kept them away from the country west of Taylor River; I was afraid they might want to repeat the climb to the top of Cement Mountain, and I wasn't sure any of us could do it again. They wanted to be rough and tough, real Wild West, old-time cowboys. That's what they thought I was. They thought I was the roughest, toughest son of a bitch in the woods. Compared to a lot of other guys in this country I'm not, but I was good enough for them, and they were happy.

# 7

## ⸻all ⸤udes

IN SOME WAYS, big game hunting, which I always thought of as Act IV in the drama of outfitting, is the climax of the entire play. As well as being the most dangerous and exciting act, it's also the most profitable. In three months, an outfitter makes about 80 percent of his income, and can turn a failed year into a successful one.

The various big game seasons run from somewhere around Labor Day, early in September, to just before Thanksgiving, nearly three months later. Between those dates, state wildlife commissions cram a number of shorter seasons: bow season and black powder season (which often overlap at least some portion of one another); two or three deer and elk seasons (again with some overlap); antelope season, mountain lion season, bighorn sheep season; the fall bear season.

You don't hear much about it, but some outfitters complicate matters even more by conducting two versions of their hunts—one that doesn't provide clients with female companionship and one that does. The "B" hunt is the traditional kind, where clients go out to kill wild game; but there's also something known as the "A" hunt, which is built around sex supplied by prostitutes imported from cities like Las Vegas and Dallas and Los Angeles. Typically, the women are recruited with promises of a working vacation—lots of sunshine, fresh air, and meals cooked to taste. They fly to the nearest large city, where the outfitter picks them up and packs them into camp with the rest of the gear. Sometimes "A" and "B" hunts are combined: clients hunt deer and elk by day, and spend their nights with the women.

Even on "B" hunts, though, I often picked up clients at the airport–high-dollar guys who'd bought or been comped a hunt–demanding to know where the action was. Some of them had been on "A" hunts in the past, or they'd heard of them, and were hard to convince that there wasn't going to be any action. Sometimes, when they insisted, I admitted that there were ranchers' daughters available in the valley, but pointed out that "their daddies have long guns."

It was a phrase that never failed to cool the ardor of even the highest-dollar dude. The truth was that Stu and I never fooled with that sort of thing. There's the law, of course–"transporting women for immoral purposes"–but in my case, the bottom line was that even before we were married, Marilyn wouldn't have stood for it. Exploitation of women like that is something she wouldn't tolerate, and I don't blame her. Then there's the local situation. Word gets around, and in a small community, once you establish a reputation for that kind of thing, it's hard to live down. I've been called a lot of things in this valley, but "pimp" isn't one of them, at least not to my face.

When that first combined deer-and-elk season opens, you see some strange sights. In a lot of little Western towns, the population can double and triple in a matter of days, and the armed portion of the population increases more than that. Law enforcement officers avert their gaze from holstered pistols and sheathed hunting knives and the arsenals of rifles racked in the rear windows of pickup trucks. Hunters are a scruffy lot, the men sour and unshaven after their cross-country journeys from the flatlands, the women frazzled. They buy licenses, groceries, beer and whiskey, camping gear, clothing. They check into motels where they sleep everywhere, often six and eight to a room, and exhaust hot water taking showers. They investigate the local bar scene and get into whatever they can find in the way of small-town trouble. Often this means no more than standing around on street corners making suggestive remarks to local women, or getting drunk in bars.

Hunters may be a boon to merchants, but to the ordinary citizen, it's like being invaded by a guerilla army. They arrive heavily armed, and many of their weapons and much of their equipment pay tribute to the various American wars of this century, ranging from the First World War to Desert Storm. Their mandatory blaze orange clothing–hats, vests, jackets, shirts, and trousers, even orange coveralls and boot packs–makes the resemblance to an invading army even more striking. Suddenly the natives, in their workaday clothes, begin to look unusual, and are shocked to realize that, overnight, they've become a minority in their own town.

A lot of outfitters take little responsibility for their clients, but I believed it was my job to work with them from the first contact– whether it involved selling them a package at a sports show, or answering a phone call–until they drove away or boarded a plane for home. I tried for at least three contacts between the time I met them and the time they arrived. I figured outfitting was a lot like college recruiting, where it's easier to hang onto the students you've got than beat the bushes for new ones.

Sometimes it was four to six months between the initial contact and a client's arrival. By then the 25 percent (or less–sometimes much less) down payment had been spent a long time ago. Many clients simplified the process by phoning to ask questions. Others I wrote to, telling them what to bring and what to expect. I always sent a copy of the menu, asking if they had any special diet requirements. (I never actually had any requests for special food. I don't know what I would have done about them if I had, but it seemed like a nice touch.)

Whenever possible, I met hunters who arrived by plane at the airport. Whether they stayed at the resort, or at a motel in town, I checked them in, briefed them on the area where we were to hunt, and impressed on them the importance of their emergency kits. I made sure they understood game regulations, had hunting licenses, blaze orange clothing, good boots, and plenty of socks. They usually responded by asking a million questions– about the country, the weather, the animal sign I'd seen, how the hunting had been.

At a rifle range in town or at the resort, I studied their marksmanship and supervised while they sighted in their weapons. All kinds of guns showed up—everything from expensive German Mannlichers to World War II Italian surplus rifles. Sometimes clients arrived with guns they'd never fired. Some of them had never fired a gun in their lives. When this happened, I conducted a crash course on the care and handling of weapons and the principles of marksmanship.

I also tried to learn something about them. Had they hunted or fished before? Could they ride? What kind of physical condition were they in? What did they do for a living? No matter what happened, I never got very far from teaching school, so I built a small corral beside the big one as a classroom to demonstrate how to pack panniers, saddle horses, and adjust tack. My theory was that the more they understood about what was going to happen, the less dependent on me they were likely to be—in educational jargon, I was "empowering the pupil."

I also believed it was important to get clients talking about themselves. I'd tie a knot, and maybe one of them would say, "That's a nice clover hitch," and I'd say, "How'd you know a clover hitch?" Or I'd tell them how important what they were going to do was—how we were going to have a hell of an adventure together, that we were going to do what the old-timers had done when they settled this country. Or I'd tell them they were doing something rare—that probably not one in a thousand people who lived in their home towns had done what they were going to do.

Sometimes I kidded them, too. "Where are you going after you leave us?" I'd ask. "You must be taking two or three trips, with all this stuff you've got."

It was a routine I developed over a period of years, and it seemed to work. Whenever I felt impatient with them, I tried to remember that, with a little less luck, I could have been any one of them. They might be dudes, but they were doing the best they could, and they were paying top dollar for the privilege. Sometimes, when I varied my routine with repeat customers, they complained, reminding me I'd left something out. Other clients, like schoolchildren who don't want to learn, refused to become involved. If I offered them a rope to tie or a blanket to hold, they backed away. That was okay, but they were missing something important, something I was willing to give them but they weren't willing to take.

Basecamp was a long ride and required a lot of equipment to sustain a party of clients and wranglers and guides, as well as their horses and mules, for a week. I encouraged everyone to bring what I called "dehydrated beer"—just the alcohol without all that water— in other words, whiskey. They say a shot of whiskey equals one beer. (Or is it a six-pack?) Anyway, there's something about whiskey that goes with hunting and living outdoors. Guys have tried to run dry camps and gone broke. I always found that sitting around a campfire at night with a glass of whiskey is kind of companionable.

The ride out of Harmel's started between eight and nine AM, and I tried to make sure the dudes had a good first hour. It was important that any pain or fear they felt wasn't communicated to their mounts, and it's amazing what attention to details will do. Starting with a bad experience can ruin the whole trip, and I knew that the only way they were going to come back again was because the first time had been fun.

In spite of my best efforts, though, it was an unusual bunch that wasn't fighting fatigue and aching, cramping muscles before we were halfway up the long haul to basecamp. Finally, over the pines, we'd start seeing vast, bare swells looming above the 10,500- foot level that marks timberline. That time of year, Forge Peak and Hartline Ridge stood trimmed in snow, and in the wind, long banners of powder drifted and swirled yellow-and rose-toned in the failing light.

Reining in my horse, I'd turn in the saddle and announce: "That's where we're going to be hunting tomorrow, gentlemen. Up there." Then I'd put my horse in motion, and behind me I'd hear the dudes stirring, muttering under their breath: "Oh, shit," and you could hear their assholes going *click, click, click.*

Not many clients were ready for the rigors of life in the high country late in the year, but some were less well prepared than others. Occasionally alcoholics showed up for a hunt, and they always caused problems. One guy filled his canteen with whiskey and sneaked drinks all the way up the trail to basecamp. The wrangler trailing the string saw him dipping into his canteen, but assumed the guy was after water. Because he was big and clumsy, with a ruddy complexion, I didn't make the connection, either, though I noticed him swaying in the saddle on switchbacks.

We were descending the trail into camp when I heard a loud noise—it sounded like *thump*, and then *whump, whump, whump*. When I looked back, he'd rolled off his horse, hit the ground, and just kept rolling right down the slope to his tent. The slope was steep, grown up in scrub aspen, with rocky outcrops among the weeds. Anybody conscious would have broken half the bones in his body, but there wasn't a mark on this guy. He was dead to the world. We carried him into the tent and laid him out on a cot and let him sleep. When he woke up next morning, he didn't even know where he was. And he was fine, said he didn't even have a headache, and was ready to hunt.

In hunting camp, I always operated by a set of rules I announced the first night around the fire. After supper, with the clients mellow on steak and whiskey, I told them what was expected. One of the most important rules concerned liquor: they could have it, but if they took a drink in the morning, they couldn't hunt that day. "You can drink," I used to tell them, "and you can hunt—but you can't do both." Occasionally there were objections, but experienced hunters appreciated my caution—they'd been out in the woods before with drunk hunters and didn't want any more of that. Novices accepted the rule as a matter of course.

Another rule was no loaded guns in camp. Every evening they checked their weapons at the cook tent, where I stored them in an Army surplus rifle rack. Another rule was no loaded guns on horseback, so each morning, before they mounted, I made certain every breech was empty—though some of them didn't like that, either. They pictured themselves riding across the mountains, flushing deer and elk in front of them, but it never happens that way. You can't come within a mile of big game on a horse. Deer and elk hear them and skedaddle—they've learned to associate the smell and sound of horses with rifle fire. Besides, most horses will buck your ass off if you start shooting around them. These moving pictures of cowboys riding along shooting are taken with them on horses trained for that sort of thing.

Two of my favorite scenes in Western films concern horses and gunfire. One is from Max Evans's novel *The Rounders*, where a cowboy, angry at a cow, rides it down and tries to shoot it and shoots his horse instead. Actually, I think the scene was left out of the film version because it was too realistic for Hollywood. The other scene is from *Jeremiah Johnson*. Robert Redford and Will Geer, playing a pair of mountain men, see an elk, and Redford rests his rifle across his horse's saddle to shoot. The first time I saw the picture, I thought: "Here comes some more of that old Hollywood horse shit." But at the sound of the shot, the horse rears, knocking Redford and his rifle flying. I loved it, because that's the way it would really happen.

Most outfitters use horses on a hunt for two reasons: to expand the range of the hunter and to gain altitude. The real hunting is done on foot, after the horses have been tied or hobbled. Because they lacked the patience to sit still, I took most clients on a slow, one-step-at-a-time stalk through the woods. Clients able to still-hunt I stationed beside game trails or the edges of clearings, though sometimes they failed to stay there. Once I took a party into the country above the Chinese Wall, south of Ohio Pass. The weather was bad, but I left several hunters beside a game trail while I worked my way above and tried to drive the game back to them. They had orders to wait until noon, but wind and snow wiped them out, and they retreated to camp after a couple of hours.

Meanwhile I'd tracked a bull elk along the trail to within twenty yards of where they were supposed to be waiting. When I got back to camp, one guy was laying for me and started to complain about the lack of game. Instead of arguing, I led him up the trail to the blind, where he'd been waiting, and showed him the elk tracks, but it didn't do any good. He told me it was my fault, that the elk should have been there sooner.

You do the best you can, but guiding hunters can be frustrating. Sometimes you know the game's moved through your area, and there's nothing you can do about it. You know they're gone, but you hunt anyway. Then sometimes they'll fool you, circle back, and there's deer and elk everywhere. You hear outfitters brag they've got a 60 or 70 or 80 percent kill rate, but I always figured if they had, they're shooting the animals themselves.

A more realistic number, I would say, is something like 50 percent. The average kill rate on elk licenses is much less than that, some say as low as 8 percent. That means that guided hunters are getting a lot more than their share. A good outfitter—a guy who knows what he's doing—will present shootable game to hunters 90 percent of the time, so that whatever it costs, paying an outfitter is the cheapest part of the hunt. Without a guide, most clients don't last more than three days in the woods, and they have a miserable time—they're cold, they don't eat right, they get lost or tired, and quit.

I always believed that modern city people simply lack the patience necessary to be good hunters. You hear stories of early-day Eskimo seal hunters, who would watch a hole in the ice for three days without moving. They had the tenacity and the patience it takes, and they trusted their judgment to be able to pick the right hole. Their families were waiting for them, so either a hunter brought back game, or they all starved.

Once the hunt started, the image I tried to create for myself as an old-timer, an expert and authority on packing and riding and hunting, paid off. What it comes down to is trust. If clients don't trust you, it just won't work. They have to believe you know what you're talking about, because one of the ultimate acts of faith one human being can show another is to wake up at four AM in a camp you rode into after dark, get on a horse you can't see, and be told to ride up a pitch-black trail—and when you pass a rock that grazes your boot, count to five, and turn your horse up the hill. I know I wouldn't do it, not for some wild-eyed gebronie I'd just met, but thousands of hunters do it every year and live to tell the tale.

I remember taking a guy out hunting at four o'clock one dark, dead cold morning. He was following me on horseback along an icy trail, and after a while I heard him breathing—deep, fast breaths, like he was running hard and couldn't get enough air. When I stopped to let him ride alongside, he was shaking so hard I could hear his jacket rustling. All his life, he told me, he'd been terrified of horses; now he was hyperventilating, and between breaths I heard his heart pounding like it was about to explode.

If I'd had a paper bag, I would have put it over his head to help him control his breathing, but all I could do was talk to him. I told him he had nothing to be ashamed of, that everybody was afraid of something, and that it was all right. I squeezed his shoulder and talked to him like you'd talk to a dog or a little kid. After a while he calmed down enough so we could go on, but I was amazed that, in spite of his phobia about horses, he'd come out and tried to hunt.

One of our favorite hunting camps was at the bottom of a steep, forested hill that we had to climb in the morning, while it was still dark. Before starting up, I'd tell the clients to put their arms across their faces and hang onto their hats. In spite of my warning, though, branches would whip them off, and I'd hear the folks yell, "Hey, I lost my hat."

"That's okay," I'd tell them, "Steve'll pick it up," and I'd yell back, "Steve, get that hat," and Steve would yell, "Right."

When we got to the top, the clients would ask Steve for their hats, and he'd say, "Hats? What hats?"

"I thought Jim told you to get my hat?" And Steve would say "*Hat?* Oh, I thought what he said was 'Look at that.' I couldn't see no hats in the dark."

I couldn't help but laugh. It happened every year. None of those dudes ever made it to the top of the ridge with a hat.

By the third day, everybody was pretty well beat and needed rest. The ride into camp, and then several days hunting at altitudes above 10,000 feet, always took a toll. Just anticipating the hunt usually kept clients from sleeping the first few nights. Finally, after all that exertion, they'd start acting like zombies. All I had to do was tell them, "Go over there and do that," and they'd say, "Yeah, yeah," and stagger off to collapse in their tents.

I might be on the ragged edge myself, but I'd never let on. "Can't kill no game in camp," I'd tease, but by that time they were so tired they didn't care. Actually, the one thing I used to worry about was running out of gas myself—I mean me, personally. I was afraid I'd get so far, and when I had to go farther, I wouldn't be able to do it, I'd just lie down in the snow. I was pushing myself all the time, operating at the edge, and there were all these people counting on me. I worried about what they'd do—whether they could make it back down to the resort on their own, or whether they'd die with me in the woods.

Sometimes snowstorms closed the Denver airport and Monarch Pass, over the Continental Divide, backing up incoming clients for days. Because an outfitting business operates on a tight schedule, all my plans would have to be rearranged as clients, eager to get started, strayed into the resort at all hours of the day and night. Once I had two parties on my hands, both scheduled to go in different directions, and only half enough horses to take them. Mounting one group on every animal we had, with all the camp equipment aboard, I started up the Butterworth Trail in the snow. Then, three miles out, at the foot of the first steep switchback, I stopped the column and announced: "Gentlemen, this trail's getting too dangerous. I can't risk your lives by taking you any farther. Everybody dismount." Shuffling around, they gathered in a group. "The horses can't handle a trail like this," I explained. "Take your rifles and sleeping bags, some peanut butter and jelly and bread. We'll walk the rest of the way."

"How far is it?" the clients wanted to know.

"Not far," I assured them. "Just three switchbacks."

I led the way while a wrangler took the horses back to camp to pick up the other party waiting to go in the opposite direction. I'd told him what I was going to do the night before. He said I'd never get away with it, but I told him, "You just watch me."

We walked for hours, the dudes gasping, hanging on to their gear and sweating in the icy wind. "Not much farther," I called. "Here we are on switchback number two."

"You said that last switchback was number two," they chorused.

"No, no, that was switchback number one. This is switchback number two."

Half a dozen switchbacks later, one guy cornered me and said: "You mean to tell me I'm paying you eighteen hundred dollars for this?"

I'd told them it was only another couple of hundred yards, but the truth was, it was more like five miles.

That night was a cold camp. I'd set up tents and cots earlier, but had planned to pack food and stoves in with the clients. The storm blew itself out, but campfires did little to break the cold, and the hunters spent a miserable night curled up in their sleeping bags, eating peanut butter and jelly sandwiches. Next morning tent ceilings sagged with ice formed from their breath. I dipped a pickle bucket of water from Forge Creek to make coffee, and before I could get to camp, ice skimmed the surface. The clients, who'd never seen water freeze that fast, poked at it curiously.

"Would you gentlemen care to wash up?" I asked. While they stared, I broke the ice and dabbed some water on my face, then told them to eat their next round of peanut butter and jelly sandwiches, because the hunt started in fifteen minutes. I knew I was pushing them pretty hard, but what else could I do? I always figured outfitting's a lot like whoring—it's money up front, and satisfaction is definitely *not* guaranteed.

By the end of the hunt, though, every one of them told me it had been the greatest experience of his life—even the guy who was worried about his eighteen hundred dollars.

When the pack train with all the camp gear finally arrived, the dudes were in heaven. They thought they were staying at the Radisson Hotel in Denver; they just didn't know things could get that bad—or that good. Maybe I short-changed them and should have tried to make up the difference, but I don't know how I would have done it. As far as I was concerned, it was a matter of that's-just-the-way-it-is. There wasn't any use putting three things instead of one on the menu after the supplies finally arrived; besides, I was having fun with the peanut butter.

I remember one late-season elk hunt that pushed me to the limit, though. It was cold and getting colder, and we were on the trail before I noticed that the zipper on my down jacket was broken. We were hunting Fossil Ridge in weather as bad as I'd ever seen. For five days the wind never let up. Blowing ice crystals seared our faces and numbed our hands; you could hardly hold a rifle, much less pull a trigger. At night the tent walls sagged with ice. The clients—wrapped in sweaters, down jackets, wool hats and scarves, down mittens, and boots—watched me hunt in my flapping jacket. Finally, the last night in camp, a Canadian doctor told me: "I've hunted in every province in Canada; I've hunted in Alaska and China, and I thought I'd seen some tough guys in my time, but you beat all. How cold does it have to get to make you zip that goddamn jacket up?"

I never told him I was wearing a Thinsulate vest under my shirt and that it had probably saved my life.

Occasionally women came along to hunt with their husbands or boyfriends, which was fine with me. If anything, it always seemed to me that women made better hunters than men. Usually they're better shots than men: They take their time and make sure of what they're shooting at. When you tell women to do something, they've got enough sense to listen and try to do it.

One woman from Oklahoma came because she was convinced her husband wasn't really hunting. Every fall he and his cronies disappeared, claiming they were bound for elk hunting in Colorado, and every year they came home with nothing to show for their efforts. They passed it off as bad luck, but she'd heard rumors about "A" hunts and suspected they were after a different kind of animal.

When she told me her suspicions, I explained what was wrong with her husband and his friends. Instead of hunting the way they were supposed to—the way I had tried to teach them to hunt—they did things their way. They insisted on walking instead of still-hunting, tramping through dead leaves, talking, smoking when they were on a stand, "sound-shooting" at some unseen noise when nothing better offered itself.

When I described what to do, she listened, then stationed herself beside a game trail. After waiting a couple of hours, she killed a big six-point elk with her first shot. Her husband and his pals couldn't believe it, but I loved it. She even had me take pictures of her and the elk with her camera, because she knew that when they got back home, the men would start lying about who actually killed it. Later she sent me a picture and had me write what happened on the back and return it to her, because that's just what they were trying to pull.

One of the heaviest snows on record in the Gunnison country fell about the middle of November during the third hunting season that year. I was in basecamp on a saddle running north from Carbon Peak toward two higher mountains, Whetstone and Axtell. Weather the first two seasons had been beautiful, clear and dry, but game had stayed high, and hunters all over the basin had struck out.

My camp was nearly five miles above the road, but I decided to take a chance the weather would hold and use it again. In camp were half a dozen clients, a guide named Dan, and a retired telephone company executive named Hobe who used to wrangle for me sometimes in the fall. Actually Hobe was a friend rather than an employee, and his wrangling was more a hobby than a job. The day before the season opened, the weather was so warm that after we reached camp, I stretched out on a bed of dry grass in the meadow and took a nap.

Opening day was clear and warm. We hunted north, walking the slopes of Mt. Axtell, but saw no sign of game. Toward evening, clouds began covering the sky, and a wind rose, droning in the tops of the pines. By dark we were getting high winds in camp. On top of Axtell it sounded like a runaway freight train, and I knew it must be blowing a hundred miles an hour up there.

We ate dinner listening to the wind. By the time we got into our sleeping bags, big wet flakes were falling hard. I set my alarm clock to wake me every hour and got up and beat the snow off the tents so they wouldn't collapse. It was coming about a foot an hour, and when we woke up next morning, it was five feet deep. It had gone from nothing to five feet overnight. I never saw it fall any faster up there.

My first problem was feeding the clients; my second was finding feed for the stock. Because there'd been so much grass when we started, I hadn't brought hay with us, and now, with snow that deep, the horses and mules were helpless. You get six to eight inches on the ground, and horses won't forage–if they can't see grass, they don't believe it's there. Mules are a little more resourceful, but five feet is too much for them, too. Elk, of course, will beat through it, but horses and mules will stand there and die.

After breakfast, I saddled Willie, one of the mules, and punched a trail down to the road. It was hard going, and every mile of the way I regretted betting on the weather holding for the third season. Back in camp, I saddled the strongest horse in my string, Joker, and broke the trail out again. By the time I returned to camp, I'd covered twenty miles. Nothing moved in the whole country. Everything was buried. Across the valley, the only thing breaking the drifts was the tops of the rose bushes. Wind still roared over Axtell, and across the saddle it was blowing about thirty-five miles an hour, filling the valley with snow boils.

Archaeologists used to think Indians cleared out of the Colorado mountains in the winter, that it was too cold for them. Now we know that wasn't true, but we're pretty sure they didn't venture into the high country to hunt, not in winter. In those days, there probably wasn't game up on top anyway. White men have driven the animals out of the valleys with their hunting, but in those days game probably stayed down low, and the Indians, who were nothing if not practical, stayed there with it.

Back in camp, I saddled Willie again, and with two pack horses made it down to the ranch where we'd left the trucks and horse trailers. The rancher was busy trying to shovel out, but he let me have as much hay as the horses could carry.

Next morning, with the wind still up, the hunters were getting bored and wanted to look for elk. Of course there weren't any; elk have more sense than to move in a storm like that. I told them to forget it and rode back to the ranch to reopen the trail and resupply. I was riding through some aspen, on my way back to camp, when a calf the roundup crew had missed that fall suddenly appeared in the trail. Willie spooked, started bucking, and threw me. I was wearing pack boots that didn't fit in the stirrups and never had a chance to stay with him.

As soon as I hit, I knew I was hurt, so I got back in the saddle right away, while I still could. Later, after the season was over, I had my back x-rayed, and the doctor told me I'd broken a spur off the side of my spine. If I'd been in town, he said, he would have put me in traction. At the time, though, all I knew was that the muscles were in spasm, and by the time I reached camp, I couldn't dismount without help. Hobe and a couple of hunters caught me when I rolled out of the saddle and carried me into the cook tent. One of them, a doctor, fed me a handful of la-la pills until the muscles relaxed and I could start breathing again.

That trip, having a doctor along was a godsend. Earlier, when Hobe had been getting ready to leave the resort to join us, he was leading a young mare into a horse trailer when some kid dropped a tarp in front of her. She reared, slamming Hobe against the trailer and splitting his ear open from top to bottom. When Hobe rode into camp, with blood all over his shirt, the doctor had made himself useful by sewing him up. We made a pair, that hunt, because between us and various falls the clients took, we kept that doctor busy patching and sewing in the cook tent.

The storm continued, the temperature fell. Several times a day Hobe and Dan boosted me into the saddle, and I rode Willie down to the road and back to reopen the trail. There were six or seven feet of snow on the flat, and the drifts were bottomless. With coffee and whiskey and la-la pills, I kept going. Normally Hobe and Dan and I would have done nothing more in our tent than sleep, because it had no stove and the air was twenty below zero. Gradually wind piled snow against the walls, constricting the space inside, so none of us could stretch out in our sleeping bags.

The third morning, with the wind still raging, the clients again insisted on going hunting. One of them had been walking around camp and told me he'd found elk tracks. I went to look and found tracks leading from one tree to another. What he'd seen were squirrel tracks, so I had to break his heart. I told him those weren't elk tracks, not unless they were little, bitty tree-climbing elk.

By now, though, I had a rebellion on my hands. We were four days into the hunt and the hunters hadn't fired a shot; in fact, they'd hardly been out of their tents. Above the roar of the wind, I heard them arguing. Finally they marched over in a body with an ultimatum: either they hunted or they were riding out. I was lying on a cot, trying to rest my back. "You can do what you want," I told them, "but I ain't hunting, because there's nothing to hunt. And I ain't going nowhere, not till that wind stops—and it *will* stop." I don't know if they'd just gotten used to the noise, but that got their attention. They started looking at each other.

"Listen to it," I said. "Do you have any idea how hard it's blowing? Or what would happen if you got out in the open, where it could really hit you?"

Up on top of Axtell, it sounded like an air raid. It was a regular jet stream, and had to be blowing well over a hundred miles an hour. In the open, those guys wouldn't have lasted fifteen minutes. They listened for a while, and we all looked at each other. Finally one guy said: "How hard does it have to blow before you get worried?" And I gave him my famous line: "Yesterday."

That really set 'em back. Their eyes got big and they went back to their tents. After that I didn't hear much out of them.

Next morning, when we woke, the storm was over. The wind had stopped, the sunshine across the snow was blinding. We were eating breakfast when we heard a wild, hammering roar: *Whoop! Whoop! Whoop!* It was an Army helicopter, a Vietnam-era Huey in camouflage paint. The Army was justifying its peacetime budget by doing good works among the civilian population, arriving to evacuate stranded hunters. Swooping low, they announced their intentions through a bull horn, but I waved them off. The noise was scaring the stock, and I wasn't about to abandon the camp or give up the hunt. After all that riding, I had a good trail down the mountain, the county was plowing the roads, and I knew the elk would be on the move.

At the ranch, we loaded everything in the trucks and stock trailers and headed back to the resort. A lot of outfitters were finished. Once the storm lifted, their hunters were in such a hurry to get home they just blew out of the country. But we had a perfect base at Harmel's, and that afternoon I took my hunters into a gulch north of the resort, and every one of them killed a bull. We walked right into the middle of a herd; they were yarded up in the snow like cattle and couldn't move. There wasn't a bull left. Spikes—the young ones, with antlers just starting to grow—were legal at the time, so we took them, too.

In terms of results, it was the most successful hunt I ever led: the kill rate was 100 percent. Not that it was something I was proud of; I just felt like we'd earned it. The truth is, the longer I was in the business, and the older I got, the more I realized that killing game isn't really what hunting is all about. There's a lot of pressure in that kind of situation and it sets up a tension in camp: who's going to kill and who's not; who's going to succeed, and who's going to fail.

That's the kind of macho game you hear some outfitters playing downtown in the bars. They come in bragging about their kill rate, promising dudes they'll get them into elk—"You're going to kill an elk; it's a done deal." I got to where I'd tell clients, "You hunt steady with me for three years, and you're probably going to kill an elk." For me, the important thing about hunting is the experience of being out there. The game, when it comes, is really just a bonus.

As it turned out, the success my hunters enjoyed following the storm wasn't unusual. The out-of-state guys had gone home, but with all that snow, local hunters who knew the score turned out in exceptionally large numbers. It's illegal to shoot from the pavement—or with one foot in the barrow pit, as a guy once told me—but that didn't stop them. Deep snow trapped herds close to the roads or penned them up in the woods. The slaughter got so bad that the Division of Wildlife thought about canceling the rest of the season. They couldn't get it done in time, though, and a lot of animals were killed. North of Gunnison, in the Almont triangle, hunters shooting into a herd of elk stampeded them through the camp and killed everything that moved—cows and calves, bulls and spikes—right there among the tents. When the herd fled down a draw, other hunters opened fire, turning the animals back through camp, where still more were killed.

I heard what happened and rode over to take a look, and it was a massacre. People had gone crazy. I heard that guys had been so excited at seeing all those animals, and hearing all that gunfire, that they'd started shooting at each other. There was game down everywhere. The snow was covered with gut piles and blood; elk and deer were hanging from trees like Christmas tree ornaments. For days afterward, you'd see cripples standing out on the road with their eyes glazed, gut-shot and dying. It was enough to make you sick.

Riding together and camping out in the high country bring people so close together that it's often hard for them to say goodbye. They don't want the experience to end, and at the same time they're relieved it's over. It's as though they've been tested, and they're curious to know if they passed. There are always unspoken questions: How did we do? What did you think of us? I used to play on this feeling when we were riding out. I'd tell them, "We're coming down on the road. Sit up straight! Show them who we are!"

With few exceptions, trips ended with a dinner at the resort. I'd hear the clients talking on the trail behind me—"Let's buy Jim dinner tonight."

It was always fun, though it wasn't always what you wanted to do. You'd rather have soaked in a hot tub and patted mama on the ass, but you did what you had to. My world was up there; theirs was down below, at the resort. They wanted to get me on something like their own ground to see what I looked like and how I acted. Was I really as crazy as I let on sometimes, or was I a more or less responsible human being, like they were?

I acted as master of ceremonies and focused on special things that happened on the trip. "Remember how George hollered when he found that big elk down? Or how that horse stepped on Harry's foot?" And I never missed the chance to sell more outfitting. "Let's do it again next year," I'd urge. If it was a bunch of hunters, I promoted the idea of a summer nature ride or a fishing trip with the family. If families were present, I used to carry on about the glories of the high country in fall, during big game season.

"You wouldn't believe this country," I'd tell them. "It's the most beautiful place in the world. You really owe it to yourself to see it."

# 8

## The World Series Elk Hunt

WHEN YOU'RE OUTFITTING, you learn there's a whole population out there that doesn't approve of what you're doing, and they want you to know it. Conservationists, animal rights activists, vegetarians, Sierra Club granola-snappers, politically correct bleeding hearts–the list goes on and on. You try not to take them seriously, but after a while all that disapproval starts preying on your mind, and you get a sense that what you're doing, if not exactly illegal, is at least antisocial.

Not long after I moved to town, I met a college administrator I'd known for years. He was coming out of the bank while I was going in. He wore a suit and tie; I was in my work clothes and hadn't shaved in a week. A few years earlier, I used to see him around the campus when I was there on business or at receptions and dinners at the governor's mansion in Denver when he was there as a guest. We were never friends, but he was an affable, well-educated guy, and I always respected him.

Now, when he saw me, he looked surprised but stopped to talk. We shook hands. He said he'd heard I was living in Gunnison, and that we'd have to get together for dinner sometime. He started past me, but I blocked his way and said, "When?" And he turned pale, backing away and raising his hands, as though to ward me off, like I had some kind of communicable disease–like leprosy, or AIDS, or poverty.

I pushed him a little more: "What about tonight?" He huffed and puffed but finally said no, he and his wife were busy, but he'd call me. Moving fast, he went out the door, and by the time he hit the sidewalk, he was running. I remember thinking: "All right for you, my friend; I've got your number."

I never did it, of course, but for a while I had fantasies about showing up on his doorstep some night and asking what time we ate.

Another time I ran into an old friend, a guy I'd worked with at the capitol, on the 16th Street Mall in Denver. We had a drink and talked about old times, but when he heard what I was doing, I saw him freeze. He gave me a tight, cold smile, like I should apologize. Of course, that kind of attitude brings out the worst in me, so to confirm his fears, I told him two or three of my grisliest outfitting stories.

Another time somebody introduced me to a woman at a party, and when she learned what I did, she stared at me like I was some lower form of life. "You mean you're one of those people who catches elk?" she asked. "No, ma'am," I told her. "I don't know what I'd do with one if I caught it. I kill elk and eat 'em, just like you do cows and sheep and chickens that somebody kills for you at the slaughterhouse."

Sometimes, when people got after me like that, I'd tell them I'd continue the conversation only if they were vegetarians—otherwise the only difference between us was that they bought their meat at Safeway, and I killed mine myself. Fortunately I never ran into anybody who claimed to be a vegetarian.

There's also a widespread perception that outfitters operate pretty close to the edge, often selling their clients little more than blue sky and sunshine. "What's your kill rate?" was a question I heard frequently from local hunters. So you'd lie a little bit, and say, "Sixty-five percent," and they'd laugh at you. "What? You mean you're charging those dudes a thousand dollars, and nearly half of them aren't killing nothing?"

Outlaw outfitters cause you problems, too. Outlaws are guys who operate without licenses or permit areas, often advertising their services in outdoor magazines. Sometimes they'll collect half the price of the hunt as a deposit and then skip town. When the hunter shows up, he finds nothing waiting for him but an abandoned post office box. In cases like that, a lot of legitimate outfitters will volunteer to fill the hunt for the other half of the fee. Not that we do it out of pure altruism or a sense of common humanity. We're acting for what amounts to the good of the order, because it's a horrible thing to send a guy back to someplace like Lawton, Oklahoma, with a story about how he was scammed, and have him tell everybody: "Stay away from Gunnison. Those guys are a bunch of crooks up there." If word like that got around, nobody would be in the outfitting business long.

Sometimes even legal and otherwise legitimate outfitters cause everybody else trouble. I remember one guy who lugged a 300-pound bear he'd just killed and cleaned into a downtown bar and propped it up on a stool. "Whiskey for me and beer for my friend," he ordered. The bartender and the owner threw him and the bear out, but people—and not just the anti-hunting crowd—were mad about it, and I can't say I blame them.

One thing a lot of us in the business wanted to do was legitimize hunting in the eyes of the community. We wanted people to see outfitting the way we saw it—as a respectable business conducted by responsible professionals. But another fly in my particular ointment was Stu. We always had our differences, but the longer we stayed in business together, the more apparent they became.

One winter, to raise money to pay deposits on booth space at sports shows, we put together a give-away magazine promoting tourism in the area. Then, mock-up in hand, I peddled advertising space door-to-door. Stu wrote some great copy for us, we had a lot of pictures, and so we made a bundle on the magazine. Part of my pitch to subscribers, though, was that 50,000 copies would be distributed throughout the region. I prepaid a printer for a token run of 1,500, but I was scared to death that after I left town, Stu wouldn't print a single one. And I was right. He raised hell about spending anything at all on printing—"That's just throwing good money away," he told me. Because the magazine was well received, the Chamber of Commerce underwrote a number of additional copies, but I had to force Stu to print the rest of the 50,000 I'd promised.

For my work on the magazine, the Chamber voted me "Businessman of the Year" and presented me with a plaque at a dinner downtown. It was an honor I was proud of; it was a pat on the back, and it helped justify some of the things a lot of outfitters were trying to do. At the same time, the award caused some hard feelings within the outfitting community and in the long run got me into trouble.

Public recognition is important for any business, but especially a business that depends on politics. When the state licenses you and is responsible for defending the integrity of that license, you're especially vulnerable. Game and Fish, and Forest Service personnel, can be the worst bureaucrats in the world. They really jerk some of these cowboys around. They have a whole book full of rules, and they can make some poor guy's life miserable. But if you've got some standing in the community, and a few political connections, they let you alone. If you're on a first-name basis with the governor or you've taken some senator out after bighorn sheep, you don't have to tell everybody about it; the word gets around. Besides, outfitting's a referral business, and your reputation attracts a lot of customers. If people have a good time, they tell their friends— but if they have a bad time, they let _everybody_ know.

Through my work with the magazine, I met Bud Rodgers. He was a high-dollar real estate developer who'd recently moved to the valley from Southern California and was busy subdividing a ranch north of town into lots and selling them as homesites. At the time, they were just getting started digging holes in the ground, but he took a full-page ad, and when I told him how I planned to pump the whole county at sports shows, he wanted some of the action.

Rodgers was tall and pale, with the withered, washed-out look of an old-time surfing addict. I liked him, and for a while we got along fine. Both of us were conservative in our politics, and we shared an interest in the economic development of the valley. I figured nothing could be more beneficial to the image of outfitting than a connection with land development. After all, I told Rodgers, what had the winning of the West been but one of the great real estate promotions of all time? He liked the idea because it moved him from the category of hustler and speculator into the mainstream of history.

By the time of the Denver Sports Show, though, Rodgers had heard about Stu's reputation and become worried about his investment. The day the show opened, Ray Jones, Rodgers's ace salesman, walked into the booth and announced that he was there to give me a hand. I hadn't known I needed a hand, but Rodgers obviously thought I did. Jones was short and dark, a former baseball player about forty pounds over his playing weight. He'd knocked around the minors as a journeyman outfielder, interrupted by occasional calls to the majors, then gone to work for Rodgers. At the sports show, when Jones wasn't talking to me or a customer, he'd stare into the distance, as though looking for a fly ball headed his way or listening for the crack of a bat.

He was a good pitchman, but he was one of those people who makes you feel bad when you see what professional sports can do to people. His whole life was predicated on his being a pro athlete. When that was over—and it had been over a long time ago—the rest of the world seemed pretty dull by comparison. When I met him, he was a reformed alcoholic putting in his time and waiting for something to happen.

Jones and Rodgers had been friends since high school. Both had been athletes, but Jones was the guy with talent. After graduation, he played ball while Rodgers went to college and then into real estate. When Jones dropped out of baseball, he called his old pal for help.

Jones was an interesting guy, and between customers, we tried to figure out how to grab some publicity for the county. Since we couldn't afford to pay for it, we decided the trick was to con the media into giving us some of their time and space for free. We knew they'd dump public service announcements in the round file, but if we could lay a hot news story on them—something with celebrities and adventure—they'd eat it up.

I told Jones how Lander, Wyoming, promoted a one-shot antelope hunt that draws celebrities and politicians from around the world. When I was in state government, I'd helped arrange for the governor of Colorado to participate. I also knew the guy who organized the celebrity one-shot goose hunts at Two Buttes Reservoir in southeastern Colorado. And I told Jones about the way business boomed at the resort after ABC showed some tape they shot there on *Good Morning, America*.

Jones had stories, too. His involved the practice of professional athletes, in the off-season, parlaying their names and celebrity status into all-expenses-paid vacations. As a ball player, Jones had participated in celebrity fishing tournaments, where organizations invite pro athletes to catch bass or something, and pay their transportation and all their expenses. It's quite a scam, and the more we talked, the more we realized that if other people could do it, we could do it, too.

What we hit on was organizing what we called a World Series Elk Hunt. The plan was for Jones, who knew a lot of players who were still active, to contact a friend on the team that won the World Series; the friend, in turn, would invite other ball players to a Colorado high country elk hunt. It seemed like a natural. Stu and I would provide the guides and do the outfitting. Bud Rodgers would bankroll the project. And the media would cover the event, writing stories datelined Gunnison, and taking pictures of players lounging around the campfire, riding horses, and posing beside trophy-size elk hanging from trees.

Rodgers, when we laid it out for him, loved the idea, but instead of saying yes, he had us pitch it to his secretary, a tall, pale woman named Marie. She looked like a 1950s Hollywood movie heroine—somebody like Deborah Kerr or Ava Gardner—playing an ugly duckling in the first reel, who emerges in the last reel as a swan. Later, somebody told me that Marie had once been a nun, so I always thought of her as "Marie, the ex-nun." She definitely looked like she'd taken her habit off and had a story to tell.

When Marie liked the idea, Rodgers said yes, but he and Marie decided that some changes had to be made in our script. First, there was to be a drawing among their real estate customers, with the winners to be invited to join the hunt. Then Marie suggested doubling participation by adding "guest hunters"—fans who'd pay for the privilege of joining their heroes on the adventure. Stu and I talked it over. That many participants would strain our resources, we knew, but because we were charging by the hunter rather than the player, we figured the more the merrier.

We contracted with Rodgers to do the first hunt, with an option to do five more. If we could pull it off, we figured the connections coming out of sports circles would be worth a fortune. Ball players tell each other about their masseuses and their trainers, but they also talk about their guides. If the experience was a good one, we knew word would get around, and it couldn't help but do our business some good. Professional athletes make a hell of a lot more money than they know what to do with. We couldn't even imagine how they spent it all, but we were looking forward to finding out.

Our business was good that summer. I was so busy I didn't even think about baseball, much less follow the pennant races. When you're working in the high country, you pay very little attention to what's going on in the rest of the world. I never watched TV, and if I read a newspaper, it was likely to be a week old. When the players started showing up at the airport, I recognized a few names, but it was mostly older guys I remembered from my years in Denver—a couple of all-star outfielders, another guy who was a Golden Glove shortstop.

Originally the hunt was supposed to take place during the first hunting season, early in October. Instead, because the playoffs and the World Series ran on longer than usual, the hunt was postponed to the third season, six weeks later. October would have been easy—we'd had a long, warm fall—but by the middle of November, it was a different story. The weather was turning colder, and there was bound to be a lot more snow in the high country.

When the players and fans arrived, we put them through the orientation session. By now I'd worked up a pretty good shtick about terrain we'd cover, big game identification, camp safety rules, and high country survival. I distributed my standard pack containing a waxed topographic map, fire-starting equipment, space blanket, and candy bars and granola.

Orientations are important when you're leading any group, but with armed men, it's especially important to establish control early. As long they believe you know what you're talking about, that control isn't hard to get—at least it didn't used to be, when the public had more respect for professional guides than it does now. With hunters, you're explaining how to do something they really want to do, but because it's so far from their usual routine, they realize somebody has to be in charge. Athletes are especially easy. They recognize the similarity between hunting and team sports, and they're used to following instructions from a coach. In fact, hunting always reminded me of playing sandlot football when you're a kid: everybody can be jumping up and down and screaming, but when one guy says: "You go left, and you go right and run long, and you go short," they all shut up and do what they're told.

With a picture mounted on a display board, I showed them where to aim—where the "kill zone" is—when you try to knock down an elk. Deer are small enough to shock out pretty quick, but elk have enough body mass to absorb everything but the most accurately placed bullets. An elk's undercoat—the dense, heavy body hair—also works as a coagulant around wounds to stop all but the most severe bleeding. I always told hunters if they knocked one down to shoot him again, because I'd seen lots of dead elk get up and run forty miles. I told them to keep the scope on him, and if he so much as twitched, shoot him again.

Doubling the size of the hunt meant dividing the hunters into two groups. I took charge of one group and Stu the other. The younger men were going with me into a basecamp some miles to the north and several thousand additional feet in elevation above the camp I'd used during the great blizzard hunt. It was north of Carbon Peak, above the Chinese Wall, in a saddle between Axtell and Whetstone called Gibson's Ridge. Wagner's group, made up of older ball players and their fans, went into camp in Sunshine Park, above the resort.

Each party had two guides, a cook (a woman at my camp I'll call Dorothy), a camp boy, and a wrangler to handle the horses. In both camps there were two sleeping tents for hunters, a guides' tent, a cook/dining tent, and a tack tent. In addition, my party was accompanied by a pair of reporters, one local and one from the national media.

One of my first surprises was that although the guests paid extravagantly for the privilege of hunting with the ball players, the reporters traveled on the cuff. Actually, they're a lot like Catholic priests—they always have their hand out, and they've got this "I-don't-pay-for-nothing" shit down cold. They showed up in street clothes and expected to be dressed, fed, given a bag and cot, and a place to sleep at night. I suppose my resentment at their freeloading was matched by their resentment at being a party to Bud Rodgers's land promotion scheme, and the preoccupation all of us had with publicity. They knew what we were up to, and as the hunt went on, I realized that though the media's easily conned and comes cheap, it's not free. I also learned that there's nothing reporters like better than biting the hand that feeds them.

I'd gotten off to a good start with the players at orientation, but things cooled down when I saw how much personal gear they expected me to pack into camp. The hunt was billed as a seven-day affair, but you wouldn't believe the stuff they brought. We used every horse and mule we owned. I had to ride up on a pack mule. One animal carried nothing but hard booze. One big-name catcher was so outraged that he threw a fit when he discovered that the liquor stores downtown didn't have some kind of fancy French brandy liqueur he liked. It was the only thing he drank—came in little short, fat bottles and cost thirty or forty dollars apiece. They ordered a case and shipped it up to camp for him two days later.

By the time I got Wagner's party lined out for Sunshine Park, the weather had started falling apart. I led my bunch out of the Ohio Creek corrals and up the Chinese Wall trail. It was the long way around, but I wanted to avoid a ranchhouse along the more direct route because it would destroy the illusion that we were going into the big, deep darks.

It was a five-mile ride up to basecamp. By the time we got there, a thirty-five-mile-an-hour wind was blowing snow across Gibson's Ridge. I grilled steaks for supper with flakes the size of tennis balls going down the back of my neck. I had to hold the grill five feet downwind from the fire—flame was blowing straight out, it was like cooking at the end of an acetylene torch.

I'm not naturally optimistic about human nature, but if I'd expected to find men of exceptional character and intelligence among the ball players, I would soon have been disappointed. After we ate, everybody hung out in the cook tent and discussed the players' favorite subjects: first, their drinking prowess; second, their experiences with group sex. The older players contributed most of the anecdotes while the young guys sat at their feet in admiration, listening and learning.

One player, a famous outfielder winding up a long and illustrious career, boasted how he used to spend nights drinking before an important game, then doctored his hangover with beer in the clubhouse before taking to the field. The younger guys loved it. Other players described finding predatory women lurking outside ballparks and in hotel lobbies and taking them to their rooms for sex, then rounding up other members of the team and coaching staff to join the fun. To keep track of their celebrity partners, the women had them autograph stadium programs, like debutantes keeping souvenir dance cards.

I sat listening, unable to believe it—the self-hatred of women who'd do that to themselves, or the kind of men who'd take advantage of such sickness. Years ago, when I was a college dorm counselor, I'd tried to break up a gang-bang: a coed spread-eagled in the grass between the buildings was servicing a mob of eager males. Waiting their turns, the guys drank beer and cheered their buddies' efforts. When I went to help the girl, she cursed me, and the guys involved almost killed me. Friends came to my rescue, otherwise they might have done it.

A curious thing about the ball players' tales was that they did nothing to disillusion the fans who had paid to come along on the hunt. Actually, the relationship was a lot like young love: the fans couldn't seem to get enough of their heroes, and it was that way all through the hunt. No matter how close to the players they got, or how much about them they learned, the fans never got over their sense of awe. I suppose a lot of people are like that: they worship some kind of exceptional talent, and they don't see the people who possess it with the same eyes everybody else does. I was always that way about Albert Einstein: I always said if he'd sneezed on me, I would have said, "Excuse me."

The longer I was around them, the more I realized that ball players divide the world into two kinds of people—those who play ball and those who don't—and it was obvious that the only people they considered important were ball players. It surprised me, but listening to them, I realized it was the same way cowboys feel about themselves and dudes.

I hung around until ten-thirty that night, then crawled into my sleeping bag in the guides' tent. The hunters went to bed between twelve and twelve-thirty, and I turned them out at three-thirty the next morning to get ready for the hunt. My plan was to send the three youngest players—two pitchers and an outfielder (a guy who was supposed to be a hell of a hitter)—and their hunting companions with my best guide, Billy Wagner. The other guide and I were to take the older players and their fans with us.

Elevation at basecamp was between ten and eleven thousand feet. On the ground lay twelve to fourteen inches of wind-crusted snow. The temperature was right around zero—not *real* cold for November up there, but cold enough. To reach their stands, Bill's group had to climb another thousand feet inside three miles—which is bad, of course, but not a killer.

Normally, to get some sense of their physical condition, I talked to clients individually before taking them out. For the World Series Elk Hunt, I'd assumed that, because these were finely honed athletes, they were in at least as good shape as the ordinary hunter. But in the cook tent, watching a bunch of bleary-eyed, hung-over guys eating breakfast, I began to have doubts.

I'll never forget that first morning. Everybody had brought the wrong equipment: they're dressed in heavy, high-priced boots and one layer of thick clothes. If they keep everything on, they're too hot; if they take it off, they're too cold. Bill, their guide, is wearing a baseball jacket and a hooded sweatshirt, a ball cap, and he's tying on soccer shoes—the kind with these big cleats—over two pairs of wool socks. "I want to be able to move," he tells them. The players' eyes are like saucers: they can't believe it. These dudes are being seriously leveled.

At five AM, I kicked their butts out the door and told them to get after it. Hunting season opened at daylight, so we had about two hours to reach our positions. In addition to heavy clothes and boots, the hunters carried rifles that weighed about twelve pounds, extra ammunition, big knives, and a lunch. I suppose the total weight per hunter averaged about thirty-five pounds. In their stomachs was a full breakfast—nice greasy eggs, toast, pancakes, sausage, and coffee—something to bulk them up and give them a little energy.

Bill's group got about a quarter of a mile, he told me, before the players started heaving their guts into the snow from the climb and their lack of conditioning. I started to get after him about being so hard on them, but he said, "I was taking it easy on 'em, I was taking it easy on 'em!" And from what I saw with my bunch, he probably had been.

We had about 500 feet to climb in something less than two miles to reach our positions by daylight. These were older guys, but they were still supposed to be sportsmen, or so I'd been told. As it turned out, I'd overestimated their physical condition by at least 100 percent. Every fifteen minutes, I had to stop and wait for them, and so help me, I never broke a sweat.

According to wildlife biologists, there are three major elk herds in the Gunnison Basin, most of them descended from animals re-introduced early in the century from other states, after the early settlers destroyed the original population. One, the Cebolla herd, stays in the southern portion of the basin, near Lake City. Another, the Mt. Emmons herd, stays north of Crested Butte until snow in the high country pushes it south toward water and forage in the Ohio Creek valley. The Taylor Park herd, which summers north-east of Crested Butte, moves south into an area known as the Almont Triangle, above the confluence of the Taylor and East Rivers.

If it weren't for Highway 135, biologists say, the two herds would join one another, and if it weren't for the concentration of people in the Gunnison Valley, both herds would move still far-ther south. Wagner's hunters, located in Sunshine Park, were in position to intercept the Taylor Park herd; with the camp on Gibson's Ridge, my group was in an ideal position to intercept the Mt. Emmons herd.

As the sky grew lighter, Bill and I led our hunters by different routes up Gibson's Ridge. To the north, we could hear the boom of big game rifles, their echoes reverberating among the peaks, and knew that the season had opened, that the elk would be on the move. With luck, all those hunters north of us would drive the Mt. Emmons herd toward the Axtell-Whetstone country. The sky was turning pale as we climbed the slope. Finally, with the first light touching the peaks across the valley, Bill and I distributed our hunt-ers in the treeline on either side of a rise, where they couldn't shoot each other, and settled down to wait.

Time passed. Heartbeats slowed. Puffs of breath like jets of steam from an old-fashioned railroad engine marked every hunter's location. I sat waiting, for a while relieved when elk didn't appear, because I knew none of the hunters could hit anything until they'd recovered from the climb. Finally, though, when it was full light and we still hadn't seen anything, I started to worry. Circling the rise, I found fresh tracks where a dozen elk had churned through the snow shortly before we arrived.

So that was that. You miss the first morning light, and the hunt's pretty much over for the day; it's entertain-the-dudes time.

On the chance that elk might have taken cover in some dark timber below us, Bill and I worked our way down, but found nothing. Below the timber, I counted the same number of tracks I'd seen above, on our side of the ridge. Unless there were elk in the trees that had been there before it snowed, the woods had to be empty.

That night, everyone was in their sleeping bags by eight o'clock. Some of the players were thinking seriously about taking up some form of physical conditioning. Their surprise at the way Bill had dressed that morning had turned to admiration. He was about their age and a hell of an athlete himself—a rodeo athlete—and for all the millions they were making, he was in a lot better shape than they were.

The next day we hunted the high meadows along Gibson's Ridge, again with no luck. The third day, I left the older guys in camp to rest while Bill and I led the younger ones post-holing through snow to a bowl on the east face of Whetstone. This time we saw elk, but before we got within range, the herd broke south and went over the divide toward Carbon Creek. I decided to try for the Almont Triangle herd, hoping that hunters north of 135 might have pushed some animals across the road, and that they'd worked their way toward Whetstone.

Stationing hunters in a line of trees, Bill and I trotted nearly three miles downhill, then circled back again, trying to drive the elk toward the waiting rifles. Instead, the herd had stayed east of the highway, and we never cut a track.

Now it was getting sticky. Three days into the hunt, and we hadn't popped a cap. Back in camp, the newspaper guys were waiting for us. "How many you get today?" Their editors are getting after them; they can only file that "Elk Ten–Hunters Zero" story so often.

Every day, the wrangler carried dispatches reporting the latest failure down the Chinese Wall trail and returned with newspapers containing stories filed a couple of days earlier. One morning a Denver television crew came up to shoot some tape but got nothing except pictures of players clowning around, swinging rifle butts at snowballs.

At night, with everybody tucked in their bags, I saddled Morgan and rode to the top of Gibson's Ridge. Sitting against a convenient tree, I'd take a swallow of Jim Beam and smoke a few cigarettes. I could see most of the East River valley and the mountains that feed it: Gothic and Avery, White Rock and Teocalli, Crystal and Italian. At the upper end, the lights of Crested Butte resembled an electric grid shaped to the plain where Coal Creek and Slate Creek meet to form the East River.

Above town, on the mountain, mercury vapor lamps turned the ski area into an illuminated cloud filled with miniature buildings and roads and cars. South, down the valley, I could see light from the Roaring Judy hatchery. Overhead, blue stars, beds and beds of them, drifted west with the winter constellations—Taurus and the Pleiades, pursued by Orion with Sirius, the dog star, at his heels; Canis Major and Canis Minor; Gemini and Perseus in the north—all magnified to spectacular proportions by the rarified, 10,000-foot atmosphere.

While I relaxed, a family of coyotes coordinated their hunts on the ridge with yips and screeches and howls—the younger members supplying the high notes, the older ones singing bass. Finally, when cold dulled the glow generated by whiskey and cigarettes, I roused Morgan and rode down to camp for another short night and another long day.

The weather continued poor. It was a bad time to be outside. Arctic snow fronts blew through, driving other hunters indoors. Locals stayed home while out-of-state hunters left their camps and holed up in motels to drink beer, play cards, and watch television, waiting for the weather to clear.

That was a problem for us, because you count on other hunters to help you. They stir up the game and keep the herds moving. But every Texan's heard about the Donner Party, or knows the old Jack London story, "To Build a Fire," where a trapper freezes to death in a storm. As far as the general public is concerned, this is man-eating country, where everybody's a potential Alferd Packer, the Colorado Cannibal, who killed and ate a bunch of people near Lake City.

The fourth day, in spite of my theory that hunting on horses is a mistake, I decided to give them a try. At least horses provide some additional range, so we rode south to search the timbered ridges above Carbon Creek. Again we found nothing.

It was as long as I'd ever gone, and as hard as I'd ever hunted, without seeing game. There were guides' strategy talks going on, right there in front of the dudes. We're arguing and scratching our asses, trying to figure this out, because these guys are looking at us with serious intent. I'm getting an itchy feeling right between my shoulder blades. They're going to quit trying to shoot elk and start shooting guides. It's the longest these ball players have ever been away from their adoring female fans; they've got an advanced case of crotch itch. Dorothy, our cook, a nice, middle-aged lady, looks good to them; I'm afraid to trust them alone with the horses. It's getting serious.

The guides and I decided the Mt. Emmons herd must have avoided Gibson's Ridge and gone to cover south of us, on Carbon Peak. There isn't enough feed to keep a herd there all winter, but it's a natural staging area for elk entering the Ohio Creek valley. There are no tracks—not even hunters' tracks going up after the herd—but I decided to mount a D-Day Operation. I really talked it up, trying to get these guys excited, but it was a dangerous thing to do: if it didn't pay off, I knew I'd be dog-shit.

Next morning, the fifth day of the hunt, we mounted everybody in camp, even the reporters. Then the guides and I, plus an additional wrangler (a local boy named Mike) rode south toward Carbon Peak. Taking dudes out in deep snow in such rough country is dangerous, but I was desperate.

Before we started, I warned them not to dismount, but I happened to be looking back when a guy's hat blew off. We were on a shoulder of the mountain, in heavy snow, with an aspen grove below us. I saw the guy hesitate and yelled, "Let it go, we'll get it later!"

He was a dentist, some little cheese-eater from Wisconsin. He heard me, but he has to have his hat right now, so he steps off—on the downhill side—and picks it up. But when he tries to remount, he plants his foot in the stirrup, and that's as far as he gets. Before he can pull himself up, the horse, figuring he's stood there long enough, takes off down through the quakies, dragging the dentist by one foot stuck in the stirrup, like something you see in a movie.

When that sort of thing happens, the natural thing to do is try to ride the runaway down on another horse. Of course, all you do is spook him worse than ever, so while Bill circled below the aspen to head him off, I told the other hunters to freeze. Holding our breaths, we watched the dentist swing out the length of the stirrup leather while his mount dodged back and forth through the trees. I waited for that ripe-pumpkin sound when a head hits, but it never happened. The horse came out of the quakies half a mile below us and took a notion to stop, just like that. I couldn't believe it.

When Bill reached them, the dentist was stretched out in the snow, still hanging from the stirrup by his boot. Dismounting, Bill slipped close enough to catch the reins and free the guy's foot. When the rest of us got there, I looked him over, but there wasn't a mark on him. He even had change and keys in his pocket. The only thing missing was his eyeglasses. He fussed around looking for them, and then wanted me to backtrack through that half-mile of trampled snow to find them.

I assumed he would demand to be returned to camp—I know I would have—but instead he remounted and said he was ready to hunt. I never did figure out whether he was just a hell of a gutsy little guy, or if he had no idea how close he'd come to dying. The odds of your surviving a horse carrying you that far that fast, through a grove of trees, have got to be incredible.

Everybody quieted down after that. For the rest of the hunt, it was like that old stockbroker commercial on TV: I would speak, and everybody would listen. We rode through a cut and up the north flank of Carbon Peak. The country was too rough to negotiate on foot. Looking back, I can't believe I took them up there. I guess I hoped they'd all die so word wouldn't get back that we didn't kill any elk. In my mind I was doing this Walter Mitty thing where I'd return to town and say, "Hunters? What hunters? They filled their licenses and got out of here a week ago." I told Bill: "Kill the reporters first—our reputations are on the line."

To climb Carbon Peak, we had to ride up a steep, narrow, icy chute through the aspen. Bill was my best rider, so I sent him up first. Spurring his mount, slashing with the reins, he scrambled up the chute and made it to the top. "Piece of cake," he yelled down, and once the other horses had seen it done, they were willing to try. "Next," I announced.

I don't know who it was, but some crazy ball player took a shot at it. I'm yelling: "Keep after him! Don't let him quit on you!"

The last guy to try it was a young pitcher, a farm boy from Georgia who was scared to death of horses. Sensing his fear, the other players had ragged him, like chickens pecking a sick one, ever since the hunt started. In a blind one day, I'd tried to encourage him; I told him everybody was afraid of something and urged him not to let his fear ruin the experience for him. Now, when he hesitated, the guys on top machoed him into giving it a shot, and he spurred his horse all the way up.

When I joined them, the pitcher was waiting for me with the saddest puppy-dog eyes I ever saw. "How're we gonna get down?" he wanted to know. He was the only guy up there smart enough to realize that we had to get back down. I told him, "Not to worry—we'll come out another way." Only there wasn't any other way.

I got them lined out, and as we rode across a snow-covered bench, I was surprised to hear a young elk bugle—this late in the season, and he was still in rut. Right away I knew where the herd was—in a long meadow on another bench a quarter of a mile above us. We tied the horses, and I gathered the hunters and explained the situation. We couldn't stalk the elk because the snow was too crusty. Our only chance was to climb straight up the slope through the trees. If they smelled us, or heard us coming, they'd break south, across a rock slide, and escape through the timber.

"They're right up there," I said, "the whole herd. It's two hundred yards of vertical elevation. To have any kind of chance, we've got to jog up as hard as we can go." Arranging everybody in a skirmish line, with Bill and the other guide, and Mike, the new wrangler, behind, I led them up in a steady, snow-churning assault.

At the top, it was a picture out of a hunter's dream: a hundred elk from the Mt. Emmons herd scattered across the meadow, heads down, feeding in the winter sunshine. The air was so still you could see their breath. Behind me, I saw the guides and Mike, but below them the slope was empty—the ball players hadn't even come out of the trees.

I gestured the hands to freeze, but as the hunters struggled toward the top, the elk started looking around. Then the old lead cow broke into a gallop, heading toward the rock slide, and the whole herd went with her.

I'd warned Mike and the guides not to fire, but when the herd hit the far end of the meadow, Mike shot a big five-point out of the bunch. By the time the ball players caught up with us, the elk were gone. I was really pissed at Mike, but I had to admit he'd waited quite a while, and let them get way out there, before he shot. So that's what we had to show for all that effort: one dead elk … and it wasn't even a hunter that took him, it was one of the hands.

Leaving the guides to clean the bull and bring it out, we got off Carbon Peak the same way we got up—down the chute. "Watch Bill, he knows what he's doing," I told them. Not that I needed to. By now they'd figured out that this was Bill's ball park, and they were playing his game, and it wasn't some bat-and-ball grab-ass: it was life and death.

"Sit back in the saddle," I told them. "Brace your feet against the stirrups, like you're on a sled."

Actually it wasn't that bad. Once you got started, you couldn't make a mistake or change your mind. In a chute like that, a horse will slide as long as you'll stay with him. At the bottom, after we got down, I saw the little pitcher giving me this reproachful look and told him: "Yeah, I lied to you, didn't I?"

Back on Gibson's Ridge, I found Dorothy, the cook, packing her gear, demanding to be taken to town. While we were gone, Stu had ridden into camp, cursed her and fired her, and then ridden out again. Right away, I knew what had happened; he'd get like that when he was drinking hard. He'd go on a three- or four-day bender, drink himself into a rage, then look for a way to spread the poison. I calmed Dorothy down, assuring her that her services were appreciated and urging her to stay. It was my first clue, though, that something had gone wrong at Sunshine Park.

Early next morning, I left Bill in charge and started down the Chinese Wall trail and met a rider coming up. It was an emissary from Bud Rodgers with a message: he and Marie the ex-nun wanted to see me. In town, I learned the extent of the damage. Wagner and Bud Rodgers's pal, Ray Jones, who'd gone into the Sunshine Park camp with him, had fallen off the wagon together. First they shot guns in the air, Rodgers told me, then somebody put somebody in the fire. There were conflicting versions about who did what to whom, but then one of the players—the Golden

Glove shortstop–said something Stu didn't like, and Stu pulled a gun and threatened to kill him.

The players had talked things over, Rodgers said, and decided the whole promotion was a ripoff. They were ready to pack up and leave. While Rodgers was telling me all this, Marie had been absolutely silent–she'd been sitting there glaring the whole time. Now she said, "This whole business is totally unacceptable."

Rodgers might be bankrolling the operation, I realized, but Marie was calling the shots. She was mad at the way their clients– the ball players and the potential investors–were being treated, because it was bad for their business. I didn't blame her. It was bad for my business, too, but at this point there wasn't much I could do about it except thank God I had the media guys with me on Gibson's Ridge instead of with Stu in Sunshine Park.

Wagner had also quarreled with his guides. When they quit, he hired two fishing guides from another resort. Unable to find game, the new guides told everybody it wasn't their fault, that this wasn't elk country anyway. They claimed they were all just wasting their time. So it turned out the Sunshine Park hunters had had no more success with the Taylor Park herd than my hunters had had with the Mt. Emmons herd. Finally, bored and angry with life in camp, Wagner rode into my camp and fired Dorothy, then returned to the resort to do his drinking in the bar.

I tried to calm Rodgers and Marie by offering to straighten things out at Sunshine Park, but it was too late. Wagner's hunters had abandoned camp and were returning to town. When I admitted our lack of success on Gibson's Ridge, Rodgers and Marie insisted that everyone be brought down. Some of Rodgers's friends had convinced him there were elk in the sagebrush west of Gunnison, so the rest of the hunt took place there. With the players and fans eating in restaurants and sleeping warm in motels, we beat the flats for a couple of days, but the sagebrush produced no more elk than the high country had. We never even cut a track.

We'd hunted hard–as hard as I ever hunted–and in spite of all my kidding about the players, I think that in a normal year we would have killed elk. Every year you expect to average about 50 percent; with ten hunters in camp, we should have taken at least five bulls.

Another problem was that I'd had to conduct the hunt by the book. Normally, I would have increased the odds of killing something by swinging over into an adjoining area. But because my fellow outfitters were pissed about that Businessman of the Year award, and the publicity generated by the hunt, they were watching so closely I couldn't do it. The local game wardens, suspicious that what we were doing with the promotion was running some kind of contest ("auctioning off wildlife," they called it, which is forbidden by law) were also on the alert.

What we were doing, and what we were selling, was perfectly legal—"a guided hunting trip"—but I knew that both the Forest Service and the Division of Wildlife were just waiting for me to make a mistake. They know that even under normal circumstances there's pressure on outfitters to produce game. When you add celebrities and publicity to the mix, the pressure's even greater. They watch to see if you try to cut corners, because if they nail you, it's wonderful publicity for them.

After the hunt was over, Marie arranged a banquet at a hall in town. A couple of hundred people turned out to see the ball players they'd been reading about in the newspapers and seeing on television the past couple of weeks. Rodgers came wearing a ski sweater over a Hawaiian shirt, like everything was fine. Marie looked sensational. Gone were the wire-rimmed glasses, the hair pulled back in a bun. She wore a low-cut dress and enough makeup on her pale features to turn her into a Hollywood swan. Ray Jones was gone—Rodgers had shipped him back to Betty Ford for more detox.

Emceeing the show from the head table, I played down our lack of success. I raffled off autographed baseballs and tried to emphasize the lighter side by handing out funny awards. At night, watching the valley from the top of Gibson's Ridge, I'd made notes about things that happened during the day. There was a "Best Liar's Award" for a ball player fond of exaggerating his exploits. There was a "Mt. Axtell Hunting Award" that went to several hunters who thought they'd seen elk when they hadn't. The dentist whose horse ran away received the "Trick Rider Award." In fact, before the banquet broke up, I made sure that everybody got an award for something.

A final disaster crowned the World Series Elk Hunt. After the banquet, the tip money for the guides, as well as the autographed baseball raffle money, disappeared. Marie had taken charge of it, putting it in her car; then she'd left the car unlocked outside the ball players' motel while she had a drink with them. At least that's what she said. Her story was that she and the players had been drinking until three or four o'clock in the morning, and when she came out, the money was gone.

Give or take a few hundred, I figured there must have been about $5,000 involved. No one knew for sure, though, because no one, including Marie, had counted it. Apparently the cops believed her story. They conducted an investigation—they claimed they talked to everybody involved—but the money never turned up. And if they ever asked what was going on in that motel room all that time, I never heard about it. I guess the moral of the story is that you've got to keep your eye on these lapsed nuns, especially around a room full of horny ball players.

I covered the guides' tips out of my own pocket, but when the dust settled, Stu and I had lost the concession for the World Series Elk Hunt. We might have waltzed away from no elk, but the drinking and fighting and gunplay had been too much. Marie didn't help us, either.

Next year, Bud Rodgers assigned the hunt to another outfitter, a guy who specialized in quantity hunting rather than quality, and so every year he started each season with a new group of hunters. During the week-long hunt, he managed to get everybody mad at him, so Rodgers gave up the idea of a World Series Elk Hunt. Two years with nothing but problems convinced him that maybe it wasn't such a good idea after all. Besides, his real estate development was doing well, so he no longer needed the publicity.

I always thought it was too bad the hunt hadn't worked. It would have been a wonderful promotion for the valley. Or maybe it wouldn't. Attitudes toward hunting seem to be changing. Animal rights activists are raising a lot of issues you never used to hear about. The old *American Sportsman* TV show is off the air. The network quit when sponsors got worried about showing birds and animals getting killed. Now, when you see people catching fish on television, it's always catch-and-release. They put them back in the water, and the camera makes sure you see them swim away. They'll show you suffering human beings—you can see movies where a girl's flayed alive—but they won't show a dead animal, because people would raise hell. It's ironic.

# 9

# Hustling the Groceries

I'M STILL NOT SURE if there's a fifth act to outfitting, but if there is, it's nothing like the others. Eight months of the year, an outfitter's the star of his own show, a larger-than-life character who's the object of an admiration sometimes amounting to awe on the part of a parade of star-struck dudes. He's the cock of the walk, giving orders, bossing a crew of wranglers, and making life-and-death decisions for himself and everyone else. It's pretty heady stuff. But once big game season is over, and all the poor gebronies he's been lording it over go back to their lives in the real world, the outfitter goes too, leaving the stage and all his props behind.

Sometimes, when we were closing the high camps at the end of hunting season, I used to imagine what it would be like to pack in enough supplies to winter over at the fishcamp by myself. But it was a pipe dream, and I knew it. Next spring, after the snow melted, they'd find my frozen body up there—and maybe catch a glimpse of a few blue-eyed coyotes hunting in the mountains.

An outfitter moves to town because he doesn't have much choice: that's where the jobs are. Only where all the poor gebronies he felt sorry for are picking up where they left off, the outfitter's always starting from scratch. The job he had last winter, if he had one, isn't there anymore. When he reports to a personnel manager for an interview, the outfitter isn't applying for some company career track position and asking questions about vacation time and pension plans and sick leave. If it hires him, the company knows it's getting a seasonal temp, some guy who's putting in his time till spring, when the snow melts and trails into the high country open again. He can't wait to get out of there.

Prospective employers used to take one look at my résumé and show me the door. Not only was I older than I should be, they knew that I was also better qualified, at least on paper, for their jobs than they were. The last guy they wanted was some gray-bearded veteran of the bureaucratic wars who might doubt their authority or give them an argument. They wasted no time getting rid of me so they could hire some kid fresh out of college who would do exactly what he was told, no questions asked, because he didn't know any better.

That left the entry-level, minimum-wage, stoop-labor jobs: flipping burgers, cutting firewood, cleaning up restaurants, feeding cattle. I know, because at one time or another I did them all in order to survive. I always thought of this survival process as "hustling the groceries."

Because there's always snow in the high country by the end of November, getting out after the last big game season takes planning. We tried to avoid locating our third-season camps up high, and we made sure the trails to the roads and the resort were downhill. We also tried to avoid being caught with leftover food. After each of the first two seasons, I'd inventory what was left and carry up only enough to fill the holes. You never wanted to pack out much food, especially perishables; the last thing you wanted to do was get caught with forty-seven and a half bottles of mustard or syrup.

The final meals in camp were made of leftovers. Whatever food got down to the resort Stu and I kept or gave the hands, because they were setting up housekeeping somewhere. The idea was never to start next year with old food.

At the resort, we dried and folded tents and sleeping bags and stored them in the tack house along with the tack and kitchen equipment. Everything mice consider edible—which is almost everything not made of metal—we hung from the rafters. The last job was loading and transporting the stock to a low-country ranch where we boarded the animals until spring. By the first of December, everything was over for the year, and it was time to start hustling a living.

One form of hustle was to trade on your reputation by accepting invitations from former clients to visit their homes. Clients love to introduce you as "my guide" and steer you around a room to show you off to their friends. "This is *my guide*," they tell everybody, so the friends can see what kind of people they hang out with on their vacations. Everybody's in dinner clothes, sipping wine and martinis, and you're in jeans and a dirty shirt. I always wore my old Stetson, too, because I figured out right away what they wanted: the tougher you looked and the crazier you acted, the better they liked it. You'd see clients winking at their friends like: "See? What did I tell you?"

In my own mind, I justified these visits as a means of promoting the business; they offered the perfect setting for selling the service next year to a new group of clients. Stu and I would pitch Western vacations in general, with talk about Yellowstone and the Grand Canyon, but the slide carousel was full of pictures of the Gunnison country and Harmel's Resort, and our services received most of the play. Sitting around talking in somebody's darkened rec room was very cozy, something that was happening between friends—and because our clients had already boasted about their experiences, they were eager to add their testimony.

I enjoyed these occasions—they were a relief from the prospect of going out and earning an honest living—but when we finished, I was ready to move on. Wagner, though, often lingered, stretching his visits over days and weeks. I admit he made an attractive house guest. He was good looking, and women and children loved him. He practiced the required social vices: he liked to eat and drink and smoke; he told a good joke; he kept whatever hours his hosts required, no matter how irregular. At the same time, there was a hint of danger about him, a sense of unpredictability that many people found attractive.

One winter two clients from Nebraska, wealthy guys who operated a custom feed business, invited us to meet their friends and go pheasant hunting with them. One guy owned a triple-wide trailer home located in the sandhills twenty-five miles from the nearest town. We arrived on a clear, cold December afternoon and found thirty or forty people waiting to meet us. A barbecue was scheduled for that evening; the pheasant hunt was next day. The clients, remembering how much I enjoyed Wild Turkey (which I did not), had purchased a special bottle in my honor. Rather than disappoint them, I helped myself to the Wild Turkey, because I was in salesman heaven. I was selling trips we hadn't even thought up— not yet.

The country looked like pictures you see of Scottish links-side golf courses, and the barbecue was wonderful. We commenced to do mashed potatoes and gravy, barbecued beef, corn on the cob, all kinds of beans and salads. Outside, the sun was going down, and pheasants were whistling in the wheat stubble. I was sitting across the table from a potential customer, giving him an account of a successful bear hunt, when suddenly the lights went out.

Later a woman told me that Stu, who was beside me, had noticed a bubbling sound in my mashed potatoes and gravy, and reached over to turn my face to one side, so I could breathe. According to the woman, I stayed this way for several minutes, then rose and walked outside—to all appearances as sober as a judge, though a little rigid in the joints. When she asked Stu if he was going after me, he said no, I was all right—all I needed was a little air.

Next morning, I woke up in a hole. It was about six feet deep and eight feet across and looked like an oversized grave. My head hurt and my face felt stiff. When I touched it, I thought I'd torn myself up, but it was just dried mashed potatoes and gravy. I'd never passed out like that before. I laid there a while, picking potatoes and gravy from my face and wondering where I was and how I'd got there. Finally I climbed out of the hole to find the others.

It turned out that the people who owned the place had been digging a new well about a dozen yards from the trailer, and I'd fallen in. I found everybody in the trailer eating breakfast. They said good morning, like nothing had happened, and so did I. I filled a plate with bacon and eggs and pancakes, and sat down and ate breakfast, too. Our clients had told everybody what a wild guy I was, and by spending the night in the well, I'd lived up to my reputation.

After breakfast we all went hunting. It was a hell of a hard hunt, but I don't remember much about it. They told me I killed two or three birds, but I can't remember firing a shot. After that I gave up Wild Turkey and stuck to Jim Beam, because it never gave me any trouble … at least not trouble like that.

A couple of years, after big game season ended, Stu and I tried to work together at the Outfitters' Feed and Supply Store. More often, though, we went our separate ways. Stu was a natural craftsman, a guy who could fix anything or figure out how to make something without a pattern or any kind of special tools. He could take things apart and put them back together—a saddle, a piece of tack, small engines, electric motors, kitchen appliances—in a way that amazed me. Once, with nothing more than a tape measure, some canvas, and a needle and thread, we cut and sewed a cover for a twenty-foot power boat—not an easy thing to do, but a project that caused Stu no trouble at all.

It was fun to watch him work. I could do some of the things he did, but only after I'd seen them done first. Stu did them without any kind of instructions; he could visualize the finished product and create it without making a single mistake. He was incredible.

When we set up the store, we agreed to split whatever profits remained after the bills were paid. Some months that amounted to $300 or $400; other months there'd be $10 or less. Some months there wasn't even enough money to pay the bills, and since I was keeping the books, I realized the difference was a matter of how much Stu was skimming from the cash drawer.

We'd quarreled at the resort about his thieving, but keeping store together exaggerated the problem. Finally I told him okay, he could keep the books, thinking the responsibility might put him on his honor, but it didn't; if anything, he stole more than ever. Cold weather and indoor living also increased his consumption of scotch. Finally things got so bad I told him he could have the store, and I just walked away; I didn't want to have anything more to do with the place.

Stu would take an occasional odd job (he filled in as night watchman in a mine for a couple weeks), but he drew the line at working for wages. "I swore off that a long time ago," he told me. I had no such reservations, and over the years I held a lot of down-season jobs—some good, some not so good.

Probably the best, in terms of status and salary, was the winter I managed the food service operation at the Crested Butte ski area. Actually it was too good a job for a guy who really wanted to be outfitting, because it paid too much, and it had me doing too many things I'd been trying to escape from when I left Denver. All I wanted was a temporary, fill-in job, something to get me through to the next outfitting season; instead, I found myself back pushing paper and managing people.

I got the job through a series of flukes. Originally I'd applied for work as a bartender. I'd never tended bar before, at least not full-time, and I thought tending bar in a ski area, with all those strange people coming and going, would be interesting. Instead, the vice president in charge of operations told me there were no bartending jobs available, but because of my experience at the Ramble, I was qualified to manage the Paradise Warming House, a bar and short-order restaurant halfway up the mountain. Only there was a catch: if I wanted the job, I had to fire the current manager. The guy had a reputation for being wild enough to be dangerous, and the vice president was afraid to do the firing himself and was looking for a patsy.

It was all right with me. Years ago, when I was working in the Denver public school system, I'd wished I had the authority to fire any number of people; later, while I worked for the state, I'd fired dozens of people for everything ranging from incompetence to felony grand larceny. Besides, I'd been outfitting and fighting for my life at the Ramble the past year, so I walked into the manager's office, collected his keys, and told him to get out. He left without a word—probably because he hoped that, once I got a look at his books, which were in pretty bad shape, I wouldn't call the cops.

Then, about the time I had the warming house ready to open, the vice president called me again and said the area food service manager had decided the job was "just too much" for him. He'd quit, and because the vice president liked the way I'd gotten rid of the warming house manager, he wanted me to take over. I told him okay, and we negotiated another contract. I knew I had him over a barrel because it's hard to find anybody in a ski community (especially at the last minute) who has much of a work ethic. Most people are there to drink and play games and get paid for it.

As food service manager, I was in charge of the staffs, the supplies and equipment, and the entertainment for all area facilities. I felt pretty silly about it, but I shopped the local thrift stores and put together the required wardrobe—a couple of sportcoats, some blue, oxford-cloth shirts (a little frayed at collar and cuffs), a few wool ties. When I saw myself in the mirror, I felt like an actor returning to a part he'd exhausted—and that had exhausted him—a long time ago.

Managing the area food service called for many of the skills I'd used working for the state: developing budgets, supervising employees, establishing menus, checking cost control, responding to miscellaneous problems. One of my most time-consuming duties was booking and supervising entertainment at the Rafters Theater. My experience operating the Ramble proved helpful when a running feud developed between me and various entertainers and their agents and managers.

I started out trying to be a good guy, but it turned into a contest of who could be the biggest prick, me or them. The problem was that most professional singers and dancers and musicians on the circuit were deadbeats, more interested in drinking and goofing off than in performing. It seems strange—you'd think performers would want to be on stage, doing their act—but that wasn't how it worked. There were some big-name entertainers among them, but all of them were a bunch of gypsies operating strictly according to formula: do the least amount of performing for the greatest amount of money, while getting as high as possible on your booze.

To get away from them, I skied a lot, and at night joined crews packing the slopes after heavy snowfalls. Sidestepping up and down hills on skis in a foot of fresh powder has got to be one of the greatest conditioning exercises—and stress relievers—ever invented.

Another winter I worked as a baggage handler (better known in the trade as a "load engineer" or "ramp-rat") with the AMR Service Group at the Gunnison County Airport. I didn't expect to like it, but I surprised myself by falling in love with the work and the people. I met all kinds of guys there—blue-collar, white-collar, guys with M.A.s, Ph.D.s, you name it. We even won some national awards for speed and efficiency in getting planes turned around. We won a national excellence award three months in a row, though you've got to realize our competition was mostly Cuban nationals who'd been in the country about fourteen hours.

One thing I liked about the job was the variety of tasks involved. When I applied, because of my age, the manager tried to put me to work on the security machine in the terminal. But I knew checking luggage all day would drive me nuts, so I told him no way, it sounded to me like an old man's job; I wanted to go out on the ramp.

The service crew is responsible for cleaning planes on the ground, de-icing them when necessary, gassing them, loading and checking luggage, and guiding pilots onto and off the runways. Sometimes there'd be four 727s on the ground at once, and the ramp crew had to turn each of them around in fourteen minutes.

The first couple of weeks I wondered if I'd bitten off more than I could chew. The cargo holds were like ice caves, long and narrow, and so low there wasn't enough room to stand upright. The suitcases we handled weighed fifty-five to sixty pounds apiece and had to be stacked precisely, so they would all fit in the limited space and wouldn't shift in flight. Working from a crouch was exhausting. The only way I survived was because some of the guys saved my bacon. One of them, a guy I'll call Dave—he must have been about thirty-five, but he was a kid compared to me—did three-quarters of the work till I got in good enough condition to hold up my end. "Get out of my way, old man, and breathe a little," he'd tell me. I'd drag my weary butt out on the ramp, rest for a while, and go back for more.

Another job that kept me through the winter was editing a vacation magazine for the local newspaper. Another winter, or part of a winter, I worked for the Crested Butte police department as a parking marshal. Crested Butte's an old coal-mining town about thirty miles north of Gunnison. By the early sixties, it was pretty much a ghost town until some guy who'd made a bundle on Kansas wheat and oil turned it around. Since then it's been struggling to find a place in the trade as a "destination ski resort" along the lines of Aspen and Vail. In contrast to silver- and gold-mining towns, coal towns were pretty makeshift affairs. Local tax laws favor old buildings over new, so many of the Butte's former mining shacks are still occupied, though they've been gutted and renovated–very much like installing Porsche engines and running gear in Volkswagen Beetles that have seen hard use.

Today, building codes rather than necessity dictate architectural style. As a result, ski towns are free, in a collective sense, to choose their appearance. With Crested Butte, the choice has been to imitate the architecture the original coal miners couldn't afford: the silver-baron, Victorian look you find in Aspen and Telluride. Locally the style is known as "Disneyland East," and consists of wood-frame buildings painted nontraditional colors like eggplant or aqua or chartreuse, with yards of impractical window glass and lots of wooden gingerbread trim around eaves and porches.

In a normal winter, the Butte receives about eighteen feet of snow (the modern record, set in 1962, is nearly thirty-two feet). On a good night, snow falls by the pound at a rate of one foot an hour, blotting out everything in sight. I remember times when its descent was awe-inspiring; it was like being caught in a cloudburst, and you felt like you could hardly breathe. Old-timers in the area tell stories of overnight accumulations eight feet deep.

With snowfalls like that, round-the-clock plowing is a necessity. Parking marshals are responsible for enforcing an ordinance that forbids leaving vehicles on the north and west sides of the streets one night, and south and east sides the next. Speeding plows can do serious bodily harm to cars buried in snow banks. Before the parking ordinance, I remember seeing a Coupe de Ville lodged in an icy wall after a plow blade sheared away the entire left side– both fenders, front and rear doors. The Caddy looked like it had been modified for an automobile show or television commercial demonstrating the quality of General Motor's comfort and design.

As parking marshal, my job was to cruise the town in a tow truck, ticketing offending vehicles and hauling them to a cold storage lot. Next day in court I'd testify that the cars had been improperly parked. They paid me $30 for every car I impounded. They also issued me a list of cars that were not to receive tickets, for political reasons.

With some vehicles, I relaxed the letter of the law, particularly for old junkers belonging to what are known as "the C.B.D.B.s"–

the Crested Butte Dirt Balls–the imitation hippie kids working as waiters and waitresses and bartenders along Elk Avenue, the town's main street. When I found vehicles like that illegally parked, I ran the bubble and hooted the siren. Nine times out of ten, some kid would come running out of a bar or restaurant and move the car. Expensive cars, though, I considered fair game. Lincoln Continentals and Jaguars were my favorites–neither one of them has bumpers worth a shit, and I used to crush 'em up like tinfoil.

Marshaling was usually pretty dull work. I guess the most exciting time I had was helping put down a New Year's Eve riot. Shortly before midnight, fights broke out spontaneously in three of four downtown bars and boiled out into the streets. I was half-asleep, cruising the south side, when I received a call for assistance over my radio. By the time I reached Elk Avenue, the town marshal and assistant marshal, a woman, were on the sidewalk watching twenty-five or thirty men engaged in hand-to-hand combat. They were big boys, and after all the booze they'd drunk, they were feeling no pain. It looked like the Texas Aggies versus the rest of the world. Until then, I'd enjoyed marshaling, but when I saw those fights, I was ready to turn in my badge. I knew if we tried to break them up, those guys would join forces and beat the piss out of us.

When the town marshal fired a warning shot in the air, nobody even noticed. The woman marshal and I looked at each other, trying to figure out who was going to quit first, but the marshal never hesitated. Opening the back of his pickup, he let his dog, a mastiff, out. Mastiffs are a breed developed in the Middle Ages to run ahead of charging knights on horseback to take out enemy pikemen so they couldn't plant their pikes in the ground and knock the knights out of their saddles. All mastiffs are big, but this one was a monster. He must have weighed 200 pounds and was so ugly he scared you just to look at him. As near as I could tell, he appeared to have an appetite for Tex-i-cans, too. He had a big, studded collar around his neck, and when he hit the ground, he let out a roar like a goddamn lion.

"Freeze," the marshal yelled, and everybody froze. "Get your hands on the buildings," the marshal yelled. "Don't let my dog get you!"

Just like that, the fight was over. The mastiff had been sent to Denver for professional training, and when the marshal told him,

"Watch 'em," he paced back and forth, growling, while the three of us cuffed them. The cellblock at the Crested Butte jail consists of one small room, but we packed it with Texans and then turned the rest of them loose, figuring we'd made our point.

My marshaling career came to an end when I ticketed and towed the mayor's car. I knew it was his car, it was on the list they'd given me, but I'd sworn to tow cars parked where they weren't supposed to be parked, and there it was. I couldn't resist.

When the mayor called me into his office next day and ordered me to tear up the ticket, I refused.

"Maybe you don't understand how city government works?" he said. "Who do you think town marshals report to?" And when I didn't say anything, he told me: "They report to the mayor." And when I still didn't say anything, he said, "I'm afraid we're going to have to dispense with your services. Your law enforcement efforts are a little too zealous."

One winter I served as middleman—what I called a "firewood broker"—between condominium owners and woodcutters. On the outfitter office printer, I ran off some cards with my name, address, and telephone number, and the legend, "Sales, Delivery, and Custom Stacking," and distributed them door-to-door around the ski area. It was another case of hustling those high-dollar dudes. I'd pay the going rate ($50 a cord, in those days) to the guys who cut it, and turn around and sell the wood for $150. The only work I did was unloading and stacking it.

I always say you have to feel sorry for these rich dudes. They have all this money, but they can't find anybody to work for them who can meet their standards. They love service, and they put a lot of stock in appearance. I could sell them any kind of wood—good, bad, indifferent, it didn't matter—and they were happy, because they didn't know the difference. The only thing they demanded was that it look good on their porches; it had to be artistically stacked.

After snowstorms, when Highway 135 between Crested Butte and Gunnison became icy, a friend of mine named Jerry Johnson and I would go cruising in a borrowed tow truck, looking for stranded motorists. It was such good money that we used to pray for storms. Jerry would call me and say, "You ready to parlay human misery into fame and fortune? It's a skating rink up there."

Wearing our down clothes, we'd pick up the truck at a local garage (the owner provided the truck and gas in return for half the profits), fortified ourselves with a bourbon *pousse*, and took to the road. When conditions were bad, the ditches yielded as many as three or four cars a run. It was a two-man job—I handled the hook while Jerry reeled them in. The going rate was $40. For some reason, we always pronounced it "forty dollah," delivered with a pidgin-English spin, maybe to make the price more palatable.

If that was the purpose, though, it didn't work. People hated to pay us. I guess they felt like we were taking advantage of them, that being in the ditch wasn't really their fault. But it wasn't like we were ripping them off. Forty bucks was high, but they weren't going anywhere without us. They were even in a certain amount of danger, sitting there in a vehicle beside the road in an icestorm. But they were spending thousands of dollars on a skiing vacation, so maybe they thought towing them out of the ditch should be part of the price, like their lift tickets and their condos.

Stranded motorists told us hard-luck tales about why they couldn't pay cash, but we were inflexible. No, we told them, we didn't take credit cards, checks, luggage, clothes, or children as security for payment. Rather than assume responsibility for our hard-nosed attitude, we blamed everything on our fictional boss, a fellow we named Junior.

"You see this guy?" I'd call their attention to Jerry, who was big and heavy, with a full beard and granny glasses. "Well, he ain't nothing compared to Junior. Junior's as big and mean and ugly as they come: he'd bite your head off like a pimple. And Junior don't do plastic or checks; Junior just does cash—U.S. currency, American."

Of course, I'd suggest, trying to look a little crazy, we did take guns—or skis. We'd clown around like your worst nightmare of what a tow truck operator might be, playing it to the hilt. We were the tow truck from hell. If some poor guy took us up on our offer to hold his skis for security, I used to growl and bite 'em—you know, testing the fiberglass, like a pirate biting a coin to check the gold content.

Once a Texan rolled into Crested Butte in a $250,000 executive motor home, but found it impossible to negotiate the frozen streets. In spite of its weight, the huge vehicle couldn't maintain traction on the ice. The Texan had a dozen people inside, sitting around a table in the galley playing cards. On the dashboard he kept a bank pouch full of hundred-dollar bills. We negotiated a price with him on the basis of size: $100 to tow the motor home away from a stop sign and set the monster in motion down Elk Avenue. Then we watched it career out of sight, like a rudderless galleon.

After a circuit of town, to see if anybody else needed help, we went back to look for the Texan. This time we found the motor home stalled beside the pumps at a filling station. For another $100, we towed it out to the highway, a distance of about twenty yards. Then we took another tour of town and drove north, toward the ski area, to see how he was getting along. Half a mile beyond the cemetery, we found the motor home cocked sideways in the ditch. The Texan was out on the shoulder, flagging us down with another hundred-dollar bill. We were sorry we hadn't doubled the price. We needed the money, and it didn't seem to make a damn bit of difference to him what we charged or how often we charged it.

One night on the highway north of the Slate Creek bridge, we saw a Chevy Blazer spin out, rip through a barbed wire fence, and plow a hundred yards into some rancher's pasture. The driver put the Blazer in four-wheel-drive and tried to make it back to the highway on his own. The Blazer looked like a jet boat, snow flying in ten-foot rooster tails, rocking and going around in circles. We figured he was ours.

Returning to Crested Butte, we drank a bourbon *pousse*, thawed out, and returned for another look. By now the Blazer was in deeper than ever. When the driver saw us, he rolled down the window and waved. So we rolled down the glass to show him we were interested. Finally he walked out to the truck. It was a Texas A&M student taking a buddy and two girls skiing in his dad's Blazer. Their skis were racked on top. All of them had those bouffant hairdos that were popular at the time.

"I don't need a tow," the kid told us. "I could get out if I had a little jerk. How much would you charge me for that?"

"Don't do jerks," I told him, "do do tows. Tows are forty dollah."

He returned to the Blazer. We drove into Crested Butte and revived ourselves with another bourbon *pousse*. Back at the scene, when the driver waved, we didn't lower the window until he made the trip across the pasture and tapped on the glass. By now his bouffant hairdo was looking a little the worse for wear.

"How much?" he asked.

"A hundred yards," I told him, "forty dollah," and rolled the window up again.

He tapped on the glass. "Would you take a check?"

"Don't do checks … do do guns, though …"

When the Aggie finally admitted he had the money, I unhooked the cable, dragged it through the snow, and attached it to the frame of the Blazer. Jerry reeled it in, but instead of stopping when the Blazer reached the pavement, he took it to the top of the boom so the vehicle stood straight up in the air, like the prize marlin at a fishing derby. I figured the kid was going to stiff us, so before I went out there, I'd given Jerry the high-sign. With all four passengers hanging from the roof liner, I tapped on the window, and when the kid rolled it down, I told him: "Forty dollah."

He handed me two twenty-dollar bills, and when the Blazer was unhooked yelled, "You dirty mother-fuckers!" and floored it.

He didn't go a quarter of a mile before the Blazer spun out again and careened into the ditch. We just sat in the truck and waited. This time the Aggie sent one of the girls back to negotiate with us. She was pretty, red-eyed with crying, her dark, bouffant hairdo coming apart around her face, so we pulled them out for free this time.

Another winter survival technique was starting diesel trucks and busses. Their drivers, not realizing how hard they might be to restart after a thirty-degree-below-zero night, would turn them off and next morning need help. Motel owners around town knew I was in the business and would recommend my service. I also made a circuit of town in the tow truck on cold mornings, and when I found a driver grinding away at his battery, I told him: "When you figure out that thing's not gonna start, give me a call and I'll give you a hand."

The price was $50. When the call came, I'd raise a modified version of our old cook tent around the stalled vehicle's hood, fire up a kerosene space heater, and charge the weakened batteries from the tow truck's bank. It took about two hours, and it never failed. In the meantime, the driver and I would adjourn to the nearest bar. Once in a while a driver would buy you a drink, so it was a pretty good scam.

Another winter I turned cowboy—a real cowboy, a ranch hand, not just my packer's imitation—when I got a job feeding cattle on a little shirttail outfit north of town. I made $30 a day working from daylight till dark. I got lunch at the big house and a place to sleep when the roads were bad. Feeding cattle consists of chopping ice out of water tanks, shoveling hay stacks, throwing bales and forking loose hay off the heavy wooden sleighs ranchers still use in the valley.

Ranch work can be dangerous. One day I was on top of a haystack jerking frozen bales loose and throwing them down on the sleigh. A spontaneous-combustion fire smoldering in the middle of the stack had melted the hay twine on the bales above, so when I pulled on one, the twine broke. Because of the ice, the bales had been coming out hard, so I'd put a pretty good heave on that one. I was having trouble moving in my heavy winter clothes, and when the twine let go, I fell off the stack about twenty-five feet and landed on my side, with my right arm under me. I broke four ribs and spent the next few weeks trying to breathe as little as possible.

The rancher I was working for kept me on because he knew I needed the money. When the hospital released me, I asked for the bill, and they said the rancher had already paid it. A lot of guys would have told you, "Stay home till you're feeling better" and saved himself a salary. I drove the team with my left hand while the rancher did the feeding. I wasn't able to pull my weight around the place for another month.

Later that same winter, I was using a five-eighths-inch spike to tighten fence wire, winding it around and around, like a tourniquet, and then fastening the wire with a staple. When the spike slipped, it pierced the middle of my left wrist, back to front, pinning it to a post. Because I was alone, I had to pull the spike out with my right hand, and before I could get it all the way out, it slipped again, punching the hole through my wrist again. By now my arm was in shock, and there was blood everywhere. It's funny how your mind works. It was about Easter, and I thought: "I can see how they could do it to Him once, but I didn't think there was enough Romans in the world to do it twice."

I thought the spike would have cut some tendons, or broken the bone, but it went through clean as a whistle. At the hospital, the doctor told me not to use the arm for six weeks. Three days later, I was out in the corral roping a calf when I tangled the injured arm in the rope. The calf was jumping at the other end, and you talk about a guy unwinding in a hurry! I still have the scar from the spike, a white dot about the size of a dime on the top and bottom of my wrist.

Another winter I fried burgers at the A&W on the west end of town. The owner's wife, who'd worked for me when I was managing the ski area food service, talked her husband into giving me the job. It paid minimum wage, but it wasn't a bad job. Sometimes, when I got bored, I'd carry my chef's knife out front, to the tables, and ask customers how they liked their burgers. It got me some strange looks. The owner, claiming that kind of behavior made customers nervous, asked me to stop. A couple of months into the season, he told me I was doing such a good job that he gave me a dime raise.

In socioeconomic terms, I probably hit bottom the two winters I swamped out the kitchen and restaurant at the Cattleman Inn. The previous hunting season, Stu and I had broken up over another one of his shady deals. Part of the season I worked with another outfitter, but we hadn't gotten along. I'd quit and hadn't caught on anywhere else, so suddenly I was broke, with no job and no prospects. The Cattleman's owner was a friend, but when I asked for a job, he told me there was nothing available.

I told him I'd take anything, and he promised to keep me in mind if either of his two regular managers quit. Then he looked away, with a sheepish expression on his face. The swamper hadn't shown up, he said; if I was willing to do that, the job was mine. A swamper's generally some old alki who's come over the hill on his way to someplace else. Swamping's a step or two above carnival geek–the guy who bites the heads off live chickens in the sideshow for a bottle and a place to sleep. A swamper usually hangs around long enough to make a stake and then beats it down the road. I swamped the Cattleman's all winter two years in a row—and it wasn't all that bad.

Swampers vacuum carpets and clean counters in the dining room, and stove tops and ovens and floors in the kitchen after the restaurant closes. Probably their most important duty is hunting kaiser rolls under counters. About the only things the swamper doesn't clean are dishes and ceilings. The hours are ten PM to four AM. The job pays minimum wage.

Probably the best thing about swamping is that it's mighty quiet. I'd work along half asleep until about one-thirty or two o'clock, when I took the kitchen floor mats outside at twenty-five or thirty below zero to wash out the grease. That woke me up again.

Another part of the job I liked was the Cattleman Inn ghost. A former owner, who'd died of a heart attack, was supposed to haunt the building at night. I'd heard about him before I took the job, and there was something to it. Lights would go off and on, or I'd see something out of the corner of my eye that wouldn't be there when I looked. Or I'd come into a room and a swinging door would be running down, like somebody—or something—had just gone through.

I'm not normally subject to such feelings, but I always had a sense that there was extra help on hand. It was a good feeling, though, rather than anything malevolent or terrifying, but lonely, like whatever it was wanted company and didn't mind my being there. The owner told me I was the best swamper he'd ever had; I was the only one who ever stuck it through the entire season.

People ask me sometimes if hitting bottom like that ever bothered me. I tell them no, that maybe it was a price I had to pay for my sins—not necessarily all my sins, but at least some of them. Maybe it's wishful thinking, but I always thought of hustling the groceries as something particularly American. When I was a kid, I admired movies where the hero operates everywhere, and with everybody equally well, no matter what his economic or social level. Maybe it's naive, but I believe this country isn't about who you are, or who your folks were, but what you are. Henry Fonda or John Garfield or Humphrey Bogart or Robert Redford, no matter who they pretend to be, belong anywhere, whether it's in a waterfront dive or wearing a tux at the home of what Bogart used to call "some rich society dame." Guys like that are Americans because they're not victims of their circumstances, they're above them. If they use the wrong fork or shine their shoes with a napkin, the joke's not on them but on their host and hostess and all their ritzy friends. For me, part of the challenge was seeing how far down I could go and still come back up, with everything intact. Besides, when winter was over, it made the return to outfitting that much sweeter.

Of all the down-season jobs I held, my favorite was operating a sleigh-ride concession out of a barn on the Washington Gulch road, south of the Crested Butte ski resort. Stu and I were in it together and used a lot of our outfitting gear: the Clydesdales, the hayride wagons, the kitchen equipment, and one of my favorite recipes from camp. We even used my stock truck, Old Blue, to pick up and return clients to their hotels.

The sleigh-ride concession also meant working not only with Stu, but with Larry Malloy, who wrangled for us. The barn had been in use for years by a local rancher, so the first thing we had to do was clean it. We spent a solid week in there, the three of us, hauling out all kinds of packrat shit, cleaning floors, washing windows, sweeping down walls. Sometimes, in a paranoid mood, I'd wonder if the owner wasn't just using us to straighten the place out before he killed the deal.

We decorated the barn with tack, old saddles, antique farm tools and pieces of machinery. We built coat racks and arranged picnic tables on a floor covered with sawdust. A double-barrel wood stove supplied heat in such volume it would run you out, even in the dead of winter. Since there was no plumbing, we installed a pump in a shack up the hill and ran water through a garden hose, insulated by snow, down to our kitchen. The toilet was a Saniflush unit parked outside in the snow. Outside the door, we set up a steel barrel barbecue pit where I cooked a lot of dinners, sometimes at twenty below zero.

Three times a night, Stu or Malloy would drive around to motels and condos to pick people up in the stock truck. For a step up to the bed, we used a hay bale. Passengers bundled up warm and sat on bales for the ride to the barn, then filed past while I served my first-night-in-camp special: steak, mustard beans, corn on the cob and bread, and coffee or pop. While they ate seated at the picnic tables, we put on a floor show for them: the three of us harnessing the Clydesdales, hooves rumbling on the boards, frosted coats steaming in the warm air.

Those big horses were wonderful: they stood seventeen hands, weighed three-quarters of a ton, and had coats like buffalo robes. It's one thing to see horses like that outside, hitched to a sleigh; it's something else to sit beside them and see how big and powerful they really are.

Because weather and snow conditions changed rapidly, a sleigh ride booked Wednesday could turn into a wagon ride by Friday. We'd bolt the sleigh's runners to the wheel drums, but we could remove and mount the wheels in fifteen minutes flat. Our route followed the Washington Gulch road, then turned north uphill through the Meridian Lake subdivision. Passengers lounged in the hay—all of them well-fed, some of them half-greased from a private bottle, everybody laughing and talking, or just looking up at the stars. Kids had hay fights, women got hay in their hair and their fur coats. During the holiday season, we sang Christmas carols, me getting a song started and then shutting up to listen. When the weather was good and the road was easy, I'd invite people to join me on the wagon box and drive the team. Kids loved that.

The only lights we'd see were in some of the homes around the subdivision. By starlight, or with a moon, the aspen took on a pale, luminous glow. We decorated the horses' harness with bells, and they jingled softly—something people living in the neighborhood, as well as our customers, loved to hear. I always thought it was the bells that made the hayride, and that anybody who would drive a team at night without bells ought to be shot. To the east, Mt. Crested Butte loomed across the valley, and when a full moon rose over its shoulder, it looked so big and close you could reach out and put it in your pocket.

The sleigh was your standard Gunnison valley hay sled, the kind local ranchers have been feeding their cattle out of for generations. Filled with hay, it held twenty people comfortably and outweighed the team that pulled it. As a result, you had to be careful on curving, downhill stretches, where it was easy to upset. On icy grades, the horses had to sidestep like dancers, traversing back and forth across the fall line to break the sleigh's speed and keep it from walking out around them. It amazed me how well they did it; it seemed like they instinctively knew how.

When there was wind, snow at the far end of the route could drift four and five feet deep across the road. We built a snow fence to slow the drifting, but some of the passengers actually took a combination sleigh ride and hike. I'd stop the team and say, "Looks like we've got a small problem here, folks. Why don't you just step down while I get us through this next stretch?" We'd do it in stages. They'd walk a little way, climb back on, and I'd drive a little farther and say: "Whoops, everybody out again," and before you knew it, we'd be down on the lower road, jingling along toward the barn.

We had no liquor license, but at the end of the ride, we sold toy-sized bottles of whiskey and rum. Then Larry dropped people off in Old Blue, picked up the next group, and we repeated the process. It was so much fun that sometimes I used to think of it as a license to steal, but it wasn't. We cleared $60,000 in two months, but people got their money's worth. We charged them $12.50 apiece, and they couldn't even eat at a restaurant downtown for that—plus we gave them a sleigh ride, too. Sometimes customers came back and did it again. I don't think I ever heard anybody bitch about being cheated.

Now that I'm no longer in the outfitting business, sometimes I'll be downtown shopping around Christmas, and I'll think about those days. Loudspeakers will be cranking out Christmas carols, and I'll remember shopping one Christmas Eve when I was hustling the groceries. Marilyn and I weren't married, then, and I had a fifty-dollar bill in my pocket—that's all the money I had. A client had sent it to me as a present, otherwise I'd have been broke. I bought her a pair of bedroom slippers, a filigree locket, and four roses—it was the end of the fifty dollars, and all the flowers I could afford. She gave me a pair of shearling slippers. She was working as a secretary at the college, taking classes, and on weekends hostessing at the Cattleman's. I went home dead broke, but it was the happiest Christmas of my life.

# 10

## Getting Out of the Business

LATE ONE FALL, Stu, Bill Wagner, and I were striking the last hunting camp. The clients were gone and the guides and wranglers were already down at the resort, waiting to be paid off. Clouds veiled in the mountains, snow the color and consistency of thin mush covered the ground. As we folded tents and packed panniers, mud and leaves piled up inches thick under our boots, throwing us off-balance so that we staggered around like drunks when we moved. Sometimes we'd hear sleet rattling in the distance, like somebody turning on a shower. We'd stop to listen, holding our breath, wondering if it was the beginning of the storm that would close the high country for the year, or just one more warning that it was time to get our asses out of there.

We'd cut the groceries pretty fine that fall: eggs and bread and that was it. No bacon, no butter; no salt or pepper; no canned tomatoes or pork-and-beans. Even the coffee was gone, fed last night to the departing guides and wranglers. Worst of all, we'd run out of whiskey. Now, sitting on a log, with water trickling off our hats into plates of cold scrambled eggs, I said: "You know what we ought to do? We ought to ride over to Doyleville and rob the goddamn bank."

Doyleville never was much more than a wide place in the road. Today there's less to show than ever—a couple of ranch-houses and some sheds scattered along the south side of the highway, about twenty miles east of Gunnison. Without the signs—one facing east, the other west, located several hundred yards apart—you'd have trouble guessing there was supposed to be a town there at all. I always milked the name for three syllables rather than two, *Doy-le-ville*, but the suggestion about robbing the bank there struck a chord with Stu and Bill. We got to ciphering about where the nearest whiskey store was and decided it had to be in Ohio City, across Fossil Ridge, in the Quartz Creek valley. There's not much more left of Ohio City than of Doyleville: a restaurant (closed much of the year), a filling station, a bar, and a scattering of summer cabins, many of them for sale, most of them deserted by late November.

Saddling the horses and loading our burros—Juan and his sister, Two—Bill and I followed Stu over Fossil Ridge along an old route known as the Horsethief Trail. This was the trail used in the 1880s and 1890s by outlaws riding through Colorado between New Mexico and Montana. After crossing Cochetopa Pass to the south, the trail follows Quartz Creek, then branches at Ohio City to follow a couple of different routes north into Taylor Park, where four tumble-down cabins, known as Horsethief Ranch, still stand. Old-timers claim that, at different times, the ranch harbored outlaws ranging from Butch Cassidy's Hole in the Wall gang to remnants of Billy the Kid's gang fleeing New Mexico after the Lincoln County War. Riding down Gold Creek, we passed the campground where, in 1898, a posse shot half a dozen horse thieves and recovered a herd of stolen horses.

It was a tough ride, but when whiskey was involved, Stu was like a beagle on point. We spent three hours in the saddle and came out on a county road within a hundred yards of the only place within thirty-five miles where you could buy a drink.

Tying the horses to the old porch supports, we went into the bar—only to discover that none of us had any money. We all carried guns, though, so the woman bartender served us whiskey; but when we ordered more, she wanted to be paid. Small and dark, she had center-parted hair and wasn't bad-looking, at least not to three guys fresh out of hunting camp. According to stories we'd heard, she was what's known as a black widow—one of these women who bump off their husbands to collect the insurance money.

We tried our best to negotiate another round, but no matter what was said, whenever voices were raised, a large malamute beside the bar would issue a warning growl. "That's Buck," she told us, in a loose-guitar-string twang out of Oklahoma. "He don't cotton to strangers."

Phoning the resort, which was about seventy miles away by road, I told a wrangler to bring the stock truck and some money to the rescue. "And hurry," I told him. "We're hungry and dying of thirst."

The woman, who overheard my end of the conversation, decided maybe we weren't as disreputable as we looked, and poured a second round.

By this time we were starving to death, especially Billy, but all there was to eat in the place were frozen pizzas. Made out of cheese and cardboard, they had names like *"Tom's Frozen Pizza, Fresh and Delicious."* So adding pizza to the tab, we microwaved something that the label claimed was sausage and pepperoni and laid it on the table to cool. Meanwhile Buck, the malamute, had never taken his eyes off the pizza since it came out of the freezer. Now he leaped on the table, wolfed it down in a couple of gulps, and returned to his place by the bar. When the woman smiled, Billy, who had a nice, dry sense of humor, looked at her and said: "Well, I ain't gonna fight him for it. How many more do you think he can eat before we get one?"

We talked her into serving us another drink, but when the stock truck arrived, we had another problem. In his hurry to start, the wrangler had snatched a hundred-dollar bill from the cash drawer; now the woman bartender claimed she couldn't make change. We talked it over, but all we could think to do was drink it up.

About $50 into the bill, Stu and I began arguing about which of the burros, Juan or his sister, Two, was fleeter of foot. The rain had stopped, so we unpacked the burros and staged what we called the first (and would be the last) annual Ohio City Burro Race.

We'd used them as pack animals for years, but we'd never tried to ride them. It didn't take us long, though, to figure out that burros don't like to be ridden. They're pretty good little animals—they'll stick close to camp, and they can make a living on very little grass—but they don't like you sitting on them, and they don't follow instructions worth a damn. As a result of the race, I realized that you want to be careful of these stories about Jesus entering the city on the back of an ass, because it's not as easy as it sounds.

The wrangler, the black widow bartender, and Bill, along with the population of Ohio City (there must have been seven or eight people), gathered in the street to watch. There's no way you can straddle a pack saddle, so we took them off and rode bareback. I was up on Juan and Stu was on his sister, Two. The course was down Main Street, about a hundred yards to the finish line at a dilapidated machine shed on the south edge of town.

Using his .44 Magnum, Bill started us. The crowd cheered, and away we went down Main Street, shouting and spurring and hanging on. One thing we learned right away is that burros don't steer worth a damn; the only way to get them to change direction is to spur them on the side of the head opposite from the direction you want them to go. Another thing we learned is that burros don't stop worth a damn, either. A truck delivering natural gas backed into the street, cutting us off, and the burros just kept going. Stu managed to guide Two in front of the truck, but I took the back route and almost went under the wheels. It was a close call, and by the time I got Juan lined out again, Wagner was well ahead of me.

I always argued that it was a photo-finish, but Stu insisted he'd won. We did agree, though, that it was time to celebrate, but when we tried to lead Juan and Two inside the bar, to have a drink with us, the black widow objected, and Buck, the malamute, took her side.

Back out in the street, two women from Pueblo, a town over on the Eastern Slope, who'd been watching the race, introduced themselves. They were bottle blondes wearing pastel-framed glasses and dangling earrings that looked like Midwestern fishing lures. Their husbands had gone off somewhere and left them with instructions—intended ironically, no doubt, given the nature of Ohio City—not to get into trouble. Since we looked like the only trouble available, they asked to take our pictures, then had us take pictures of them. Then we all posed with the burros, striking lewd poses so they could show their husbands they'd managed to find some action, even in Ohio City.

When the hundred dollars was finally gone, we loaded the burros and camping gear on the stock truck for the trip around to the resort, then rode our horses back over the top. We could have gone with the wrangler, I guess, but none of us wanted to end the season in a stock truck, not when we could ride the Horsethief Trail again.

Thinking back, it's hard for me to believe that, at the time of the race, Stu and I were nearly fifty years old. Bill Wagner was over thirty, with a wife and two kids. That made Stu a grandfather twice over, and I was old enough to be one. But there we were, two guys our age acting like a couple of kids. For me, I guess that was part of Stu's charm; he made me feel young again.

After that, whenever things got a little seedy, we used the phrase about robbing the bank at Doy-le-ville as a standing joke. That next winter, for example, Stu and I were camped in a broken-down ranchhouse near Jack's Cabin, south of Crested Butte, when the phone rang. It was a New York lawyer calling to collect a debt he claimed we owed. Stu had placed an ad in a vacation magazine, but their advertising department never sent a copy and the magazine never sent a tearsheet as proof that it had run. Stu had refused to pay; now the magazine had turned the debt over to a law firm to collect. Somehow the lawyer had traced us to the ranchhouse.

Actually, it was a pretty impressive piece of detective work. Stu took the call. "Yep," I heard him tell the lawyer, "I'm putting you down in the book," and he made the lawyer spell the name of the firm till he got it right. It was four or five names long, and Stu wrote them on the wallpaper by the phone. I couldn't figure out what he was doing until he said: "Yes, sir, I've got you down in my book. We're snowed in right now, but as soon as the passes open, we're going to ride over and rob the bank at Doy-le-ville, and you will be paid. Your name is in my book."

They never called us again.

When we first went into business together, before Stu started drinking so hard, it seemed to me that as partners, we were ideally suited. Because of my accounting background, it might have made more sense for me to run the business side while Wagner handled the field work. Instead, each of us did what we preferred to do—Stu kept the books, and I dealt with the outdoor side. I was the traveling recruiter, the contact man who pitched outfitting to the dudes and worked with the guides and wranglers. Stu, though, had made a lot of money selling farm machinery, and in spite of the failure of his resort, he was an able businessman, with a good head for numbers. It took a while for me to figure it out, but I finally realized that Stu had an ulterior motive for staying near the books ... and the bar at the resort across the road from the office.

Stu also had a flair for words, written as well as spoken. Over the years, he designed all our advertising, wrote the copy, answered phone calls, and took care of the correspondence. He was always what I call a Barnum-and-Bailey kind of guy: tough-minded, a gambler, with a strong sense of the dramatic. I found him complex and interesting, one of the most interesting guys I ever met.

From the beginning, though, there were things about him that bothered me. There was a cruel edge to his practical joking, and a guardedness about his past that didn't fit the carefree cowboy front he usually showed you. Over the years, drinking in bars or sitting around a campfire, we talked a lot. You'd think in all that time you'd find out everything you wanted to know about a guy—maybe more than you wanted to know—but not with Stu. Parts of him were off-limits: what he really thought about the high-dollar dudes we worked with, for instance, or how he felt about his childhood. I'd talk about how things were for me as a kid, complaining about my dad and how he'd treated me, but Stu never opened up. The first time we met, sitting in the bar at the Ramble Inn, he'd told me about his mother's abandoning the family, and how his father couldn't support them. He'd talked about living with his rich aunt and uncle, and where he'd gone to school, but nothing beyond the bare facts.

The better I got to know him, the more it seemed like it wasn't just his father and mother that had let him down, it was the whole world. There wasn't any trust or compassion in him. He looked out for himself and what he considered his, but that's as far as it went. If you were inside that circle, okay; if you weren't, watch out, because you were fair game.

Sometimes it seemed that, as far as he was concerned, I was just like everybody else, another outsider. But at other times, I wasn't. One evening, while I was riding alone in the high country, a bear spooked Morgan, and he threw me. The horse ran off toward the resort, but instead of following him, I walked the shorter distance down to the highway. Because it's suicide to ride that country in the dark, Stu and I had agreed that if one of us failed to return by nightfall, the other one wouldn't attempt to find him until morning. The one thing we weren't going to do, of course, was call Search and Rescue. It was different with the clients—we'd have called for help for them, if we had to—but not for ourselves. The missing guy was supposed to get up someplace high, if he could, and start a fire, so the other one could find him when he went looking.

It was still dark when I reached the highway, and it took me a couple of hours before I finally managed to hitch a ride. It was the middle of the morning before I reached the resort and asked for Stu. The wranglers told me that the night before, when Morgan came in, Wagner had saddled Buddy and ridden out to find me. I was beat, so I sent a wrangler after Wagner to bring him back. That night, when he showed up, I told him, "Listen, I thought we had an agreement?"

"We do," he said, "but I knew you'd have done it for me."

I thought about that for quite a while, wondering what I'd have done if the shoe had been on the other foot. Maybe I'd have gone, I realized, and maybe I wouldn't. The agreement we had made sense, but sense wasn't really the issue.

Over the years, things from Wagner's past had a way of showing up. Once a couple of young guys, farmers who'd worked for Stu at his farm machinery business in Texas, joined us on a hunt. Around the campfire, during his absence, one of them said to me: "You better kind of watch yourself. He cuts a deal pretty close." Before he could say any more, or I could ask what he meant, Wagner returned and nothing more was said.

Another time I met a guy from Wagner's part of Texas, a hardware store owner. When I asked if he knew Stu, his face turned beet-red and he started cursing. He told me that Wagner, whom he'd considered not only a regular customer but also a friend, had never paid for half a dozen shotguns he ordered before he left town. "The son of a bitch ordered them, and then took off and left me holding the bill," he said.

I'd hear things like that and they'd hurt. I'd think: "That's not the guy I know; Stu wouldn't pull a stunt like that." But in a way I knew he would. It was like he was some kind of Jekyll-and-Hyde character out of a book. He just wouldn't add up and make sense to me.

Another thing that bothered me about Stu was that he was always hard on horses. He used them pretty heavy, always on the edge. The weights he packed were about a third more than anybody else packed, and he wouldn't ease off. Sometimes we quarreled about it, but when I'd say something, he'd tell me that's what they were there for and to mind my own business.

As Wagner continued drinking, his jokes became rougher and more violent. They seemed less a matter of teasing people or testing them, than pushing to see how far they'd go. This was true for me as well. We never came to blows over it, but both of us knew that if we ever did, it would be the end of our partnership. In spite of that, Stu couldn't keep himself from putting the pressure on me.

One summer we took a bunch of Texas cattlemen on a ride into the country below Forge Peak. These weren't your ordinary dudes; these guys were outstanding horsemen and hunters with years of experience in the outdoors. They knew what they were doing, and all of them were capable of putting a couple of cocky outfitters to the test. The third night out, we pitched our tents in a meadow we called Bootstake Camp after a circle of stakes we'd used, years earlier, to dry our boots after getting caught in a hard rain. Because the meadow was a favorite campsite, we'd left the stakes to mark it.

After dinner, we started drinking and gambling in the cook tent. It was high-stakes poker, the kind Wagner liked and wasn't very good at. A lot of money changed hands. Finally I got sleepy, and since I'd already dropped more than I could afford, I carried a tarp outside, spread it over my bag, and went to sleep.

Meanwhile, in the tent, Stu started bragging to the Texans about one thing and another. Finally he claimed that his horse, Buddy, had eyes like a cat and could actually see in the dark. When the Texans made fun of the idea, Stu bet them $50 that he could put Buddy right over the top of me at a gallop; Buddy wouldn't touch me, Stu told them, and he wouldn't break stride.

The Texans covered Wagner's money and went outside to watch. Stu tied on a halter on Buddy and mounted bareback. It was a cloudy night, with no moon or stars showing, and they agreed it would be a fair test of the horse's night vision. Riding to the end of the meadow, Wagner wheeled and came back at a dead run.

I was sound asleep but roused enough to hear the rumble of hooves and feel the ground tremble. I had no idea what it was, but I sat up just in time to see Buddy right on top of me. Before I could think about moving, he hit me—put a hoof right in the middle of me and knocked me flying.

Somehow Stu kept Buddy from falling. At the other end of the meadow, he turned and rode back while I rolled over, gasping, arms wrapped around my stomach, too weak even to curse. "You damned fool," Wagner yelled at me, dismounting in front of the Texans. "If you'd just laid there, I'd have made fifty dollars."

I was hot. If I'd had the strength, I'd have jumped him right there. But while I sat there, one of those big Texans got to telling it—how Wagner said he could have made $50 if I'd just laid still— and I laughed harder than anybody. That's the way he was. He could get away with things that anybody else would have been killed for.

Occasionally I got back at him. Once, when he was bringing the horse herd to camp—riding bareback, with nothing but a halter to guide his mount—I jumped out of a tree, howling like a mad Comanche, or at least what I figured a mad Comanche howled like. The herd stampeded, with Wagner riding for his life. When he finally got his horse turned and came back with the herd, everybody was laughing. He was laughing, too, and smiling that big smile of his, like a kid who'd just won a race.

One thing it took me a while to figure out was that Stu resented the high rollers we dealt with. We needed those guys, but he could never forgive them for having what he wanted. There was a lot of envy on his part, a lot of jealousy. He never talked about it, not even to me, but losing the resort really hurt him. I don't think he ever got over it. He was one of those guys who's always looking to pull off some kind of deal, something so big it'll put him on easy street. The resort had been the best chance he'd ever have. He was the kind of guy who wants to throw thousand-dollar bills around and say, "Come on, guys, the party's on me," and he could never afford do it.

Over the years, Stu's drinking became a serious problem. God help me, I used to drink with him myself; I've got that on my conscience. But if it hadn't been me, it would have been somebody else, or nobody else, because it really didn't matter whether he had company or not. I tried to talk to him about it, but it just made him edgy. He drank scotch, Highland Mist, a couple of quarts a day. Once he told me he was going to switch to beer, but it was just a line, he never switched. He drank a little beer in public and saved his scotch drinking for later. Finally, toward the end, scotch kept disappearing from the bar at the resort. He was stealing it. I don't know, maybe he figured if he wasn't paying for it, drinking it didn't count.

The more he drank, the more our lack of money bothered him. After his bankruptcy, the banks wouldn't lend him a dime; everything the business bought, and therefore just about everything we owned, was in my name. He started overcharging customers when they made deposits with their credit card numbers. He'd run the numbers through the machine twice; then, a month or so later, when clients received their bills and called to complain, he'd claim it was the secretary's fault and promise to straighten things out. Only we didn't have a secretary; Stu handled everything himself. He'd stall as long as he could, then refund the overcharge. In the meantime, he'd use the same technique to overcharge other clients to pay off the earlier ones.

Things got crazier and crazier. He started stealing money from the tip jar in the office. The jar would be full of coins and bills guests put in after a ride; fifteen minutes later it would be empty. When the wranglers complained to me, I talked to Stu about it, but he denied it. He said the kids were lying. Finally, when one wrangler threatened to go to the sheriff, Stu showed up with the money, claiming he'd found it under a rock beside the corral.

When I was conducting fraud investigations for the state, the first thing I learned was that most thefts are caused by lack of internal controls. Sooner or later, money left lying around is going to turn up missing; the temptation's just too great. Most people are honest or want to be honest. The ones who aren't—the ones who prefer to do it wrong—are the exception. I knew a guy who used to steal Baby Ruth candy bars and hide them from his kids. He'd go off by himself and eat them on the sly. There's something sick about that, but who knows what there was in his background that caused him to do it? He was like a dog that bites you if you come near his dish when there's food in it, even though it was you who put it there. He literally bites the hand that feeds him.

Another problem with Stu was that he hated to pay the help. Payday never happened on payday. He could never make himself let go of the money. I'd come back from up on top, and the kids wouldn't have been paid. I'd tell him, "Stu, one thing you don't want to do is fuck with the payroll," but he always had some kind of excuse. The kids would just waste it or he had some debts to pay; it was always something.

One fall, just before hunting season, I went to Mexico for a couple of weeks' vacation. When I got back, ready to start the season, the stock was gone. There wasn't a horse or a mule on the place. Wagner had cleaned out the corral and sold every animal we owned. When I walked in the office, he was sitting at the desk with a bottle of Highland Mist in front of him.

"What happened?" I asked. He didn't say anything, just looked at me with his pale gray eyes, like we were playing another game of level-the-dude, and this time I was it. He told me his creditors had been after him again, so he'd sold the string and paid them off. Just like that: no apologies, no explanations; nothing about renting stock, nothing about trying to work the upcoming season. It was over and we were done, take it or leave it.

He asked if I wanted a drink. I said okay and sat down. It was funny, but I felt like I'd watched this scene before, in so many movies, that I'd played it myself: two guys sitting across a table from each other with whiskey in front of them. One's cheated the other one, but you'd never know it to look at them. In a minute, they'll pull their guns. One of them will kill the other, then finish his drink and walk away. I even thought about doing it. Stu and I were both carrying, and I was mad enough. He knew it, too. We watched each other, smoking cigarettes, but neither of us made a play. Finally, when I finished my drink, I got up and left. It was a case of kill him or forget it, so I forgot it. I decided it wasn't worth the rest of my life.

The breakup had been coming for a long time, but I hadn't seen it, probably because I hadn't wanted to. The winter before, while we were operating the sleigh-ride concession, Stu had run the sleigh over me. We were doing a barbecue for a real estate promotion, and he showed up late. I was hooking up the horses. I knew he was drunk, but I didn't know how drunk. I said, "Hold 'em," and got down behind the horses to hook up the sleigh—and he didn't hold 'em. They got away from him and pulled the sleigh over me. I rolled between the runners, but maybe, in a way, that was really the end of it. You can overlook a lot of things, but after that I knew I had to get away. It's just going to get worse, I told myself; you better get out before they carry you out.

Next day Stu came up to me and said, "Hey, I was drinking too much last night. Sorry." But that doesn't describe it. There are a hundred ways a guy can get hurt out there, if he isn't careful. Stu was turning into one of those guys who can't be careful. I saw a movie once, another Western, and there was a scene that stuck with me. A bunch of cowboys are breaking horses, and one of them is thrown, an old-timer. He breaks his back, they carry him into the bunkhouse, and he lies there and dies, and that's it. No family, no nothing. That's the end of him.

At the same time, breaking up our partnership was one of the hardest things I ever did. If you're lucky, you may have four or five close friendships in your lifetime. When you lose one of those friends, it's something you never get over; it's like dying a little yourself.

When I told Marilyn what happened to the horses and mules, she thought maybe I could salvage some of them. She wanted me to go around the valley and tell the ranchers and outfitters who'd bought the stock that it hadn't been Stu's to sell. Maybe by spring I could have recovered enough of it, at some kind of price, to make a difference. But finally I figured what the hell: it had to end sometime, it might as well be now. Besides, I knew my career as an outfitter was coming to an end. I'd planned on about ten years of midlife retirement, and I'd gotten eight. That wasn't bad, I thought. For every dime it cost me, I'd had a hundred thousand dollars worth of fun. I was just lucky it hadn't cost me anymore than it did.

I know Stu's out there somewhere today waiting for me to ask him for that money he owes me, but I'm not about to give him the satisfaction. Let him wait.

My last trip as an outfitter took place the following summer when the manager at Harmel's called to ask a favor: his head wrangler had quit, could I fill in on a late-season ride? At first I told him no. I felt like I'd made my peace with outfitting; I felt that going back again, after I'd put away my spurs, would be tempting fate.

During the year, I'd applied for a position as assistant business manager at Western State College, down the valley in Gunnison. The process of application and interviews had taken months, but out of nearly a hundred applicants, they had chosen me. In a way, it was as big a career change as I'd made eight years earlier when I started outfitting. I wasn't getting any younger and it was good to know something like that was still possible for me. It was also nice to have my theory confirmed about landing back on my feet after dropping out of the real world for a midlife retirement.

I'd signed my contract with the college and was set to start work in a couple of weeks. The new president, a bright guy from back East, wanted to put an educational program in place that included a lot of things I believed in. With my background in the public schools, in budgeting, and in state politics, I believed I could help him get some important things done.

In the back of my closet, I found some clothes that had escaped the fire outside the Ramble Inn years ago, and had survived my winter managing the food service at Crested Butte Mountain Resort. The ties were too wide, the coats were too loose, and no amount of starch restored life to the shirts. I had to cinch the pants tight with a belt to keep them from sliding off my hips.

Marilyn helped me pick out the rest of my wardrobe at the local J.C. Penney's. By then we'd been going together for quite a while, and I was ready to try marriage again, and she'd agreed to try it with me. The Outfitters' Feed and Supply store was a thing of the past—I'd told Stu it was his. Old Blue, the stock truck, was gone, a gift to a rancher friend who'd given me a job when I was down and out last winter.

But the manager at the resort kept after me, telling me what a hole he was in and reminding me that I owed him a favor. Finally I talked it over with Marilyn, and we decided I should go. I could repay the favor, I'd make a few hundred bucks doing something I loved to do, and best of all, I'd get one more look at the high country before the new job at the college ended my outfitting career once and for all.

For a while everything went fine. In fact, until the morning we broke camp and started back down to the resort, the trip was just about perfect—so good, in fact, that a guy might have second thoughts about quitting. The clients were the kind of people I enjoyed working with: a dozen young professionals from the Los Angeles area, all athletic, well-educated, and self-sufficient in the outdoors.

We went into the old fishcamp on Diamond Creek, and the weather was perfect. During the day, everyone rode and hiked and fished, or else lounged around camp, reading and talking, or taking naps. At night, after dinner, we sat by the campfire, talking and drinking a little whiskey, then turned in early.

Two members of the group were doctors, one of them a specialist in emergency medicine, the other an ophthalmologist. With them were their girlfriends, two young nurses. The emergency specialist was a deep water sailor; he'd crewed on a number of sailboats cruising between California and Hawaii and had some wonderful stories to tell. He'd also served as the doctor for several international expeditions to Africa and South America that had been featured in *National Geographic* magazine.

My staff consisted of two wranglers to help with the horses and look after the clients. One was my old friend, Larry Malloy; the other was a young guy I took along to camp-boy and pull packs. Once the camp was set, my only serious responsibility was keeping everybody fed and making sure they all stayed happy. About the only thing that went wrong was that, about midway through the week, we started running out of candy. I never took along more of anything than I thought we'd need, so I always watched my supplies pretty close. That way, if I saw I'd guessed wrong, and we were running short of something, I rationed it.

At first I thought a mouse or a ground squirrel was raiding my cupboard, but it turned out that one of the nurses (the girlfriend of the emergency specialist) had a sweet tooth. She was always dropping by the cook tent to talk or have a cup of coffee, and for a while I thought it was a case of her finding me as attractive as I found her. But that was just a case of wishful thinking on my part, because after she left, I'd find something missing–sugar cubes, honey, candy bars, chewing gum. One afternoon, while my back was turned, she even cleaned out my supply of baker's chocolate.

When I realized what was going on, I tried to discourage her by kidding her about her appetite for sweets, but it didn't work. She was young and cocky, extravagantly pretty, with dark hair and big, dark eyes. She was the nurse of your dreams, the kind who could make a patient want to live just by being there at his bedside–the kind nurses in big-city hospitals are supposed to be, but never are. Whenever I looked at her, I thought of the English actress, Jean Simmons, in *The Big Country*. She knew she was going to live forever, and she was going to do it on her own terms. "For a thousand dollars," she told me, when I got after her about the chocolate, "I would think you could afford enough candy for a week."

Probably she was right. They were paying a stiff price for their week's vacation, but that wasn't my business, and I didn't let it bother me. Whenever I was out with clients, I tried to project a sense that I was comfortable with what we were doing, and that no matter what happened, I felt at home. I wanted them to feel like we were all involved in the experience together and that I was enjoying myself as much as they were. In a way, of course, I was. That's part of the reason why I pulled some of the strange stunts with people that I did–to kid them along, to let them know that we were all out there to have a good time. But the truth was something I'd learned a long time ago: that you can never relax, not really; not till you've got your clients tucked in bed at night, and not till you've brought them back, safe and sound, to the resort.

The last morning, when we broke camp, I realized that I was feeling the same way about leaving that guests often felt: it had been a wonderful trip, we'd had a great time together, but I was glad it was over. It surprised me. I'd never experienced anything like that before, but I put it down to the fact that, in taking one more trip after I'd made up my mind to quit, I was pushing my luck.

I'd been over the trail to the resort a hundred times in every kind of weather—rain and sleet, sunshine and snow. Today it was perfect: not a breath of wind, not a cloud in the sky. The sun was warm and the horses were in a good mood, knowing they were headed back to the corral. We were riding across the mesa when I noticed that the little sweet-toothed nurse had tied a knot in her horse's reins. She was also leaning forward in her saddle on the downhills, too interested in what was going on around her, or too careless, to ride properly. So I stopped and lectured her about sitting back, and I made her untie the reins. She didn't like it. She'd watched people ride with their reins knotted all her life, she said. I agreed that people did it all the time, but told her it was a bad habit—a dangerous habit—to get into. So with me and every-body else watching, she untied the knot and we rode on, but she wasn't happy about it.

We'd done all the hard parts—ridden the bogs, traversed the steep slopes—when the trail crossed Diamond Creek for the last time. The ford itself was a sun-washed sand and gravel bar, like a carpet of gold, under about eight inches of fast-flowing water. But above and below the bar, the current had scooped a couple of deep, muddy holes. I forded the creek and kept riding, turned in the saddle to watch the others. Four more riders crossed without trouble, but suddenly the nurse's horse, approaching the ford, de-cided he wanted a drink, and instead of following the trail into the creek, he stepped sideways off the bank into the upper hole. Caught leaning forward, the nurse pitched over his head, and her foot caught in the reins, which she'd retied, pulling him down on top of her.

The whole thing happened so fast it was like a series of still pictures—*click, click, click*—and there wasn't a goddamn thing I could do about it. Horse and rider disappeared, and when he came up, his eyes were rolling. Rearing, he plunged up and down, gone crazy, jerking her from the water and throwing her back. When his hooves crashed right in the middle of her, I thought, "Okay, that's a broken hip"—and when he came down again, he caught her right in the face, and I thought, "I hope he killed her clean."

I don't know how I got there, but all of a sudden I was in the water, slashing the reins to cut her free. By then the horse had reared at least ten times. As soon as the reins parted, he plunged away downstream, water flying. He hadn't been trying to hurt her, of course; he was just trying to get the hell out of that hole, and she was in his way.

I dragged her out and carried her to the bank. The iron shoes had laid her scalp open, broken her jaw, cut the cartilage across her nose, and slashed one eyelid so clean it might have been done with a sharp knife. I could see the eyeball inside, like one of these white marbles you play with when you're a kid–a "milky." I figured she was deader than hell and thought: "There goes the store."

When the doctors and the other nurse rushed to help, I got out of the way, and they went to work on her. Doctors like those two never travel without a regular candy store, and they knew just what to do. It was the perfect combination–granted that if it had to happen, it couldn't have worked out better–because if there was ever a time when you needed an emergency room specialist, this was it, and the ophthalmologist was just right for the damage around her eyes.

The nurse was conscious but in shock, soaked with mud and bloody water. "We're not going to move her," the boyfriend told me. "It'll take three-and-a-half hours to get medical help in here," I reminded him.

So we moved her, propping her in the saddle in front of Larry while I rode hell-for-leather to the trailhead and the nearest telephone. All the way down, I wondered whether the million-dollar insurance policy the Forest Service requires would cover the damage. By the time the rest of them reached the road, the ambulance was there, and they headed down the canyon to Gunnison, siren screaming.

Next day, when I went to see her in the hospital, I took a bunch of flowers and the biggest candy bar I could find, one of those big Swiss chocolate bars full of nuts and raisins. Because her jaw was wired shut, she couldn't do anything with it, but it was my way of apologizing for getting on her butt about that sweet tooth. Maybe, I thought, if I hadn't pushed her about the candy, she wouldn't have resented my trying to straighten out her riding, and she wouldn't have retied those reins.

It was also the only way I could think of to apologize for something that was, at least in part, my fault. Because the truth was that I had relaxed. The sun had been shining, the birds had been singing. It was my last trip, and we were an hour or so out of the resort. If I'd been paying attention, I would have noticed those reins, and I would have taken the bridle off and led her down.

Nothing ever happened with the insurance. Nobody sued me or the resort. Everybody in the group had heard me warn her and seen her untie those reins; even the boyfriend knew she was legally at fault. Later, talking to him, I found out it had happened before, a couple of years earlier. She'd been riding a motorcycle without a helmet and had smashed up the other side of her face, so this was not her first event.

The doctor and nurse came back the following year—they wanted to do another trip with me—but by then I was out of the business and not about to tempt fate again. To return the favor, the nurse brought me a candy bar, another one of those big Swiss chocolate delights. We ate it in my office at the college and talked about the trip and the accident. Looking at her, you couldn't tell that anything had ever happened. She moved just like she had always moved, and that beautiful face was as beautiful as ever. It was an incredible recovery, I thought, until the boyfriend told me no, it was major reconstructive surgery. He had a reciprocal arrangement with a plastic surgeon friend on the West Coast, and the guy had repaired the damage—from the inside, leaving no scars—without charge.

All of us had been lucky. We'd been careless, and we'd gotten away with it. The clients, of course, didn't know any better, but I did. The high country's beautiful, but I learned a long time ago that it's a trap. Nine times out of ten, you walk in and steal the cheese, like Jerry the mouse in the old cartoons, but if you keep coming back, it finally catches up with you. You get away with it so long that finally you start thinking there's nothing to it—and all of a sudden the trap snaps shut.

The fact is that I was responsible for the nurse in more than just a legal sense. She'd escaped, but her accident had been one more sign that my outfitting career was over. I'd had a good run for my money. I'd written a lot of good scenes, and some good acts; I'd met some wonderful characters, and I'd given what I knew was the performance of my life. But I'd never quite got it right, and by now I knew I never would. Life isn't art, and outfitting, no matter how hard I'd tried to make it one, isn't a play. It was time for me to move along, to start over somewhere else, and I was looking forward to it.